"Introductions to philosophy come in all shapes, sizes, and especially content. It did not take long to recognize two things that separate Jason Crowder's from other such volumes. First, he takes very seriously the Christian philosopher's duty to apply his stock and trade in the context of Christian revelation. For Crowder, philosophy is not a discipline that operates independently of God's Word, but with Scripture verses tacked on at the end. Rather, he organizes his philosophy in the context of God's words to us. Second, he is convicted that good theology and philosophy must be applied to life. After thinking well, what manner of persons ought we to be? How can these truths be applied in real life situations? I recommend this volume, especially as it exhibits these two strengths."

—Gary R. Habermas, PhD
Distinguished Research Prof. & Chair, Dept. of Philosophy, Liberty University

"Here is a scholarly, highly readable, and biblical treatment of philosophy. Those who value careful thinking and tight logic will find much to feast on in this book. I particularly appreciate how Crowder demonstrates that philosophy is relevant to daily Christian living. Highly recommended."

—Ron Rhodes
Founder & President of Reasoning from the Scriptures Ministries;
Author of over 70 books on sharing the gospel message and defending Christianity

"Most people outside of academia shy away from subjects that seem inaccessible to them. Anything perceived as too heady or high-minded gets relegated to an apathetic heap and discarded as irrelevant. Dr. Crowder has done a good service to the Body in *Philosophy, Who Needs it?* by pulling down essential, practical, and historic truths from the supposed ivory tower seat and making them, not only approachable, but desirable as well. As one who earned his college degree in philosophy as a professed atheist and who now pastors a local fellowship, the value of this introductory work cannot be overstated."

—Eddie Exposito
BA in Philosophy (University of New Orleans);
Pastor of Sovereign Grace Fellowship (Slidell, LA)

"Every generation of American Evangelicals needs a new set of prophetic voices to extend into the present the historic line of voices calling us back from the anti-intellectual betrayal of Jesus' Great Commandment (to love the Lord our God with all our mind) to which we are prone. Jason Crowder has stepped up to that plate and hit a solid line drive. Lovers of truth and good Christian thinking can be grateful."

—Donald T. Williams, R. A.
Forrest Scholar at Toccoa Falls College, President of the International Society of Christian Apologetics; Author of nine books including—*Mere Humanity: Chesterton, Lewis and Tolkien on the Human Condition* and *Reflections from Plato's Cave: Essays in Evangelical Philosophy*

"*Philosophy, Who Needs It?* is far more than a basic introduction to philosophy. Crowder answers the question why to all doubters of the importance of philosophy for the church and especially the pulpit. Beyond the why, he explains philosophy with the perfect balance of depth and explanation. I wish I had this book years ago. An extreme blessing."

—Eddie Coakley
Senior Pastor of Trinity Baptist Church (Cayce, SC)

"In the church there is too often an unnecessary division of those who feel that advanced education and studies in complementary disciplines such as philosophy are unnecessary at best, and detrimental at worst, and those who place philosophy above the authority of Scripture. Jason Crowder calls his readers to the correct perspective: The Bible is the highest authority, and the study of philosophy can complement and enhance one's understanding of that highest authority. I agree with him at this point and encourage others to take the time to read this work and see if they too come to the same conclusion."

—Rick Walston
Founder and President Emeritus, Columbia Evangelical Seminary

"Jason Crowder has done the Christian Church a great service by writing this book. In it he shows that, if we are to love God with our minds as well as our hearts, we must think deeply about the Bible, the world, morality, and the Christian view of reality. This means that every Christian, whether he be a lay person or a minister, must be a good philosopher, as well as a good theologian. Jason can help us begin this intellectual journey as he introduces us to philosophy (i.e., the love of wisdom) from a Christian perspective. In this climate of anti-intellectualism that has infected the American Church, this book will be a major contribution to the health of the Christianity in our country. I highly recommend this book."

—**Phil Fernandes**
Pastor of Trinity Bible Fellowship (Bremerton, WA);
President of the Institute of Biblical Defense

"Too many Christians believe that childlike faith means that we do not need to think about our faith. The biblical evidence, from both Jesus and Paul, reveals that the opposite is true. Everyone does philosophy, the question is whether it is good or bad philosophy. Jason Crowder provides the resource to get Christians on the path to good philosophy. *Philosophy, Who Needs It?* presents scholarly content in a manner which the layperson can understand and apply."

—**Stephen J. Bedard**
Pastor of Queen Street Baptist Church; Director of Hope's Reason Ministries; Adjunct Professor, Emmanuel Bible College

"For many Christians, *philosophy* is a four-letter word, and any Christian who goes so far as to study philosophy is to be regarded with suspicion, if not pity. In reality, however, everyone has a philosophy of some kind, whether they recognize it or not. The only question is whether they have a good philosophy. This splendid book is an invitation not merely to good philosophy, but to *Christian* philosophy: philosophy directed by the word of God and pursued to the glory of God. So come on in, the water's fine!"

—**James N. Anderson**
Associate Professor of Theology and Philosophy;
Academic Dean, RTS Global, Reformed Theological Seminary

"While attending a pastors' conference, I was struck with the following thought: pastors need to be taught the Bible, and they need to be taught how to think. This is true not just for ministers but for all genuine believers in Jesus Christ. Jason Crowder has produced an invaluable field guide to Christian philosophy which should prove most useful to readers who strive to love the Lord with all their MIND."

—**David W. Bailey**
Pastor of Cottondale Baptist Church (Cottondale, AL);
Author of *Speaking the Truth in Love: The Life and Legacy of Roger Nicole*

"Dr. Crowder's *Philosophy, Who Needs It?* is an eminently practical work. Someone of moderate intelligence, who has never taken a class in philosophy or read a book about the subject, could teach this book's contents to a Sunday School class or youth group without becoming confused himself or confusing anyone who is paying attention. Ordinary Christians without academic attainments or aspirations need to know about this subject and its relation to their faith. For that audience, this book is ideal."

—**Dennis W. Jowers**
Professor of Theology & Apologetics, Faith Evangelical College & Seminary

"In our day when much of the visible church is susceptible to and promoting many false doctrines, a book like *Philosophy, Who Needs It?* is much needed. This is a thoroughly biblical view of philosophy and will help any Christian learn to reason better and gain a greater understanding of truth. Applying the apostle Paul's directive in Romans 12:1–2 for having a renewed mind, this book will be a great help for the Christian learning to discern truth from error. Well done!"

—**Joe Tolin**
Pastor of Grace Fellowship Church (Gulfport, MS)

"In a culture steeped in anti-intellectualism, Crowder's book offers a challenge to those who would be faithful to Christ. Part of what it means to follow Jesus is to develop intellectual virtue—to be good thinkers—which in turn, leads to a life well-lived. In *Philosophy, Who Needs It?* Crowder provides a biblically informed introduction to philosophy, expertly showing the tight connection between pursuing the truth and pursing Jesus as the source of truth."

—Paul Gould
Assistant Professor of Philosophy & Christian Apologetics,
School of Theology, Southwestern Baptist Theological Seminary

"Crowder's book captured my interest from the beginning and sustained it until the end. Judging from the wide range of resource material and the depth of thought, a lot of work and research went into the making of this informative and stimulating book. The philosophical ideas and concepts are well supported by Scripture. The book should have a wide readership at many levels: personal, small group studies inside and outside of the church, and as a college textbook. There are many nuggets of truth in this book that made me grab my notebook and write them down for further thought and reflection. Get the book, read it, and enjoy it. You will be glad you did."

—Edward Lyrene
Retired Southern Baptist Minister and Pastor

"Jason Crowder has produced a very readable and practical primer on philosophy. While admitting the dangers and limitations of philosophy, he nonetheless demonstrates its benefits and even necessity for Christian discipleship of a biblically grounded and theologically informed pursuit of philosophical inquiry. *Philosophy, Who Needs It?* will be a great resource for Christian pastors, students, and laypersons."

—Steven B. Cowan
Assistant Professor of Philosophy and Religion, Lincoln Memorial University;
Co-author, *The Love of Wisdom: A Christian Introduction to Philosophy*

"The author has given us a superb introduction to, and a biblical rationale for, the study of Philosophy. Further, he has clearly outlined and defended Christianity's great need to continually pursue the intellectual development of its mind. This important release could not have been more timely for our postmodern age."

—Pastor Jerry Marcellino
Audubon Drive Bible Church in Laurel, Mississippi;
Co-founder of FIRE (The Fellowship of Independent Reformed Evangelicals)

"Every person is a philosopher, but few can articulate their philosophy of life or possess a sufficient understanding of the influences on their thinking. In *Philosophy, Who Needs It?*, Jason Crowder guides readers toward a greater knowledge of the nature of philosophy and aids them in developing a Christian view of life. Anyone giving careful attention to this book will walk away with a mind and heart more thoroughly shaped through Christian truth."

—Scott Slayton
Lead Pastor of Chelsea Village Baptist Church (Chelsea, AL);
Blogger at One Degree to Another (scottslayton.net)

"In order to communicate effectively with the world regarding 'the way, the truth, and the life,' Christians should be conversant in how to approach truth and knowledge. Dr. Crowder's book provides an excellent, accessible introduction to philosophy that readers will find relevant, useful, and properly balanced with Scripture. This is the book on philosophy I can recommend to all Christians regardless of their level of experience."

—Eric Odell-Hein
President, Columbia Evangelical Seminary

"We are living in an emotionally-driven culture that has not often paid clear thinking its due. Such a situation is putting the proverbial 'cart-before-the horse.' The result is numerous people on a wide path paved by unexamined experiences or under-evaluated truth claims. It could be argued that the issue is not that we live in a society where intelligence is lacking, but instead that comparatively few people know how to think. Jason Crowder's *Philosophy, Who Needs It?* comes to the rescue helping readers to get at the meaning and application of knowledge. Crowder approaches his topic as a Christian who believes that faith is foundational for understanding truth. He writes in a winsome style that is compelling, convincing, and challenging. *Philosophy, Who Needs It?* will be useful for high school, college, and graduate students as well as for anyone who wants to better understand the vital role of philosophy in properly evaluating the world in which we live from a biblical perspective."

—Ray Rhodes Jr.
President of Nourished in the Word Ministries;
Author of *Family Worship for the Reformation Season* and numerous other books and articles

"Jason Crowder has written an excellent resource for parents, church leaders, and anyone who is interested in pursuing and defending truth. This practical and scholarly work shows how faith in God complements our God-given ability to think. As Crowder's pastor, I appreciate the way he utilizes proper biblical hermeneutics, church history, personal stories, and everyday illustrations to equip philosophers from all walks of life with discernment. He provides the necessary tools for sorting out and engaging the clamoring voices of formal and informal philosophers who assert their unbiblical, relativistic, politically correct views. This book is a must-read for Christians who want to effectively show and tell others that Christianity is the only logical and sustainable worldview."

—James R. Albers
Pastor of Celebration Baptist Church (Wichita, KS)

Philosophy, Who Needs It?

Philosophy, Who Needs It?

A Layman's Introduction to Philosophy

JASON D. CROWDER
Foreword by Winfried Corduan

WIPF & STOCK · Eugene, Oregon

PHILOSOPHY, WHO NEEDS IT?
A Layman's Introduction to Philosophy

Copyright © 2016 Jason D. Crowder. All rights reserved. Except for brief quotations in critical publications or reviews, no part of this book may be reproduced in any manner without prior written permission from the publisher. Write: Permissions, Wipf and Stock Publishers, 199 W. 8th Ave., Suite 3, Eugene, OR 97401.

Wipf & Stock
An Imprint of Wipf and Stock Publishers
199 W. 8th Ave., Suite 3
Eugene, OR 97401

www.wipfandstock.com

PAPERBACK ISBN 13: 978-1-4982-1979-2
HARDCOVER ISBN 13: 978-1-4982-1981-5

Manufactured in the U.S.A.   02/23/2016

Unless otherwise indicated, all Scripture quotations are from the ESV® Bible (The Holy Bible: English Standard Version®), copyright © 2001 by Crossway, a publishing ministry of Good News Publishers. Used by permission. All rights reserved.

Scripture quotations marked HCSB are taken from the Holman Christian Standard Bible®, Used by Permission HCSB © 1999, 2000, 2002, 2003, 2009 Holman Bible Publishers. Holman Christian Standard Bible®, Holman CSB®, and HCSB® are federally registered trademarks of Holman Bible Publishers.

Scripture quotations marked (NIV) are taken from the Holy Bible, New International Version®, NIV®. Copyright © 1973, 1978, 1984, 2011 by Biblica, Inc.™ Used by permission of Zondervan. All rights reserved worldwide. www.zondervan.com The "NIV" and "New International Version" are trademarks registered in the United States Patent and Trademark Office by Biblica, Inc.™

To my parents, Dale and Jan Crowder, for raising me in a Christian home and for sacrificing through the years to make sure that I got everything I needed, including an extensive education.

To my beloved wife, Rebekah, thank you for your endless support and encouragement through my educational, ministry, and teaching endeavors, and who is probably more excited that this project is finalized than I am.

To the memory of Dr. James Walker Bryant (1936–2014), thank you for being such a great influence and mentor in my early days of my formal philosophical and theological training at the University of Mobile.

Contents

Foreword by Winfried Corduan | ix
Preface | xiii
Acknowledgements | xv
Abbreviations | xvii
Introduction | xxi

Part One: Prelude to Philosophy and Its Value for the Christian

Chapter 1
What is Philosophy? An Examination into Its Nature | 3

Chapter 2
Biblical Justification for Philosophy:
Reflection on the Faith-Reason Relationship | 17

Chapter 3
Christianity and Philosophy:
Influence of Philosophy within Christianity | 38

Part Two: How We Come to Know Things

Chapter 4
Insights on the Operation of Revelation:
Philosophy of Divine Revelation | 47

Chapter 5
What is Truth? Developing a Biblical Perspective | 61

Chapter 6
Truth Leads to Freedom: Distinctions of Biblical Truth | 74

Chapter 7
Truth and Falsehood: How Do We Know What is True? | 90

Chapter 8
Truth or Truths? Confronting Truth-Claims | 103

Part Three: Philosophy and the Gospel

Chapter 9
How Shall We Live? Living in and Engaging a Pagan Culture | 123

Chapter 10
God's Mandate and the Christian Thinker:
The Solution to the Madness | 136

Part Four: So What Now

Chapter 11
Concluding Thoughts: Only Scratching the Surface | 155

Bibliography | 171
Subject Index | 189
Ancient Documents Index | 201

Foreword

I AM DELIGHTED THAT Jason Crowder has provided us with this book. For a long time now, I have maintained that there are two kinds of theologians, namely those who are aware of the philosophy underlying their theology and those who are mediocre theologians. Let me clarify what I mean by these words.

First of all, I am not limiting the label *theologian* to people who are pursuing theology as a vocation, and are teaching and writing professionally in this area. I am including any person who is making an effort to understand and express the teachings of the Bible in a coherent fashion, and I will refer to such people as *thinking Christians*. The Bible is the Word of God, which comes to us in sixty-six books, written in different languages from different human points of view, yet expressing a single message: the story of our redemption by God's grace. When we put that story together in a clear and intelligible way, we are theologizing, though possibly on a rather minimal level. I am including statements as simple as, "In order to be saved, you must accept Jesus Christ as your Lord and Savior." This statement is not a precise quotation from Scripture, but we know that it is what the Bible teaches; we may even see it as the culmination of the message of the entire Bible from Genesis through Revelation. Still, we, the human beings who are not divinely inspired authors, are making such assertions as we declare the gospel within our life-world. We may like to be thought of as theologians or we may disdain the label, all thinking Christians are—if only by this minimal definition—theologians.

Also, again invoking a minimalist understanding, we cannot avoid taking recourse to philosophical concepts, though we may not realize or admit that we are doing so. All thinking people have a way of understanding their lives and surroundings by means of concepts that combine to make up their worldview. A worldview, following the very literal meaning of the term, is the grand perspective by which we try to make sense of everything that we know and experience. It provides the philosophical categories that regulate our thinking. As mentioned above, it frequently does so without our even being aware of it. For example, for some people a worldview consists purely of materialism; they believe that the only thing that is real is physical matter and that nothing exists or can possibly happen outside of the material world. People who hold such a worldview may insist that there is nothing special to it, that every rational person should subscribe to a materialist worldview.

In general, Christians have a view of the world that includes: what it means to be a human person (the *body* and the *soul*), the existence of an infinite Creator (*God*), the self-disclosure of God (*revelation* and *the Bible*), the actions of God within the world (*the supernatural, redemption*), and many similar items. But when we come to a more specific analysis of what these terms actually may mean to a person, it very likely turns out that two Christians, equally committed to the truth of the Bible and to a Christian worldview, have somewhat different interpretations in mind. For example, when we ask a question such as, "What is a human being?" we will soon discover that the words bring up different images for various Christians. Some people believe that they are entirely identical with their souls, which are construed as independently existing, ghostlike beings that are for a time entrapped in their bodies. Others may claim that it takes a body and a soul together as a unit in order to be completely human. Leaving aside the question of which of these two options—or perhaps some other one—is true, the point is that thinking Christians must have something in mind when they are using terms like *soul*, and their total concepts are not going to be entirely based on only scriptural content. The integration of some philosophical conceptions is inevitable.

I am saying, then, that thinking Christians not only will have a *theology*, no matter how undeveloped, but also an underlying set of philosophical concepts, again possibly quite minimal, that undergird their theology. Many people may bristle at the idea that they are relying on any philosophical concepts and insist that they have no worldview other than biblical content. Whatever we might call a *worldview* may appear to them to be simply common sense. However, they do not see that their *common sense* rests on a different worldview compared to what people in other cultures and places consider to be *common sense*. For example, it is considered to be a trait of American thought in general to take a philosophically pragmatic approach to solving problems. In overly simplistic terms, the dictum, "If it works, then it must be true," holds sway. For people in some other cultures, what is true is defined by the decrees of human or divine authority figures, and any pragmatic concern as to whether a belief actually has a positive impact on a person's life is thought to be irrelevant.

Ideas such as these have led some people to embrace relativism, a position according to which there is no objective truth. Then any belief may wear the badge of *truth* if it is considered to be true within one worldview, while another belief, though inconsistent with the previous one, receives the same honor if it, too, is accepted as true in some other worldview. But, as Jason Crowder shows in this book, relativism is a position that is impossible to hold, and theological content provides no exception.

For the thinking Christian, the source of truth and the final authority for what is true is the Bible. Thus, relativism cannot be an intentional outcome because the Bible is the standard by which all beliefs should be measured. We do not need to belabor the reality that human beings are fallible and that two Christians may actually hold incompatible beliefs, each of them thinking that they are relying on biblical content. Crowder takes account of this fact and analyzes it; I just want to emphasize that our failure, or possibly our inability, to maintain a standard entails neither that there is no standard nor that the standard does not apply.

So, now, let me sum up what I have tried to say so far:

a) Thinking Christians are at least minimally trying to correlate biblical teachings with each other, thereby creating a *theology*;

b) Their *theology* cannot help but be formulated in the terms and philosophical concepts of their worldview, no matter how rudimentary they are; and

c) Regardless of the worldview that may influence a person's theology, the final authority for what is legitimately included is the Bible.

Taking these three propositions together, it becomes clear that thinking Christians need to be able to discern between those beliefs that are truly based on the Bible and those that are generated by philosophical perspectives. Believers who do not pay attention to their conceptual presuppositions are likely to include thoughts and ideas in their theology that are not based on the Bible and may impede their understanding and teaching of the biblical message. That is the reason why I started out by saying a little crassly that theologians who are unaware of their philosophical presuppositions are likely going to produce a mediocre theology.

Foreword

In short, we cannot get around utilizing philosophical concepts in expressing our faith in a way that makes sense while being faithful to the message of the Bible. Philosophical ideas that are contrary to the Bible obviously are not going to be of any help here. On the other hand, committing ourselves to philosophical concepts that are suitable to understand what God has revealed means far more than just packaging abstract thoughts in some suitable metaphysical concepts. We must learn to think biblically.

This thought takes us to come to one of Crowder's main contributions to this topic: He stresses that to think biblically entails to live biblically.

How do we bring off such a feat? A good start is to read the book to which these thoughts are just preparatory. Jason Crowder teaches us that the person whom I am calling the *thinking Christian* is a Christian who is aware of the role of philosophical concepts but far more importantly, one whose philosophical ideas are grounded in the objective reality of God, and who, thus, is not just a *thinking* Christian, but a Christian whose entire life is based on the reality of God as he has revealed himself. Crowder teaches us in this book how we should live in light of the philosophical and theological truths that he has shared with us.

Crowder's writing brims with notes and references, a witness to thorough scholarship, which also allows for solid interaction with his conclusions by pursuing the extensive background material he has used. Though not tying himself to any single person or movement, there is no question that his anchor points are Augustine and some of the leading presuppositionalists of the twentieth-century, such as Gordon Clark and Carl Henry. I trust that any readers who do not share that specific tradition will not simply resurrect the debates of the last century but understand the motivation behind the selection, namely to bring our thoughts into line with God's self-revelation. The point of this book is not to make an argument concerning apologetic methodology but to clarify the proper role of philosophical thinking in a theology that touches on every single aspect of our lives. Crowder's reflections are both personal and applicable to all of us who take seriously the notion that our beliefs should be based on divine revelation.

Winfried Corduan, PhD
Professor Emeritus of Philosophy and Religion
Taylor University
Author of *Handmaid to Theology*
November 28, 2015

Preface

As I began my doctoral studies in philosophical theology and apologetics in the fall of 2006, I was shocked by the number of friends and ministers who thought I was wasting my time and money pursuing such a degree. Some of them still do not understand that the call to the ministry includes a call of preparation for that great work. Unfortunately in this day and time, an anti-intellectual sentiment within Christianity still exists.

Yes, it is unfortunate that this mindset exists when a number of godly men in the twentieth-century devoted seasons of their ministry fighting this perspective. Off the top of my mind, some individuals come to mind: Harry Blamires, Os Guinness, Arthur Holmes, T. W. Hunt, J. P. Moreland, Mark A. Noll, James W. Sire, R. C. Sproul, and John R. W. Stott. These are just a handful of people who have written on the importance of developing the Christian mind.

Christianity is not a blind faith—a baseless and irrational leap into the dark—as some of its critics and skeptics like to claim. However, believers who fail to take seriously the command to love the Lord with all their mind do often lend unwitting support to the charges of those who see religion as unreasonable, ridiculous, and without warrant. There are times when a believer says something that is less-than-rational about the Christian faith. To err is part of the *fallen* human condition. But there is a sufficient difference between erring unintentionally and doing so intentionally. For a mature believer not to be able to explain one's faith in the most straightforward way is shameful.

There are elements found in philosophy that can assist Christians in being able to explain their faith to those around them. One does not need to master the topic to glean from it. This project consists of finally capturing on paper thoughts that I have been formulating over the years and the revisiting of several of the papers that I wrote while pursuing my Doctor of

Preface

Theological Studies degree in philosophical theology and apologetics with Columbia Evangelical Seminary under the supervision of Rick Walston.

Philosophy is considered the handmaid of theology. It is, therefore, essential that Christians have a proper understanding of what philosophy is. More importantly, believers ought to have an appreciation for philosophy because of its relationship to theology.

This work is not a complete work on the topic of philosophy and its relationship to the Christian faith. A single book or several books cannot contain all that can be said and has been said through the ages on these topics. In fact, I am not convinced that a multi-volume encyclopedia the size of *Encyclopedia Britannica* could contain all that can be said in this area of study. This project will hopefully be an encouragement for those wrestling with the role that philosophy should have in the Christian's life.

To some degree, everyone is a philosopher. Each of us thinks about and reflects upon various issues in our daily lives. We consider the pros and cons to the countless decisions that we have to make before we render a final verdict. Some individuals do this to a greater degree than others. There are some individuals—such as William Lane Craig, Winfried Corduan, Greg Ganssle, Douglas Groothuis, J. P. Moreland, and Alvin Plantinga—who devote their lives and ministries to the pursuit of Christian philosophy. Being a professional philosopher is not required for reading this book. To glean from this work, you simply just need to have a curious mind.

Through the years, I have had individuals tell me that philosophy is a waste of time for Christians and its study should not be pursued. This is not the case. The exact opposite is actually the case; all followers of Christ ought to have a basic understanding of what philosophy is and its value for everyday life.

It is my desire that the content within this book is glorifying to God and edifying for your Christian walk. In the recent months, my Christian motto has become: *Coram Deo Vive*. The proper translation of the Latin phrase is: Live in the presence of God. I hope that this motto becomes the axiom for your Christian walk as well.

Soli Deo Gloria,
Jason D. Crowder
Reformation Day 2015

Acknowledgements

I WOULD LIKE TO thank Rebekah, my beloved wife, for the countless times that she proofread this manuscript, heard me talk about this endeavor, and wondered when I was going to get sleep at times. I also am grateful for the very helpful comments and insights that I received from a graduate student of Columbia Evangelical Seminary, Elizabeth Johnston, and from Brian Orr, an alumni of the institution preparing for a research PhD in theology, who both proofread this material. The insights and corrections of these three have been valuable.

In mid-August 1995, I began my post-high school educational pursuits that would be continuing over twenty years later. Individual professors stand out more than others. One of those professors is John Buaas, who I first took a class with in Spring 1996. Through the years we have stayed in touch thanks to Facebook. I never imaged that we would be colleagues one day. Nearly twenty years later, we are when I started working for Butler Community College as an adjunct in January 2014. I am thankful for his willingness to assist me with cleaning up some of my awkward phrasing, which I could smooth out on my own.

Additionally, my appreciation and gratitude needs to be expressed to Winfried Corduan for his encouragement and insights in the beginning stages of this project and his continual support and encouragement to its completion. I am also indebted to Douglas Groothuis for his encouragement in the early days of this project and for graciously allowing me to talk through some of the content found in the second major division of the book. I am grateful to Greg Ganssle for recommending that I reach out to Doug Blount to see if he would be willing to review a portion of chapter 7. And I am thankful that Doug Blount graciously offered to review my remarks concerning William James. It is truly a blessing to have influential scholars supporting and encouraging up-and-coming scholars.

Acknowledgements

I must also thank my editor, Matthew Wimer, at Wipf & Stock for being willing to take a risk and having faith in me to allow this project to move beyond a dream. In the early days of the project, he graciously answered countless clarifying questions that I had on ensuring that I was formatting the manuscript properly in its layout. And at the end of the project, he graciously gave me flexibility to seek a balance of endorsers between scholars and ministers. Additionally, I would like to thank the entire Team at Wipf & Stock Publishers who assisted with moving this work from a manuscript to its final form.

Last but not least, I am grateful beyond words that God called me into his fold at a very young age and for those who allowed God to use them as his vessels to introduce me to the truth. Through the years, numerous people have assisted with developing my philosophical and theological mind. Those individuals know who they are. I thank the Lord for your faithfulness to your callings. As a result, this work in the end is a collective work, but any error or faults found are entirely my own.

Abbreviations

CLASSICAL AND ANCIENT CHRISTIAN WRITINGS

An. post.	*Analytica posterior* (*Posterior Analytics*)
Apol.	*Apologia* (*Apology of Socrates*)
Civ.	*De civitate Dei* (*The City of God*)
Fid. symb.	*De fide et symbolo* (*Faith and the Creed*)
Mag.	*De magistro* (*The Teacher*)
Metaph.	*Metaphisca* (*Metaphysics*)
Lib.	*De libro arbitrio* (*Free Will*)
Poet.	*Poetica* (*Poetics*)
Pol.	*Politica* (*Politics*) or *Politicus* (*Statesman*)
Praed. sanct.	*De Preaedestinatio Sanctorum* (*On the Predestination of the Saints*)
Praescr.	*De praescriptione haereticorum* (*Prescription against Heretics*)
Resp.	*Respublica* (*Republic*)
Serm.	*Sermones*
Theaet.	*Theaetetus*
Tusc.	*Tusculanae disputations*
Trin.	*De Trinitate* (*The Trinity*)
Util. cred.	*De utilitate credendi* (*The Usefulness of Believing*)
Ver. rel.	*De vera religione* (*True Religion*)

Abbreviations

REFERENCE WORKS AND PERIODICALS

ANF	*Ante-Nicene Fathers*
BDB	*The Brown-Driver-Briggs Hebrew and English Lexicon*
CDP	*Cambridge Dictionary of Philosophy*
DLGTT	*Dictionary of Latin and Greek Theological Terms*
DRP	*Dictionary of Religion and Philosophy*
EDBT	*Evangelical Dictionary of Biblical Theology*
EDNT	*Exegetical Dictionary of the New Testament.* Edited by Horst Balz and Gerhard Schneider. 3 vols. Grand Rapids: Eerdmans, 1990.
EDT	*Evangelical Dictionary of Theology*
JBC	*Journal of Biblical Counseling*
JETS	*Journal of the Evangelical Theological Society*
NDBT	*New Dictionary of Biblical Theology*
NDT	*New Dictionary of Theology*
NIDNTT	*New International Dictionary of New Testament Theology.* Edited by Colin Brown. 4 vols. Grand Rapids: Zondervan, 1975–78.
NIDOTTE	*New International Dictionary of Old Testament Theology & Exegesis.* Edited by Willem A. VanGemeren. 5 vols. Grand Rapids: Zondervan, 1997.
NPNF1	*Nicene and Post-Nicene Fathers*, Series 1
SBJT	*The Southern Baptist Journal of Theology*
StudAr	*Studia aristotelica*
TDNT	*Theological Dictionary of the New Testament.* Edited by Gerhard Kittel and Gerhard Friedich. Translated by Geoffrey W. Bromiley. 10 vols. Grand Rapids: Eerdmans, 1964–76.

SCRIPTURES

Hebrew Bible / Old Testament

Gen	Genesis
Exod	Exodus
Lev	Leviticus

Abbreviations

Num	Numbers
Deut	Deuteronomy
Josh	Joshua
Judg	Judges
Ruth	Ruth
1–2 Sam	1–2 Samuel
1–2 Kgs	1–2 Kings
1–2 Chr	1–2 Chronicles
Ezra	Ezra
Neh	Nehemiah
Esth	Esther
Job	Job
Ps (*pl.* Pss)	Psalm(s)
Prov	Proverbs
Eccl (or Qoh)	Ecclesiastes (or Qoheleth)
Song	Song of Songs
Isa	Isaiah
Jer	Jeremiah
Lam	Lamentations
Ezek	Ezekiel
Dan	Daniel
Hos	Hosea
Joel	Joel
Amos	Amos
Obad	Obadiah
Jonah	Jonah
Mic	Micah
Nah	Nahum
Hab	Habakkuk
Zeph	Zephaniah
Hag	Haggai
Zech	Zechariah
Mal	Malachi

New Testament

Matt	Matthew
Mark	Mark
Luke	Luke
John	John
Acts	Acts
Rom	Romans
1–2 Cor	1–2 Corinthians
Gal	Galatians
Eph	Ephesians
Phil	Philippians
Col	Colossians
1–2 Thess	1–2 Thessalonians
1–2 Tim	1–2 Timothy
Titus	Titus
Phlm	Philemon
Heb	Hebrews
Jas	James
1–2 Pet	1–2 Peter
1–2–3 John	1–2–3 John
Jude	Jude
Rev	Revelation

VERSIONS OF THE BIBLE

ESV	*English Standard Version*
HCSB	*Holman Christian Standard Bible*
NIV	*New International Version*

Introduction

"Brothers, do not be children in your thinking.
Be infants in evil, but in your thinking be mature."

—1 Cor 14:20[1]

NAIVETÉ IS NOT A Christian virtue. Christians must know what they believe and why they believe those truths. They need to respond to those who question or criticize their faith. Understanding other perspectives enables the believer to defend Christianity.

Christians must live and think differently from those in the world. Apostle Paul writes, "Do not be conformed to this world, but be transformed by the renewal of your mind, that by testing you may discern what is the will of God, what is good and acceptable and perfect" (Rom 12:2). Paul commands believers to "take every thought captive to obey Christ" (2 Cor 10:5). Jesus and Peter teach on the significance of the believer's mindset. Jesus says to "love the Lord your God with all your heart and with all your soul and with all your mind and with all your strength" (Mark 12:30). Peter tells believers to prepare their minds for action (1 Pet 1:13). Believers should develop a distinctly Christian perspective and critical thinking skills. Using philosophy assists in fulfilling the mandate to love God with one's mind.

Furthermore, Christians should anticipate being asked about the hope and joy that they have in their lives. Believers must always be prepared to give an answer to anyone who asks (1 Pet 3:15). They ought to grow in their spiritual walk (1 Cor 3:1–4; cf. Heb 5:12–14; 1 Pet 2:2). Christians

---

1. Unless otherwise noted, all Scripture quotations are from the ESV.

should be able to give a response that makes sense logically. Likewise, they should be capable of distinguishing between biblical truth and false teachings (1 John 4:1), which is related to the ability to rightly divide the Word of God (2 Tim 2:15). Christians need to be able to give a succinct account of the gospel message and have the ability to elaborate upon the summary at length when necessary.[2] Paul begins the book of Galatians the way he does for this very reason. He spends time dealing with what the gospel is and why it matters (Gal 1:6—2:10).

Marked discrepancies exist between the thought processes of the followers of Christ and others. The Christian mind does not war against Christ (Rom 8:7). Christians have the mind of Christ (1 Cor 2:6). Therefore, *foolishness* and *deceived* do not describe the believer's thinking processes (Rom 1:21–32), nor does *alienated* and *hostile* (Col 1:21). Christians seek the wisdom and instruction from God (Prov 1:7: Rom 3:18) and acknowledge the treasures of wisdom and knowledge offered by Christ (Col 2:3). Furthermore, they should not walk "in the futility of their minds. They are [not to be] darkened in their understanding, [are not to be] alienated from the life of God because of the ignorance that is in them, due to their hardness of heart" (Eph 4:17–18).

Who needs philosophy? Everyone does. All will face situations in which its application is helpful. For example, during campaigns, politicians tend to give false generalizations, provide unwarranted conclusions, and over promise. They also distort their opponents' views and words. Oftentimes nothing more than half-truths appear. How does one separate truth from error? How does one determine the best choice amongst two or more options? Philosophy can assist here. Philosophy touches on all areas of life. It also deals with the big questions. Who am I? What is the meaning of life? What is good and evil? What is ethical and unethical?

Philosophy is not simply a hobby or an elitist pursuit by ivory-tower intellectuals. It is for the average person. Philosophy promotes clear and consistent thinking. Thus, philosophy should have an important place in the Christian's life.

According to Ecclesiastes 1:9, "there is nothing new under the sun." For those who have not read anything on philosophy before now, the concepts are completely foreign and new. For those who are familiar with

---

2. This is referred to as a touchstone proposition within Christian philosophy. It is a proposition in which if any of it is found to be inconsistent the statement must be rejected. For more information on this concept, see Groothuis, *Christian Apologetics*, 92; Halverson, *Concise Introduction*, 384; Nash, *Faith and Reason*, 47.

Introduction

these concepts, hopefully, you find this treatment refreshing because of its presentation.

Why another book on philosophy? More specifically, why another work examining the relationship that philosophy has with Christianity?[3]

First, when properly understood and utilized, philosophy is the handmaid of theology. Philosophy permeates theology, whether biblical or systematic.[4] Understanding theology becomes easier and more comprehensive when one knows the essentials of philosophy, which allow certain concepts to be conveyed within the context of theology. To some degree, everyone is a philosopher. Likewise, everyone is a theologian, whether a good, mediocre, or poor one. As followers of Christ, we all do theology. Philosophy enhances the study of theology.

Second, classic and stagnant concepts need new life breathed into them from time to time to show that they are still relevant. People should not be afraid or fearful of these ideas.

Third, some individuals desire to know about philosophy. They want to be introduced to Athens and then decide later if they want to stay awhile. For example, a retired US Army sergeant first class wants to learn more on the topic because he assists with the Gideons International ministry in lower Alabama. His patriotism moved him to drop out of high school during the Vietnam conflict. He wants to strengthen his confidence when sharing his faith. This book serves as a practical approach to philosophy instead of a technical one.

Philosophy, Who Needs It? approaches the topic of philosophy as a layman's introduction to the subject. Since this book is not exhaustive, it serves as a starting point. Hopefully, the work encourages believers to do further reading on the topic.

Philosophy, Who Needs It? is divided into four major divisions, with each portion functioning with a specific goal. Part one serves as a prelude to philosophy by describing what philosophy is and laying out its intrinsic value. The section also provides biblical justification for the use of philosophy and the influence on Christianity. Part two examines how people learn information and how they should evaluate the material's trustworthiness. Philosophy provides objective tools for testing the validity of truth-claims.

---

3. This is a topic that I am currently pursuing in-depth with the University of the Free State as my research PhD dissertation.

4. Corduan, *Handmaid to Theology*, 10; De Mowbray, "Philosophy as Handmaid," 1–37.

Introduction

Part three continues the thoughts from the previous section by looking specifically at philosophy and the gospel message and also touches on how Christians should defend their faith. Practical applications on applying philosophy to everyday life conclude the book.

Grab a notebook and a pencil to take notes. Along the way, jot down questions that come to mind and thoughts that you might want to research further. Once you are ready, begin the journey into *Philosophy, Who Needs It?*

PART ONE

Prelude to Philosophy and Its Value for the Christian

1

What is Philosophy?
An Examination into Its Nature

> "'Behold, the fear of the Lord that is wisdom,
> and to turn away from evil is understanding.'"
>
> —Job 28:28

"NOTHING IS MORE HIGHLY esteemed among men than philosophy," according to Philip Mauro.[1] When beginning a study into a new or unfamiliar subject, having a basic understanding of its content is helpful. A definition is the best place to begin any discussion. Many philosophers have problems defining philosophy with a specific, straightforward definition. But as we move towards a better grasp of the word, a description reveals itself in the term's etymology, which is the study of the history and origins of words.

History ascribes Pythagoras of Samos with introducing the terms *philosophy* and *philosophers* to the ancient Greek world.[2] Pythagoras combines two Greek words, *phileo* and *sophos*, to form a single concept—philosophy. *Phileo* means to love, and *sophos* denotes wisdom. Hence, most philosophers can agree upon *the love of wisdom* as a conventional definition.

---

1. Mauro, "Modern Philosophy," 5.
2. Diogenes Laërtius, *Lives of Eminent Philosophers*, 1.1.8; Cicero, *Tusc.*, 5.3–4.

On some level this elementary definition suffices. But the explanation lacks a full scope of what philosophy is. From here, trying to arrive at an agreeable definition gets more muddled.

MOVING TOWARDS A MORE CONCRETE DEFINITION FOR PHILOSOPHY

A consensus exists among philosophers that there is no airtight definition for philosophy beyond the traditional one, which expresses everything the subject covers. The problem of obtaining an all-encompassing definition is, in some manner, due to philosophy touching upon nearly every aspect of human life and all topics of study. A survey of ancient Greek philosophical writings reveals biology, botany, law, mathematics, physics, psychology, and rhetoric are just a few of the subjects originating from philosophical discourse. Philosophy does not have any specific material of its own, which bewilders the situation further. As a result, we cannot distinguish the term with regards to a particular area of investigation. Additional problems arise in deriving a more concrete description; for example, the content and character of philosophy changes throughout history.[3] At one point in time, God was an acceptable given in philosophical thought, and today the existence of God is questioned rather than assumed. Still further, a problem rests in whether philosophy is simply the evaluation of concepts and presuppositions or if more than this exists.[4]

Look closer at the traditional definition for philosophy—the love of wisdom. Defining *wisdom* presents a challenging task since one may not know what constitutes wisdom. *Merriam-Webster Dictionary* defines wisdom as:

- knowledge that is gained by having many experiences in life
- the natural ability to understand things that most other people cannot understand
- knowledge of what is proper or reasonable: good sense or judgment

In other words, wisdom is the proper understanding and right application of knowledge about the nature of reality. A wise person, therefore, lives accordingly by applying what the individual learns to real-life situations. Do

---

3. Bonjour and Baker, *Philosophical Problems*, 1–3; Russell, "Value of Philosophy," 107–13.

4. Geisler and Feinberg, *Introduction to Philosophy*, 14–17.

not simply equate wisdom to having knowledge. Having wisdom is much more than mere knowledge of facts and various other bits of information. I am confident you can think of someone who you consider to be book smart but who does not have a bit of common sense.

Remember a wise person applies what is learned to everyday life. Solomon personifies wisdom throughout the book of Proverbs to illustrate this point. For example, let us look at Proverbs 4 to see why we must apply knowledge to life:

> Hear, O sons, a father's instruction, and be attentive, that you may gain insight, for I give you good precepts; do not forsake my teaching. When I was a son with my father, tender, the only one in the sight of my mother, he taught me and said to me, "Let your heart hold fast my words; keep my commandments, and live. *Get wisdom; get insight; do not forget, and do not turn away from the words of my mouth. Do not forsake her, and she will keep you; love her, and she will guard you. The beginning of wisdom is this: Get wisdom, and whatever you get, get insight. Prize her highly, and she will exalt you; she will honor you if you embrace her. She will place on your head a graceful garland; she will bestow on you a beautiful crown."*
>
> *Hear, my son, and accept my words, that the years of your life may be many. I have taught you the way of wisdom; I have led you in the paths of uprightness. When you walk, your step will not be hampered, and if you run, you will not stumble. Keep hold of instruction; do not let go; guard her, for she is your life. Do not enter the path of the wicked, and do not walk in the way of the evil. Avoid it; do not go on it; turn away from it and pass on.* For they cannot sleep unless they have done wrong; they are robbed of sleep unless they have made someone stumble. For they eat the bread of wickedness and drink the wine of violence. But the path of the righteous is like the light of dawn, which shines brighter and brighter until full day. The way of the wicked is like deep darkness; they do not know over what they stumble.
>
> My son, be attentive to my words; incline your ear to my sayings. Let them not escape from your sight; keep them within your heart. For they are life to those who find them, and healing to all their flesh. Keep your heart with all vigilance, for from it flow the springs of life. *Put away from you crooked speech, and put devious talk far from you. Let your eyes look directly forward, and your gaze be straight before you. Ponder the path of your feet; then all your ways will be sure. Do not swerve to the right or to the left; turn your foot away from evil.* (Prov 4:1–27, emphasis added)

Rightly applying what one learns to one's life will assist in avoiding dangerous pitfalls. People have difficulty in being consistent with how they apply what they learn. At one point, the learned material might be applied correctly. But at a different time, the individual may not apply it correctly or simply not think about it.

While definitions are helpful, a true, concrete definition is not required for someone to have a basic understanding of what philosophy is.[5] Digging deeper into the nature of philosophy unveils insights into the development of a more concrete definition for the term.

What is the Source of Philosophy?

> All men by nature desire to know. An indication of this is the delight we take in our senses; for even apart from their usefulness they are loved for themselves; and above all others the sense of sight. For not only with a view to action, but even when we are not going to do anything, we prefer sight to almost everything else. The reason is that this, most of all the senses, makes us know and brings to light many differences between things.[6]

Aristotle unequivocally states human beings have an innate desire to know the unknown, which is the source of philosophy. Everyone longs for a sense of wonder, to marvel at the mysteries of the world.

Within philosophy, a sense of childlike wonder exists. Our sense of curiosity starts at an early age. One of the chief characteristics—if not the primary and most distinctive trait—of toddlers is their love for asking questions.[7] A toddler's questioning can be endless. Sometimes a simple answer is sufficient while other times it is not. Children desire answers to their simplistic questions.

As children mature, their inquiries become more complex. Wrestling with abstract ideas, adolescents want resolution to complex questions. A simple one-word response is no longer sufficient; they want to know more. "When I was a child, I spoke like a child, I thought like a child, I reasoned like a child. When I became a man, I gave up childish ways" (1 Cor 13:11). Furthermore, adults continue to search for meaning behind their questions.

---

5. Moreland and Craig, *Philosophical Foundations*, 12.
6. Aristotle, *Metaph.*, 1.1.980a21–27.
7. Cole and Cole, *Development of Children*, 323.

What is Philosophy?

From infancy through adulthood as the human mind develops, it becomes keener in various areas.[8] Just as the human mind matures through questioning, philosophy arises from the workings of an inquisitive mind, which is bewildered, astonished, and amazed by seemingly simple things or things that seem entirely impractical.

A perplexing problem remains—where to seek out knowledge and understanding. But this problem does not keep people from looking for new information and continuing to seek understanding of the world around them and of themselves.[9] One's search for knowledge and understanding is a lifelong journey, which has many roads with numerous paths. Some excursions are rewarding, and others are strewn with bitter dreams. For some individuals, the desire to learn has little influence or impact, and for others it plays a vital role. Matthew Stewart illustrates this point well by distinguishing between philosophers who merely desire to argue their philosophies with those who desire to live their philosophies. Those individuals who merely want to argue their viewpoints are satisfied once they finish their disputations. On the contrary, those who want to live their philosophies never see the journey to obtain new things as being complete. They are always at work.[10] Despite the fact this desire may not be strong for all, it is nevertheless still present. The yearning for knowledge and understanding is more prevalent in some stages of life than in others.

An individual is not born with all knowledge. A person, however, is born with the capacity to acquire it. As a person matures, a greater sense of what it is the individual wants to know and understand develops.[11]

People philosophize simply because of their desire to know the knowable,[12] and using their sensory faculties supports this fact.[13] Harold Bloom states people read and reflect upon things because of their desire for wisdom.[14] People care more about the learning process than focusing

---

8. For more on the stages of cognitive development, see Boole, *Laws of Thought*; Braisby and Gellatly, *Cognitive Psychology*; Dewey, *How We Think*; Goldstein, *Cognitive Psychology*; Leahy and Harris, *Learning and Cognition*; Thomas, *Counseling and Life-Span*.

9. Reynolds, "Quest for Knowledge," lines 1–5.

10. Stewart, *Courtier and the Heretic*, 54.

11. Burnyeat, "Aristotle on Understanding," 97–139; Lear, *Aristotle: Desire*.

12. Aristotle, *Metaph.*, 1:1:982b11–25.

13. Ibid., 1:1:980a21–27.

14. Bloom, H., *Where Shall Wisdom*, 284.

on specific content to learn, particularly when younger.[15] As one matures, focus shifts to learning specific content because of career advancement.

Each human desires to know what can be known, according to Aristotle.[16] Philosophy keeps alive humanity's sense of wonder and awe through seeing familiar things from an unfamiliar perspective.[17] As an individual begins to philosophize, the person realizes even the simplest things in ordinary, daily life can lead to confusion and that things seeming minute prove very significant. For example, think about the tilt of the earth. If the axial tilt changes by just a few degrees, season lengths change, farming patterns are altered, food supply fluctuates, ocean levels change, and economic structure changes. To continue towards a concrete definition for philosophy, we need to consider the following question: what is the goal of philosophy?

What is the Purpose of Philosophy?

Philosophy does not stop with the sense of bewilderment and marvel. Initial amazement leads to the formation of questions that guide one's curiosity. Sometimes a simple answer will suffice, and other times it does not. Philosophy connects itself closely with the quest for truth. In some regards, truth captures an unconstrained element—truth is an immutable absolute.[18] Philosophy strives passionately for additional knowledge. While hoping to bring some insight into the complexity of life, the chief aim of philosophy is the pursuit to see the bigger picture. Philosophy is committed to determining the truth. "Since all truth is God's truth, and since philosophy is a quest for truth, then philosophy will contribute to our understanding of God and His world."[19]

What Philosophy Is

Philosophy encapsulates the critical investigation of concepts of human inquiry. A stagnant body of knowledge does not depict philosophy. Philosophical thought is a continuous, reflective process that integrates new

15. Schaeffer, D., "Wisdom and Wonder," 641.
16. Aristotle, *Metaph.*, 1.1.980a27—981a12; Aristotle, *An. post.*, 2.19.
17. Russell, "Value of Philosophy," 110.
18. This concept will be developed further in another chapter.
19. Geisler and Feinberg, *Introduction to Philosophy*, 22.

information. Hence, it needs to be understood as an intellectual and cognitive pursuit. K. Scott Oliphint defines philosophy as "a theoretical activity that seeks to make sense out of the world in order to make sense of our place in it."[20] This endeavor allows one not only to reflect upon but also to analyze critically and evaluate various facets of life. Mastery of a single idea is not the primary goal. Grasping an association of ideas is the essential goal. Just because a satisfactory resolve in one era can be helpful in the historical juncture, it may, however, be found problematic in the next. For example, religious beliefs and practices once were accepted as philosophical norms; now they are not. Thus, philosophy is the description of the very nature of reality—expounding how humans ought to think and act within the world.[21]

No brief definition communicates what philosophy is. Philosophers suggest people study philosophy in detail to comprehend what it is. Studying a topic leads an individual to a better understanding.[22] To get a better grasp on the subject, a person needs more information.

ACQUIRING A DEEPER UNDERSTANDING OF PHILOSOPHY

An individual's pursuit of obtaining knowledge of the unknown frequently leads to more questions than answers, which may lead to frustration. The frustration that may occur relates to any area of obtaining new information; in other words, it is not unique to philosophy. The twentieth-century information explosion illustrates this point. Vast volumes of knowledge and information are now only seconds away by a few clicks on the internet. With all the material available at any given moment, life's most basic spiritual questions remain unanswered by human wisdom.[23]

The Challenge of Philosophy

At his trial for heresy for encouraging his students to challenge the accepted beliefs of the day and to think for themselves, Socrates proclaims life is only

---

20. Oliphint, *Christianity and the Role*, 5.
21. Geisler and Feinberg, *Introduction to Philosophy*, 17.
22. Bonjour and Baker, *Philosophical Problems*, 1.
23. MacArthur, "Only Source of Wisdom," lines 1–4.

worth living if it is examined.[24] Philosophy's basic and enduring challenge lies within those words. Critical thinking—which is clear, comprehensive, and correct—is philosophy's challenge. Thus, the essential challenge of philosophy is to think logically.[25] Specific requirements are necessary to achieve logical thinking.

First, clarification of thought must prevail. Connecting the dots in someone's thinking is not always easy to do. When I was finishing up my studies with Columbia Evangelical Seminary, my wife, Rebekah, proofread some my papers while we were dating. She repeatedly told me to connect the dots for the reader. In my mind, the content was crystal-clear. But from her perspective, the material was muddy water at best. Difficulty surfaces when one spends too much time focusing on a minute point, instead of looking at the bigger picture. To illustrate this, it is not uncommon for the ambiguity of an argument to lie in the definition of a single word. Over the course of time, definitions take on new or different meanings than they originally held. For example, when a present-day reader sees the title *The Gay Science*[26] on the bookstore shelf, the individual naturally is going to have the modern-day definition for *gay* come to mind. When the philosopher wrote his work, the word gay did not mean what it does today. This is why it is vital to define keywords when they are not being used in a conventional manner. We can avoid unnecessary confusion by defining our terms. Studying philosophy contributes to a person's capability to organize one's thoughts and issues more clearly, to deal with questions of value, and to extract what is essential from masses of information.

Having the ability to think critically goes beyond having clarity in thought, one needs to reason correctly as well. This is why logic is intertwined with the study of philosophy; *logic* assesses the rules formulating and governing how we know things. An individual needs to present one's arguments in a manner where it is thought out critically and stated so it is a solid and strong position. If the argument is flawed, the person has failed to think correctly. This does not mean the thought is completely wrong. It simply means one must revisit it to fix any flaws before a catastrophic error in the reasoning occurs. This, of course, presumes it is still possible to repair the argument. Some arguments, however, are so inherently flawed that an individual cannot fix them. To illustrate this, I will give an example

24. Socrates in Plato's *Apol.*, 38a.
25. Geisler and Feinberg, *Introduction to Philosophy*, 69–71.
26. Nietzsche, *The Gay Science*.

of two arguments. One will not have any logical issues, and the other will have a flaw in its reasoning. Argument 1: Since I am not lying, I must be telling the truth. Argument 2: Since I am under oath, I need to tell the truth to assure I do not commit perjury.

Can you determine which argument contains the flaw? The first argument does. This option assumes the individual has to be telling the truth since the person is not lying. The logical flaw here is referred to as begging the question or circular reasoning. It is plausible that the person is stretching the truth to make it sound more believable than unbelievable. The second option acknowledges the fact it is possible the person could lie while under oath. Furthermore, logic allows one to reduce thoughts to their logical forms where the ambiguity and fallacies can be either discovered in another's arguments or eliminated from one's position.[27]

Lastly, since philosophy is not limited to any particular body of knowledge but rather embraces knowledge generically, it is essential an individual thinks comprehensively about knowledge—integrating all knowledge into a single philosophical system, a *weltanschauung* (worldview). What is a worldview? According to James W. Sire, a worldview is "a set of presuppositions (assumptions which may be true, partially true or entirely false) which we hold (consciously or subconsciously, consistently or inconsistently) about the basic makeup of our world."[28] A thorough worldview will address the purposes and presuppositions of life. It will capture the sense of wonder that endures within us, which is the beginning of philosophy.[29] We never cease to question or investigate our surroundings. There are three questions every generation continues to ask and worldview must answer. The first probe is the question of origin: where did I come from? The second deals with the question of purpose: why am I here? The final one asks the question of destiny: where am I going? Philosophers do not come to the same conclusions to these three probing inquiries. But the same basic questions, nevertheless, about the meaning of life consistently come up. Likewise, if we were to pose these questions to our friends, a variety of answers would be given. While examining the purposes of life, the presuppositions that lie behind them are also investigated. Often an individual is unaware of the basic premises that form one's life and thoughts because

---

27. A later chapter will go into more information on logical fallacies and how to detect them.

28. Sire, *Universe Next Door*, 16.

29. Plato, *Theaet.*, 155d2–4; Aristotle, *Metaph.*, 1.1.982b11–25.

family and society embed them almost unconsciously at an early age into a child. A good worldview will in a non-contradictory fashion account for all the facts of experience and express itself where it is consistent throughout its explanation.[30]

Religious skeptics tend to question the legitimacy of religious authority, along with various religious beliefs and practices. With this said, it should not be shocking when skeptics charge Christians as having blind faith. Christians have added fuel to the charges of skeptics by speaking of their faith illogically.[31]

Philosophy presents a unique challenge for followers of Christ. A Christian has a specific obligation to study philosophy because it will challenge and contribute to a better understanding of the individual's faith. As Geisler and Feinberg note, "the result of such a challenge should not be the loss of faith, but the priceless possession of a well-reasoned and mature faith."[32] If the loss of faith does occur, it is not the fault of philosophy. Rather, it is the fault of the church for sending an individual out into the world who is incapable of thinking effectively for oneself.[33]

All ideas have consequences, and at times those consequences are serious.[34] If the Christian is unaware of the contemporary philosophical thought, rather than being exempt from its influence, the individual may be devoured by its cunningness. Philosophy offers a specific challenge for the believer because there are negative and positive aspects to philosophy. It aids in the refutation of opposing beliefs, which is its negative aspect. Philosophy also assists in the formation of a Christian worldview, which is its positive aspect. In the New Testament, Paul illustrates in 2 Corinthians 10:5 these two aspects: "We destroy arguments and every lofty opinion raised against the knowledge of God [negative aspect], and take every thought captive to obey Christ [positive aspect]."

---

30. Cosgrove, *Foundations of Christian*; Dockery and Thornbury, *Shaping a Christian Worldview*; Geisler and Watkins, *Worlds Apart*; Nash, *Worldviews in Conflict*; Naugle, *Worldview*; Noebel, *Understanding the Times*; Sire, *Naming the Elephant*. This concept will be discussed in greater depth later in the book.

31. Samples, "Faith and Reason," line 2.

32. Geisler and Feinberg, *Introduction to Philosophy*, 22.

33. Koukl, "Value of Philosophy," lines 68–70.

34. Sproul, *Consequences of Ideas*; Tarnas, *Passion of the Western*; Weaver, *Ideas have Consequences*.

What is Philosophy?

Christians need to have knowledge of philosophy so that they are not at the mercy of the non-Christian in intellectual matters.[35] The challenge, then, is for the believer to engage the non-Christian in establishing the Christian worldview as a valid system of truth, as well as showing the inconsistencies of other worldviews.

Philosophy is demanding and challenging. Most things in life are. Nothing in life comes without struggles, just like nothing is truly free. A cost hides behind freedom and free items. Someone pays the price for others to experience certain rights and privileges. When it comes to philosophy, an individual must personally invest to get a return on investment. What intrinsic value does philosophy have?

The Value of Philosophy

An individual should not conclude philosophy is impractical or meritless because it lacks immediate and tangible results.[36] Philosophy profoundly influences the formation and development of both institutions and thoughts that impact society. Ideas discussed in the classroom ultimately influence the shape of society's policies. Thus, one should not underestimate the importance of philosophical thoughts' impact on civilization.[37] Abraham Lincoln is attributed to saying "the philosophy in the classroom in one generation will be the philosophy of the government in the next."

Its study can liberate individuals from the grasp of prejudice and narrow-mindedness. Philosophical inquiry teaches one how to distance oneself from one's beliefs and the beliefs of others where the individual can view them with a healthy degree of scrutiny. By studying philosophy, one learns to read and listen more critically, which allows a person to be less susceptible to propaganda. As a result, the ability to distinguish sound argumentation and evidence from total absurdity is gained.[38]

Studying philosophy develops the reasoning skills and enhances problem-solving capacities. It encourages one to develop sound methods of doing research and analysis. It also aids in how an individual analyzes

---

35. Geisler and Feinberg, *Introduction to Philosophy*, 73.

36. Russell, "Value of Philosophy," 107–9.

37. Geisler and Feinberg, *Introduction to Philosophy*, 20. For more information on how philosophical thought has impacted society, see Sproul, *Consequences of Ideas*; Tarnas, *Passion of the Western*.

38. Geisler and Feinberg, *Introduction to Philosophy*, 20–21.

concepts, definitions, arguments, and problems. It trains one how to construct properly clear formulations and sound arguments. Philosophy assists an individual in distinguishing fine differences between viewpoints and in establishing common ground between opposing positions.

As a result, studying philosophy enhances an individual's communication skills, as well as one's ability to persuade others. Verbal and written communication is improved since the person is capable of expressing and defending coherent views on complex issues through articulating well-constructed, systematic arguments. Additionally, one eliminates ambiguities and vagueness from one's speech and writing. Not only does an individual learn to build and defend one's views, the individual discovers how to appreciate opposing positions and to anticipate counter-arguments.[39]

There is intrinsic value gained from studying philosophy. Unfortunately, philosophy's value is not often self-evident. One finds philosophy's worth through doing philosophical reflection. A question still lingers that brings additional insights into what philosophy is: are there any divisions within philosophical study?

The Major Branches of Philosophy

If you were to open any of the textbooks presently used in an introduction to philosophy course, you might be overwhelmed by the numerous divisions mentioned. Historically, philosophy is comprised of three main branches, which cover the core areas of life: natural, ethical, and dialectic. "Natural philosophy occupies itself about the world and the things in it; Ethical philosophy about life, and the things which concern us; Dialectics are conversant with the arguments by which both the others are supported."[40]

As philosophy develops, these categories change slightly. Natural philosophy morphs into physics and metaphysics, which discusses the issues of cause and effect found within reality.[41] Ethical philosophy primarily remains intact but encompasses the critique of values beyond those just found in morals.[42] Philosophers eventually change the name of this branch

---

39. Kvanvig, *Intellectual Virtues*; Kvanvig, *Value of Knowledge*; Wason and Johnson-Laird, *Thinking and Reasoning*.

40. Diogenes Laërtius, *Lives of Eminent Philosophers*, 1.1.13.

41. For additional information on natural philosophy, see Aristotle, *Metaph.*; Coffey, *Ontology*; Hasker, *Metaphysics*.

42. For additional information on ethics, see Bonhoeffer, *Ethics*; Davis, J. J., *Evangelical*

of philosophy to axiology (the study of value) because aesthetics and social-political philosophy emerge into the equation. Aesthetics deals with the evaluation and critique of beauty and art.[43] Social-political takes into account people living in a community.[44] Dialectical develops into logic, the processes of reasoning.[45] Epistemology emerges from logic. This field of study questions knowledge, truth and falsity, belief, and certainty.[46] These three broad divisions of philosophy give genesis to the other fields found listed in modern primers.[47]

CONCLUSION

Despite the lack of a universally agreed upon definition for philosophy, the question of what philosophy is can be answered through the examination of its nature. Philosophy, in essence, is the systematic study of ideas and issues, a reasoned pursuit of fundamental truths, a comprehensive understanding of the world, and so much more. Philosophy touches every

---

Ethics; Geisler, *Christian Ethics*; Holmes, *Ethics*; Lewis, *Abolition of Man*; Mitchell, C., *Ethics and Moral Reasoning*; Murray, *Principles of Conduct*.

43. For additional information on aesthetics, see Aristotle, *Poet.*; Munson, *Art and Music*; Schaeffer, F., *Art and the Bible*; Thiessen, G., *Theological Aesthetics*.

44. For additional information on socio-political, see Aristotle, *Pol.*; Augustine, *Civ.*; Baker, *Political Thought*; Grudem, *Politics According to the Bible*; Plato, *Pol.*; Plato, *Resp.*; Skillen, *Good of Politics*.

45. For additional information on logic and philosophy, see Bonevac, *Simple Logic*; Clark, *Logic*; Fisher, *Logic of Real Arguments*; Geisler and Brooks, *Come, Let Us Reason*; Polythess, *Logic*; Quine, *Methods of Logic*; Quine, *Philosophy of Logic*; Tidman and Kahane, *Logic and Philosophy*; Thompson, *Habits of the Mind*; Watts, *Logic*.

46. For a more in-depth description of epistemology, see Cook, "Epistemology," 225–26; Dew and Foreman, *How Do We Know*; MacGregor, "Epistemology," 220–21; Moser, "Epistemology," 273–78; Wood, *Epistemology*.

47. Even though I list the three main branches as Diogenes Laërtius catalogs them, this ordering is not concrete. Other philosophers flip the ordering in the second and third points. For example, Plato and Augustine both prefer to put epistemology before axiology. Regardless of how I or anyone else arranges the ordering of the major branches of philosophy, it is essential that everyone sees them as "facets of philosophy as a whole or three lenses through which we view that one discipline," as Randall Bush of Union University remarks in an exchange of emails with me. He is absolutely correct here on how people need to approach the study of philosophy. And one could argue that putting epistemology before axiology is more beneficial since it can aid in avoiding later philosophical problems that arise in the Enlightenment during the seventeenth and eighteenth centuries.

domain of human existence in some form or another. Indeed, philosophy is in a sense inescapable: human life confronts every thoughtful person with some perplexing questions, and nearly everyone is guided by idealistic assumptions, even if subconsciously.

Thus, studying philosophy is not an easy task. For an individual to understand philosophy, the person must have dedication and endurance because it embraces and encompasses numerous subject matters. Some individuals often deem philosophy as impractical and worthless because people do not easily see its value. Once one studies philosophy, its worth is understood. The study of philosophy enhances one's problem-solving abilities, the ability to understand and express abstract and difficult issues, and the ability to persuade others through well-constructed arguments.

Knowing what philosophy is aids in determining whether it has a place in the Christian's life. The next chapter elaborates further on this issue: the challenge of philosophy for the Christian. Chapter 2 approaches the topic by giving a biblical justification for Christians to study and use philosophy in their daily lives and through reflection on the faith-reason relationship.

2

Biblical Justification for Philosophy
Reflection on the Faith-Reason Relationship

> "We destroy arguments and every lofty opinion raised against the knowledge of God, and take every thought captive to obey Christ."
>
> —2 Corinthians 10:5

"God places no premium on ignorance."[1] Nowhere in either the Old or New Testament does Scripture tell believers to live their faith in ignorance. Faith may be more praiseworthy than reason because "without faith it is impossible to please God" (Heb 11:6). On the other hand, reason—a rational faith—may be more dignified because it examines the Scriptures to find truth (Acts 17:10–15).[2]

God compels Christians to use their intellectual capacities for his glory (Matt 22:37; Mark 12:30; 2 Cor 10:5; 1 Pet 1:13). At the same time, believers need discernment against worldly wisdom (1 Cor 1:20–25; 3:18–23; Col 2:8). The Bible repeatedly declares God's children are called to live by faith (Hab 2:4; Rom 1:7; Gal 3:11; Heb 10:38). Christians should not and cannot

---

1. Geisler and Feinberg, *Introduction to Philosophy*, 74.
2. The Bereans are characterized as being more dignified or receptive to the truth than the Christians at Thessalonica, because they examined the Scriptures daily to verify the truthfulness of Paul's teaching.

try to put faith and reason against each other because a false dichotomy emerges.³

Biblical warrant exists for the use of philosophy by Christians. Paul reasons with others from the Scriptures (Acts 14:14–17; 17:2, 22–31). In Philippians 1:7, Paul defends and establishes the gospel of Christ. Paul warns against false doctrine and teaching, and then he calls believers to contend for the faith (1 Tim 6:3–6, 11–16). Workers who receive God's approval stand firm in the faith. They need not be ashamed as they rightly handle Scripture and thus safeguard the church (2 Tim 2:14–16). Paul, in Titus 1:9, charges Christians to refute unsound doctrine. Christians need to be ready to give a defense for the hope they have (1 Pet 3:15).

How can an individual effectively refute false doctrine if the person is not capable of recognizing deceitful teachings? Simply put, those who do not see errors cannot refute them. Flawed teaching can only be refuted by those who recognize it and are adequately grounded in the Christian faith to respond. C. S. Lewis correctly notes:

> To be ignorant and simple now—not to be able to meet the enemies on their own ground—would be to throw down our weapons, and to betray our uneducated brethren who have, under God, no defence but us against the intellectual attacks of the heathen. Good philosophy must exist, if for no other reason, because bad philosophy needs to be answered.⁴

ESTABLISHING THE BIBLICAL BASIS FOR STUDYING PHILOSOPHY

Christians find biblical support for philosophy in the relationship between faith and reason. In Christian thought, however, tension between the two exists. The issue is rather simple. Should reason ground faith, or should faith govern reason?⁵

3. This topic is discussed in detail later in the chapter.
4. Lewis, *Weight of Glory*, 58.
5. Traditionally, philosophers address the issue in epistemology. Today, however, they discuss the friction within the area of philosophy of religion as well. Philosophy of religion is a modern branch of philosophy that examines issues related to religion and religious belief. For further information on this topic, see Evans and Manis, *Philosophy of Religion*; Geisler and Corduan, *Philosophy of Religion*; Helm, *Faith and Reason*; Helm, *Faith with Reason*; Nash, *Faith and Reason*; Plantinga, *Faith & Rationality*.

Biblical Justification for Philosophy

Throughout church history, Christian philosophers and theologians have disagreed on what best represents the teachings of the Bible. Some individuals favor reason over faith and seldom acknowledge faith as having any authority in obtaining knowledge. These people are referred to as Rationalists.[6] On the other hand, another group, referred to as Fideists, believes reason was destroyed because of the Fall. Fideism argues the human intellect is incapable of attaining any knowledge using reason alone.[7] Martin Luther wavers between the two positions.[8]

Questions arise when exploring the relationship between faith and reason. How should the believer view philosophy and its use? In the second century, Tertullian captured the essence of it when he penned his thought-provoking question: "What indeed has Athens have to do with Jerusalem?"[9] In fact, thinkers have asked Tertullian's question in one way or another throughout church history. People still find the faith-reason relationship interesting and crucial. Pope John Paul II addressed the topic in 1998 because the issue is very important.[10]

Christians must have a grasp on the proper biblical teaching on the relation between the two. As with any other issue, people have varying opinions on how faith and reason relate to each other. Through the centuries, theologians have relied on four primary interpretations to show how these concepts interconnect: faith *against* reason, faith *and* reason, faith *plus* reason, and faith *supports* reason.[11]

Before proceeding into these four positions, two fundamental matters need to be addressed. First, one needs to know how the Bible views reason. And second, the nature of faith needs discussion. Without a basic foundation established by defining these two terms, all further dialogue is in vain.

---

6. Garber, "Rationalism," 771–72; Geisler, "Rationalism," 29–46; MacGregor, "Rationalism," 524–25.

7. Boa and Bowman, *Faith Has Its Reasons*, 363–447; Geisler, "Fideism," 47–64; Hasker, "Evidentialism," 294; MacGregor, "Fideism," 250.

8. Althaus, *Theology of Martin Luther*; Becker, S., *Foolishness of God*; Bendtz, "Faith and Knowledge," 21–29; Bergvall, "Reason in Luther," 115–27; Breen, "Twofold Truth Theory," 69–92; Fischer, "Reasonable Luther," 30–45; Gerrish, *Grace and Reason*; Luther, *First Lectures on Psalms*, 11:285; Luther, *Sermons on Gospel of John*, 23:99; McGrath, *Luther's Theology*; Mitchell, J., "Through a Glass Darkly," 21–50; Robbins, "Luther on Reason," 191–202.

9. Tertullian, *Praescr.*, 7.

10. John Paul II, *Fides et Ratio*.

11. Cosgrove, *Foundations of Christian*, 55–57. Even though Cosgrove uses the word *learning* instead of reason in his discussion, he implies the notion of reason.

Believers need to know how one uses these key terms regardless what the dialogue is. Misunderstandings ran amuck if people fail to define essential words.

Biblical Reflection on Reason[12]

D. Martyn Lloyd-Jones proclaims, "There is no doubt that, in one sense, the highest gift that God has given to man is the gift of the mind."[13] According to Scripture, God created humans in his image (Gen 1:26-27; 9:6; Ps 8:3-8; 1 Cor 11:7). Theologians argue human beings have the capability to reason and think logically because God made them in his image.[14] Thus, the human mind is the seat of reason and decision-making (1 Chr 17:2; 2 Chr 7:11; Neh 5:7; Job 12:1-3; Pss 19:14; 49:3; Prov 15:28; 19:21; Eccl 2:3; 8:16; Dan 4:16; 5:12; 7:1; Rom 10:10; 14:5; 1 Cor 14:14-15; 1 Pet 1:13; Rev 17:9). Humans have the ability for thinking rationally. Therefore, not only do humans discover truth but also persuade others to accept an opposing viewpoint. Even though humans are rational beings, our reasoning has limitations (Job 11:7-9; 32:11-12; 32:3; 38:36-37; Eccl 3:11; 8:16-17; Ps 145:3; Isa 40:13, 28; 55:8-9; Acts 17:23; Rom 11:33-34; 1 Cor 1:20-21).

Our knowledge does not compare to God's (Job 12:20, 24-25; Isa 29:14; 55:8-9; 1 Cor 1:18-31). The Latin phrase *finitum non capax infiniti* declares God's knowledge as being superior—"the finite is incapable of the infinite."[15] Despite this obvious limitation, human reasoning can direct individuals to God to the point where they have the ability to know him and his character (Isa 1:18-20; Acts 17:22-23, 27; Rom 1:19-20; 2:14-15; Heb

---

12. For specific nuances of Greek terms used for *reason* and its related words, see the following articles: Harder, "nous," 3:122-30; Goetzmann, "synesis," 3:130-34; Fürst, "dialogizomai," 3:820-21; Müller, "dokeō," 3:821-22; Eichler, "logizomai," 3:822-26.

13. Lloyd-Jones, *Studies in the Sermon*, 369.

14. The notion of humans being created in the image of God is a crucial topic of study. Unfortunately for the purposes here, there is not ample space to do the topic justice. However, for further reading and discussion on what the image of God means, see Berkhof, "Man as the Image of God," 202-10; Bray, "Image of God," 575-76; Erickson, "Image of God," 517-36; Ferguson, "Image of God," 328-29; Grudem, "Creation of Man," 439-53; Henry, "Image of God," 545-49; Hoekema, *Created in God's Image*, 11-101; Hoeksema, "Man, Created," 77-86; Machen, *Christian View of Man*; Sherlock, "Focus 1," 27-91; Turner, "Image of God," 365-67.

15. Muller, "*Finitum non capax infiniti*," 119.

11:17–19). As finite beings, however, we lack the capabilities to comprehend fully God, the infinite.

Even though God created us in his image, the likeness is disfigured (Gen 3:1–24; Rom 3:23). The Fall impairs our ability to reason. Describing humanity's fallenness, the apostle Paul describes people's understanding as darkened, which results in them being "excluded from the life of God because of the ignorance that is in them, because of the hardness of their heart" (Eph 4:18). According to John Piper, an individual's hardness of heart leads to irrationality and spiritual ignorance.[16] "Our self-centered hearts distort our reason to the point where we cannot use it to draw true inferences from what is really there. If we don't want God to be God, our sensory faculties and our rational faculties will not be able to infer that he is God."[17] In other words, the fallen human mind confuses the Creator with his creation (Isa 44:16–18; Rom 1:21–25).

Despite its fallen condition, the human mind can still know something of God through creation (Rom 1:19–20). But our ability to reason is fatally flawed by sin (Gen 6:5–6; 8:21; 2 Chr 12:14; Pss 5:9; 64:6; 73:7; Eccl 9:3; Isa 32:6; Jer 17:1, 9; Rom 8:5–8; Eph 4:17–19). Scripture describes the mind as hardened (2 Cor 3:14) and depraved (1 Tim 6:5). Romans 1:21 characterizes human rationality as futile, darkened, and foolish because individuals choose to suppress the truth with unrighteousness (Rom 1:18).

Christians must not dismiss or ignore the reality of sin and its effects on the mental faculties of people.[18] In Colossians 1:21 Paul declares sin as hostility in the mind. The Fall did not obliterate human rationality; the consequences drastically impact how we think. God's intention goes beyond wanting people to understand and be able to communicate. God wants people to think through their actions before they act them out.[19] We, however, lack the capability to have our minds to govern our decisions fully because of the effects of sin. Lloyd-Jones writes:

> Man, as the result of sin and the Fall, is no longer governed by his mind and understanding; he is governed by his desires, his affections and his lusts. That is the teaching of Scripture. Thus we see that man is in a terrible predicament of being no longer

---

16. Piper, "Faith and Reason," lines 75.
17. Ibid., lines 76–79.
18. Green, "Theological and Philosophical," 67.
19. Lloyd-Jones, *Studies in the Sermon*, 369.

Part One: Prelude to Philosophy and Its Value for the Christian

governed by his highest faculty, but by something else, something subsidiary.[20]

Despite the fallen state of the mind, it is not destroyed.[21] The biblical writers provide evidence of this fact. They make logical inferences to ordinary things to establish a foundation for spiritual discussions.[22] The New Testament contains examples of the use of the mind. Paul employs reason in his efforts to convert unbelievers and to encourage believers (Acts 17:2–4, 17; 18:4, 19; 19:8–9; 20:7–9; 24:25; 1 Cor 14:9). Scripture's authors exhort believers to use their minds (Mark 12:30; 1 Cor 2:16; 2 Cor 10:5; Rom 12:1–2; 1 Pet 1:13; 3:15). God can change the attitudes of the sinful mind if he wills. He can convict the mind of sin (1 Kgs 2:44; Ps 51:3; John 16:8–11). Scripture testifies how the sinful mind can be transformed (2 Chr 32:26; Job 42:6; Ps 119:36; Acts 2:37; 26:17–18; 1 Thess 1:9). It is God—and God alone—who enlightens the mind (Deut 29:4 and 1 Cor 4:6). God may, however, choose to withhold understanding as well (1 Sam 10:9; Job 38:36; Isa 32:4; Jer 24:7; 31:33; 32:39; Ezek 11:19; 18:31; 36:26–27; Rom 2:4; 2 Cor 3:14). Furthermore, Scripture teaches God brings renewal to the mind (Ps 51:10; Titus 3:3–7). When one becomes a Christian, God begins to renew the mind so that one's rationale can be trusted (Rom 6:17). Once the process starts, the believer can receive and recognize truth from God. The Holy Spirit clears the mind to enable the proper interpretation of the truth.[23]

Since the Fall mars people's reasoning, what should one make of faith? What is the point of faith? Is there any reason to express faith in something? Or since one's reasoning is flawed, does that mean faith is more reliable and trustworthy?

Biblical Reflection on the Nature of Faith[24]

Many twentieth-century scholars regard faith as simple-mindedness and treat the word unfavorably. According to these individuals, faith is "an

---

20. Ibid., 370.

21. Erickson, *Christian Theology*, 644–48; Geisler, *Systematic Theology*, 3:147; Grudem, *Systematic Theology*, 490–511; Moreland, *Love the Lord*, 59–60.

22. Moreland and Craig, *Philosophical Foundations*, 18.

23. Lloyd-Jones, *Studies in the Sermon*, 376.

24. For specific nuances on the Greek word for *faith* and related words, see the following articles: Becker, O., "peithomai," 1:588–93; Michel, "pistis," 1:593–606.

Biblical Justification for Philosophy

expression of an uncritical spirit."[25] Is the twentieth-century sentiment the proper method for understanding faith? Scripture portrays faith in a much different light by showing it in a variety of ways. Saving faith is the only type of faith which truly matters.[26]

Before discussing the nature of faith, a definition for faith needs to be established. The writer of Hebrews defines faith as "the assurance of things hoped for, the conviction of things not seen" (Heb 11:1; cf. John 20:29; 2 Cor 4:18; Heb 11:1–3, 7, 27). Faith embraces a constant outlook of reliance toward the one true God, whereby one abandons all dependence on one's strength and puts full trust and dependence in God. Faith represents confidence in God and commitment to him, his word, and his promises despite any trials or blessings that may occur.

Whether individuals want to admit it or not, lives are lived on the premise of faith. Bishop Westcott in 1916 described faith as "the absolute condition of all of life, of all action, of all thought which goes beyond the limitations of our own minds," and he continues with all "live by faith however we live."[27] For example, we do not have a guarantee the sun will rise tomorrow, yet everyone makes plans for tomorrow. Every time individuals get on an airplane, they implicitly express faith that the aircraft will stay in the sky until the pilot lands at the final destination.

The question, then, becomes: what is the object of one's faith? Faith always has an object. The believer sees God as the object of their faith. More precisely, the object of their faith is the person and work of Jesus Christ (Pss 25:1–2; 26:1; Prov 29:25; John 3:16, 18, 36; 6:68–69; 14:1, 6; Heb 11:6; 1 Pet 1:21). Unbelievers place their trust in objects of faith as well. They might place their faith in human resources (Ps 20:27; Hos 10:13), other people (Ps 118:9), themselves (Prov 28:36), or idols—whether money, a job, etc. (Isa 42:17).

By faith Christians place trust in God (2 Sam 22:31; Pss 18:2–6; 27:13–14; 1 Pet 2:23). For faith to be authentic, it cannot be second-hand (John 4:42; 2 Tim 1:5). In other words, each individual must have a personal relationship with God. We cannot be saved based on the faith of our parents or grandparents. Both the Old and New Testaments speak of the call of

---

25. Martin, G. W., "Faith," 246.

26. As crucial as saving faith is, this particular faith is not the type of faith with which this section is primarily concerned. Therefore, the notion of being justified by faith will not be examined.

27. Bishop Westcott, *Spectator*, 7.

faith (Ps 37:3–5; Prov 3:5–6; Isa 26:4; 50:10; Mark 1:15; John 6:28–29; Acts 16:30–31; 19:4; 20:21; Rom 1:5; 1 John 3:23). Faith becomes a necessity in both temporal and spiritual matters because faith contains a personal element.[28]

The Lord is the *only* true God (Ps 115:2–11; Hab 2:18–20). God alone can be trusted absolutely (Pss 9:10; 91:1–4; Isa 12:2; Nah 1:7). God's self-revelation leaves no excuse for unbelief (Pss 19:4; 51:4; John 1:10–12; 14:8–11; Rom 1:18–21; 3:1–4; 10:17–18; 16:25–27). Just as the improper use of reason is sinful, actions that do not stem from faith are sinful (Rom 14:23). A person's lack of faith and subsequent unbelief is to be challenged (Ps 95:7–8; Isa 7:9; Jer 17:5–6; Mark 16:4; Heb 3:12–18). Since God's self-revelation leaves no excuse for unbelief that in turn leaves no excuse for lack of faith, then why do people lack genuine faith?

Before addressing a lack of faith, the origin of faith must be established. God gives faith as a gift (Matt 16:15–17; Mark 9:24; Luke 17:5; Acts 3:16; 14:27; 18:27; Rom 12:3; 1 Cor 4:7; 12:9; Eph 2:8–9; Phil 1:29; Jas 2:5). As a gift, humans cannot obtain faith through their own doing or intellectual pursuits. Faith comes through God's Word or after a direct revelation from God (Exod 14:15; Josh 6:2–5; Isa 52:7; John 1:17; 2:22; 4:41–42; 17:20; 20:30–31; Acts 11:19–21; 27:23–25; Rom 10:14–17; 1 Cor 2:4–5; 1 Tim 3:15; Heb 11:29–30). A personal encounter with Christ leads to faith (John 9:35–38; 20:26–28). Knowledge of God's faithfulness (Ps 46:1–3; Lam 3:19–24; Nah 1:7; Acts 2:25–26) and achievements can lead to faith (Deut 3:21–22; 1 Sam 17:34–37; Jer 14:22).

Is there any responsibility connected with God's gift of faith? God expects Christians to grow in their faith. The Bible rebukes those who have a weak faith (Matt 6:28–30; 8:26; 14:31; 16:8; 17:20; Mark 4:40; Luke 8:25; 12:27–28; John 12:42–43; 19:38; Rom 14:1–2; 1 Cor 8:1–13). And Scripture commends and encourages individuals to have a strong faith, one growing in maturity (Matt 8:10; 9:20–22; 15:28; Mark 5:25–34; 7:29; Luke 7:9; 8:43–48; Heb 10:22). Faith grows in several ways. First, growth in faith can occur as an answer to prayer. Scripture encourages believers to pray for more faith (Mark 9:24; Luke 17:5). Second, faith grows through the encouragement of others (Num 14:6–9; 2 Chr 32:7–8; Luke 2:32; Acts 14:22; Rom 1:11–12; 1 Tim 3:2–3, 10; Jude 1:20). Faith grows stronger through times of testing (Gen 15:15; Rom 4:18–21; Jas 1:2–4; 1 Pet 1:6–7). The testing of faith is the means by which the genuineness of faith is either proved or

---

28. Hastings, *Christian Doctrine*, 15–17.

disproved (Matt 13:20–21; Mark 4:16–17; Luke 8:13; 1 Pet 1:6–7). Through the testing of faith, a believer's character develops (Rom 5:3–4; Jas 1:2–4). God promises to be there to assist his children during difficult times and trials (Ps 91:14–15; Isa 43:2; Luke 22:32; 1 Cor 10:13; 2 Cor 12:7–9; 1 Pet 5:10; 2 Pet 2:9). In 2 Corinthians 7:5–7 and 1 Thessalonians 3:2–3, we see where God's aid is through the encouragement of others. Testing of faith purifies God's people (Ps 66:10–12; Isa 48:10; Jer 9:7; Zech 13:9; Mal 3:2–3; 1 Pet 4:17).

By what means is faith tested? God uses a variety of methods to test one's faith. Discouraging and trying people can be the means of testing (2 Kgs 18:19–25; 2 Chr 32:10–15; Isa 36:4–10; Matt 9:24; Mark 5:35–36, 40; Luke 8:49–50, 53). Difficult times and circumstances can try one's faith (1 Kgs 17:17–18; 2 Kgs 4:1, 17–28; Acts 14:22; 2 Cor 11:25–27). Times of persecution further tests faith (Dan 6:10–12; Acts 8:1–4; Heb 11:35–38). God will ever allow Satan to test one's faith without permission to do so (Job 2:7; Luke 22:31; 1 Thess 3:4–5; Rev 2:10). Believers can respond to these trials in several ways. First, we can rejoice at sharing Christ's suffering (1 Pet 4:12–13). Second, we can pray for God's help (Heb 4:14–16; 1 Pet 4:19). Third, we can persevere through the trial (2 Thess 1:4; Heb 12:1–3; Jas 1:12; 5:11; Rev 2:3, 19).

With the preliminary thoughts on biblical reflection of reason and the nature of faith complete, a question remains. How should faith and reason be joined? Faith anticipates reason, which perfects faith. What is true knowledge? This is justified true belief. "The fear of the Lord is the beginning of knowledge," which can only start with faith in the Lord. Without the use of reason, faith cannot be explained in a reasonable manner. This is why faith precedes reason. For knowledge to be accepted as truth, the learning process requires faith as its foundation. In other words, faith is the only means by which human beings can apprehend knowledge.[29] Historically, Christian thinkers have held one of four chief views on the proper relationship between the two. The question ultimately becomes: what view does the biblical data support?

---

29. Martin, G. W., "Faith," 247.

FOUR VIEWS ON THE RELATIONSHIP
BETWEEN FAITH AND REASON

At times people argue faith and reason are incompatible with each other, and matters of faith do not exhibit rational thinking. This perspective presents an unbiblical understanding of what biblical faith is. The Reformers teach there are three facets of biblical faith: *notitia, assensus,* and *fiducia*.[30] Faith begins with the intellectual element of faith, knowledge (*notitia*), which involves recognition and a simplistic grasp of basic teachings of Christianity. You must place your faith in something or someone. What a person believes matters. Trusting the wrong person or believing incorrect information has eternal consequences.[31] The second aspect of faith, *assensus*, is, in essence, the awakening of the soul to the personal acceptance of the *notitia* of the Christian faith. A person must be persuaded by the truthfulness of the content, according to James and 1 John. The devil and his demons know the truth concerning Christ. *Fiducia* is the logical outgrowth of the first two facets of biblical faith. This element of faith includes the surrender of one's heart to God and the acceptance of Christ as Savior.[32] Biblical faith is never a blind, irrational faith. This being the case, faith and reason are not hostile to each other; rather, they cooperate for a biblical faith.

Christian thinkers recognize faith as an expression of reason and knowledge. But faith encapsulates more. Historic Christianity understands faith as the necessary prerequisite for all true knowledge. For example, how do you know the chair in which you are currently sitting will hold you up? You have sat in a chair countless times since childhood, and it did not collapse on you. But the first time you sat in a chair as a young child it took a small amount of faith to believe the chair would hold you. Faith is "an inescapable element of all human understanding," notes Carl F. H. Henry.[33] The Bible treats humanity as capable of obtaining knowledge and understanding it, as well as being responsible for lacking a proper comprehension

---

30. Althaus, *Theology of Martin Luther*, 43–63, 110–15, 130–36, 211–18, 429–45; Calvin, *Institutes of the Christian*, 1:542–92; George, *Theology of the Reformers*, 59, 70–71, 225–26, 326.

31. Erickson and McMaken, *Does It Matter?*

32. Moreland and Craig, *Philosophical Foundations*, 18; Ryrie, *Basic Theology*, 327; Thiessen, H., *Lectures in Systematic Theology*, 271–73.

33. Henry, *God, Revelation and Authority*, 1:169.

of it.[34] Neither reason nor faith should be ignored. Both coexist within the pages of the Bible.

Unfortunately, some Christians have the perception that philosophy fundamentally opposes Christianity and believe it pointless to discuss how philosophy aids the Christian faith. Those who argue against the use of reason see knowledge and reason as a challenge to faith.[35] As a sophomore in high school, my European History teacher introduced me to philosophy. When I went off to college, I decided to take an introductory course in philosophy my first semester. I recall sitting in Ingram Dining Hall at the University of Mobile as a freshman debating classmates on the incompatibility of Christianity and philosophy. I appealed to the same passages from the New Testament that many others go to for biblical support against philosophy: Colossians 2:8 and 1 Corinthians 1:18—2:16. Over the course of time, God showed me the errors of my thinking through several gracious friends and professors.

Faith *against* Reason

"See to it that no one takes you captive through philosophy and empty deception" (Col 2:8). Those who oppose the use and study of philosophy appeal to these words of Paul as their key biblical support.[36] The mantra of real estate is "location, location, location." As believers, context needs priority. Think of it in the mathematical formula: context^6. As you see, there are six different contexts one needs to consider when determining how a passage of Scripture means. It is never wise to take a single verse out of its context to determine its proper meaning.

Those appealing to Paul's words stop reading here, and they do not read the entire verse in its full context. Colossians 2:8 has six different contexts in which one must read the passage before concluding Paul argues against all use of philosophy. Its immediate context—the paragraph in which the verse falls—needs examining. The second level encompasses the chapter. The entire book of Colossians is the third level. The fourth level entails the rest of the Paul's writings. The fifth level broadens the scope of the entire New Testament. Finally, the entire scope of the Old Testament needs to be examined as well. Often, however, a passage's proper meaning does not

---

34. Sire, *Discipleship of the Mind*, 94.
35. Davis, J. H., "Faith and Learning," 134–35.
36. Green, "Theological and Philosophical," 80.

Part One: Prelude to Philosophy and Its Value for the Christian

need to go beyond looking at the third or fourth level. Scholars refer to this process of biblical interpretation as the principles of hermeneutics, which is a fancy word for the process of discovering an interpretation.[37]

When one reads Colossians 2:8 in its proper context, one will notice Paul argues for Christians finding their sufficiency in Christ, not in other things.[38] When one reads its broader context, one realizes the verse is not a prohibition *against all* philosophy. Paul warns us about a particular type of philosophy—empty and deceptive philosophy—which infiltrates the church of Colossae. Thus, Paul cautions the church how she cannot develop her doctrinal views and teachings based upon any philosophical system hostile to orthodoxy. Paul's warning is a caution against heresy.[39] Finally, a logical issue emerges here as well: one cannot beware of problematic philosophy unless one has an awareness of a potential problem emerging.[40] We must recognize error before being able to counter it. On numerous occasions the church has been affected by heretical teachings because individuals failed to detect and refute it. Learning how to recognize the logical errors in people's thoughts and arguments can protect against bad philosophy.

Some believers also cite the opening chapters of 1 Corinthians as scriptural support against philosophy, specifically 1:18—2:16. Here Paul argues against the wisdom of the world. He admits he did not visit the church at Corinth with persuasive words of wisdom (1 Cor 2:1–5). As a result of this, some individuals presume human reasoning and apologetics are ineffective in sharing the gospel message, according to J. P. Moreland.[41] Paul does make a contrast here but not between the rational and irrational use of human reason as some individuals argue. The contrast exists between human wisdom and divine wisdom.[42]

---

37. Theologically this process is referred to as the *Analogy of Faith*. This theological teaching states the proper biblical interpretation will be in full agreement with the rest of the Word of God. In other words, the meaning of a biblical passage will not contradict another passage of Scripture. For more on the principles of biblical hermeneutics, see Hendricks and Hendricks, *Living by the Book*; Fee and Stuart, *How to Read*.

38. Bruce, F., *Epistles to Colossians*, 94–113.

39. Ibid.; Geisler and Howe, *When Critics Ask*, 487–88; Green, "Theological and Philosophical," 80; Moreland, *Love the Lord*, 59.

40. Geisler and Feinberg, *Introduction to Philosophy*, 73.

41. Moreland, *Love the Lord*, 58.

42. Stott, *Your Mind*, 22–23.

Like Colossians 2:8, the passage must be read in context. When read in its broader context, several reasons emerge showing why they do not provide biblical warrant against philosophy. First, if Paul makes an indictment against philosophical reasoning here, he would contradict his practices in Acts 14:14–17 and 17:22–31, as well as his logical appeal to Christ's resurrection in 1 Corinthians 15. In each of these instances, the apostle Paul clearly appeals to rational and philosophical arguments. Second, when one does the proper reading on the passage, one discovers Paul does not argue against the use of philosophy or even reason. What Paul argues against is the prideful use of philosophy—autonomous reasoning.[43]

Neither Colossians 2:8 nor 1 Corinthians 1–2 give the Christian validation to ignore the use of human reason or philosophy. What these two pivotal passages speak against is the improper use of them. Christians should not partake in prideful, empty, or deceptive philosophy. Christians are to love the Lord God with their entire mind. They do this by using their intellect and understanding (Mark 12:30). These passages reveal Christ is to have complete lordship in our lives, including lordship over our minds.[44]

Another crucial issue arises with this solution to the problem. Faith *against* reason teaches Scripture is the only authority and source of knowledge. Hence, the general revelation of God tends to be ignored.[45] If God intended for general revelation to be ignored completely, he would not have given it. It is unfortunate there are individuals who concede their faith is indefensible. Those who hold such a position often say what they believe is *beyond reason* as an attempt to avoid the problem outright.[46] "If evidence for it could be given, it would not be faith but knowledge. Faith has no rational foundation, these Christians say; it is a direct and personal experience of the living God."[47]

The Bible does not ask believers to abandon the use of reason in accepting truth.[48] There is, in fact, a scriptural mandate telling people to use reason: "'Come now, and let us reason together,' says the Lord" (Isa 1:18).

---

43. Fee, *First Epistle to Corinthians*, 27–120; Moreland and Craig, *Philosophical Foundations*, 18–19.
44. Green, "Theological and Philosophical," 80.
45. Cosgrove, *Foundations of Christian*, 55–56.
46. Noebel, *Understanding the Times*, 159. See also Williams, *Life of the Mind*, 11.
47. Williams, *Life of the Mind*, 11.
48. McDowell and Hostetler, *Don't Check Your Brains*.

Since believers should not forsake the use of reason, how should the Christian understand the relation between faith and reason?

Faith *and* Reason

The second way Christian thinkers attempt to reconcile the faith-reason relationship depicts faith and reason as "merely parallel categories."[49] The approach here, in essence, sees a dichotomy between the two. Unfortunately, some Christian thinkers often insist faith and reason are completely independent of each other, lacking a connection between them. When individuals attempt to reconcile the relationship in this manner, they argue for faith and reason to remain distinctly separate.[50] Phrasing the reconciliation as faith *and* reason purports a dichotomy between the two concepts. Faith becomes one side of the pendulum, and reason becomes the other.

If faith and reason are, in fact, to be understood as opposites, then how ought the two be joined? Or are the two joined only in the mind of God, while the finite human mind is incapable of joining faith and reason?[51] If the latter is the case, then it is pointless to go any further in the discussion seeking to find a biblical understanding on how the two are related because any attempt to do so would be in vain.

In essence, faith and reason are not opposed to each other. Faith acknowledges one mode of truth, and reason reveals another source of truth. Things of faith, spiritual things, have their root in Scripture, and everything else has its roots in general revelation.[52] An unnecessary and false opposition arises when people see faith and reason as two independent categories. The established dichotomy is a relatively recent phenomenon in church history with its roots grounded in the philosophical thought of the Enlightenment.[53] In the past few decades, a renaissance amongst some to integrate faith and reason has occurred. This movement sees both faith and reason functioning as sources of truth.

Scripture does not support this approach of reconciliation. Some individuals prefer to say reason precedes faith; others argue faith precedes reason. Is there any difference biblically speaking? Does it really matter

---

49. Dorman, "*Fides Quaerens Intellectum*, 58.
50. Davis, J. H., "Faith and Learning," 134–35.
51. Dorman, "*Fides Quaerens Intellectum*," 58.
52. Cosgrove, *Foundations of Christian*, 56.
53. Ibid. See also Dorman, *Faith for All Seasons*, 9; Pannenberg, "How to Think."

Biblical Justification for Philosophy

which one comes first? The apostle Peter believes and teaches faith precedes reason and everything else ought to supplement one's faith (2 Pet 1:3–11). For some thinkers, the problem emerges because of the usage of the term *reason*, which is the language philosophers prefer. With seeking to remain as biblical as possible, perhaps I should use the word *light* because it carries a fuller grasp of what the term reason means in philosophical discourse; the term carries notions of wisdom, understanding, and knowledge.[54] But in reality, no need exists for splitting hairs over semantics. Forsaking the term *reason* in this discussion, if one acknowledges a fuller understanding of it, is pointless. Scripture always sees light as a function of faith. "For the fear of the Lord is the beginning of knowledge" (Prov 1:7; cf. Job 28:28; Ps 111:10; Prov 9:10; 15:33; Eccl 12:13). The Bible urges people to seek wisdom and understanding.

Faith *plus* Reason

Faith *plus* reason acknowledges harmony occurs between the Scripture and other areas of study. In other words, a correlation between faith and reason exists. Faith functions as a means of truth, and reason functions as another means to obtain truth. The goal of acknowledging faith and reason as both being sources of truth is to join the two together for greater truth.[55]

This way of solving the faith-reason problem acknowledges both general and special revelation. Certain truths unveil themselves in the general revelation of God, such as how the heavens declare God's glory (Ps 19:1–6). On the other hand, only God's special revelation reveals other truths, such as his specific plan to restore humanity into a right relationship with him, which is the overarching theme of the Bible. Despite the fact faith plus reason acknowledges both general and special revelation, difficulty arises on how the two relate to each other.[56] Because of this difficulty, people can call faith *plus* reason as an improper relationship.

While faith plus reason acknowledges both general and special revelation, the approach moves towards the right direction. At least this perspective attempts to reconcile properly the two concepts, even though problems emerge within its explanation. The attempt to reconcile the issue is better than the previous two attempts. A better way of understanding the relation

---

54. McComiskey, "emphanizō," 2:488–90; Brown, C., "phōs," 2:490–96.
55. Cosgrove, *Foundations of Christian*, 56–57.
56. Ibid., 57.

between faith and reason does exist. Augustine of Hippo formulates a solution to the faith-reason conflict, which many people accept throughout church history, including Anselm and Calvin.

Faith *supports* Reason

Blaise Pascal—renowned French mathematician, physicist, and religious philosopher—notes, "we know the truth not only through our reason but also through our heart. It is through the latter that we know first principles, and reason, which has nothing to do with it, tries in vain to refute them."[57] Winfried Corduan picks up the same motif when he writes:

> "Faith *that*" is the intellectual category . . . [by which] we mean an immediate assent to the truth of a proposition without any epistemological tests. As soon as a testing procedure is introduced, the faculty of reason is involved. . . . "Faith *that*" is not contrary to reason . . . "Faith *that*" is an important facet of human knowledge. We believe many things to be true on just that basis. . . . no one's beliefs are completely based on rational grounds.[58]

Both Pascal and Corduan follow in the thoughts of Augustine of Hippo on the proper understanding on how to solve the faith-reason dilemma. Augustine believed *faith is the essential prerequisite for all understanding and knowledge.* In other words, faith precedes reason. The faith supports reason position sees faith as the foundation for all pursuits of knowledge.[59]

Augustine's impact upon philosophical and theological thought cannot be overstated. His teachings are pivotal in the development of the dogma of the Roman Catholic Church, in the establishment of Christian orthodoxy, and significantly impact many of the church's greatest thinkers, both Roman Catholic and Protestant.[60] Augustine has, in essence, profoundly influenced the universal church in one way or another with his keen insights. Hence, studying Augustine's thoughts on the proper association of

---

57. Pascal, *Pensées*, 28 (*Pensée* 110) and 140–42 (*Pensée* 449).

58. Corduan, *Handmaid to Theology*, 72.

59. Cosgrove, *Foundations of Christian*, 57.

60. Augustine's teachings were vital in the philosophical and theological formation of the some of the greatest thinkers of Christianity: Anselm of Canterbury, Thomas Aquinas, Blaise Pascal, Martin Luther, Thomas Cramer, John Calvin, Jonathan Edwards, John Owen, J. Gresham Machen, Benjamin B. Warfield, James Montgomery Boice, J. I. Packer, and others.

faith and reason is beneficial, especially since he developed the solution to the faith-reason problem that has been accepted throughout church history as the proper relationship between the two. Augustine's emphasis on the philosophical problem in his homilies, sermons, and treatises highlights the topic's significance.

Augustine was fond of writing the Latin imperative *Crede ut intelligas*, which translates as "believe in order that you may understand."[61] If he did not use the phrase explicitly, Augustine implies its meaning in his thoughts.[62] The phrase summarizes Augustine's understanding of the proper relation between faith and reason. One can only wonder if Augustine came to this conclusion from the Septuagint rendering of the latter part of Isaiah 7:9, which reads, "and if you do not put your faith in, you will not live."[63]

No conflict or tension subsists between faith and reason for Augustine because faith and reason are complementary. Faith is more than mere trust. To know anything, one must have faith in something. According to Augustine, all knowledge begins on the premise of faith since faith is the necessary prerequisite for understanding. Faith serves as the foundation for all knowledge, and faith operates as an indispensable element of and for all knowledge.[64] Faith acts similar to a testimony or authority, functioning as indirect means of knowledge. Augustine pens, "there are two different methods, authority and reason. Authority demands belief and prepares man for reason. Reason leads to understanding and knowledge. But reason is not entirely absent from authority, for we have got to consider whom we have to believe, and the highest authority belongs to truth when it is clearly known."[65] While Augustine did not believe reason would cause or necessarily lead one to faith, he did believe reason supports faith in totality.

---

61. Muller, "*Crede, ut intelligas*," 85.

62. *Crede ut intelligas* appears twice in Augustine's *Serm.*, 43.7, 9. This is only one source in which the principle behind it is found. See also the following works of Augustine for additional insights into his thoughts on the subject matter: *Mag.*; *Lib.*; *Ver. rel.*; *Util. cred.*; *Fid. symb.*; *Trin.*

63. The Septuagint Greek translation is the author's. Most modern translations have the basic meaning this translation expresses. But they smooth out the reading in the latter part by stating something to the effect that one will not stand firm or be established, which is in the meaning of the imperfect tense of the last verb to live. Augustine, in fact, quotes this verse twice in *Lib.*, 1.2.4 and 2.6, and at least once in *Mag.*, xi.37.

64. Augustine, *Trin.*, 9.1.1.

65. Augustine, *Ver. rel.*, xxiv, 45.

Augustine argues further how Christians should seek to use their reasoning faculties of reason to grasp great truths and doctrines of Scripture. Hence, Augustine's principle on the proper relation between faith and reason is *Crede ut intelligas*.[66] How does Anselm of Canterbury understand the relationship?

Anselm of Canterbury followed Augustine's solution to the faith-reason enigma. Reason alone is liable to error. Faith is an absolute requirement and the criterion for all rationale. Anselm writes in the opening chapter of his work *Proslogion*: "For I do not seek to understand in order to believe, but I believe in order to understand. For this too I believe, that 'unless I believe, I shall not understand.'"[67] The principle *Intelligo ut credam*,[68] "I understand in order to believe," is no less true than the phrase *Credo ut intelligam*, "I believe in order to understand."[69] While the statements complement each other, Anselm stresses the latter as his principle on the relation between faith and reason. Anselm further notes, "While the right order requires that we should believe the deep things of the Christian faith before we undertake to discuss them by reason, it seems careless for us, once we are established in the faith, not to aim at understanding what we believe."[70] Anselm's *Credo ut intelligam* is in essence nothing more than an echo of Augustine's *Crede ut intelligas*. What about John Calvin on the matter?

John Calvin deals with the topic in the first five chapters of his *Institutes of the Christian Religion*. Calvin concludes it is impossible to have an understanding of anything, including humanity's predicament, without knowing who God is first.[71] Ted M. Dorman states, "a firm conviction of the existence and nature of God . . . is the foundation of all other knowledge."[72]

---

66. For additional reading on Augustine's theory on the proper relation of faith and reason, as well as his general theory on epistemology, see the following sources: Brown, C., *Christianity & Western Thought*, 1:93–99; Copleston, *History of Philosophy*, 2:40–90; Hankey, "Ratio, Reason, Rationalism," 696–702; Nash, *Light of the Mind*; Nash, *Life's Ultimate Questions*, 140–66; Nash, "Christian Rationalism," 79–90; TeSelle, "Faith," 347–50; Warfield, "Augustine's Doctrine," 135–225.

67. Anselm, *Proslogion*, 73 (chapter 1).

68. *Intelligo ut credam* is the formula adopted by Scholasticism. Peter Abelard adopted this principle as their motto on the correlation between faith and reason. Thomas Aquinas adopted this principle as well; however, he saw it as complementary to *Credo ut intelligam*.

69. Muller, "*Credo, ut intelligam*," 86.

70. Anselm, *Cur Deus homo*, 1.1.2.

71. Calvin, *Institutes of the Christian*, 1.1–5.

72. Dorman, "*Fides Quaerens Intellectum*," 59.

The consensus of historic Christianity is that faith is the necessary precondition for all knowledge and understanding. Therefore, the principle accepted throughout church history is *fides quaerens intellectum*, faith seeking understanding.[73]

Does this position have the support of Scripture? If Scripture does not support this understanding of the faith-reason challenge, then it does not matter if church history does. Historic Christianity has not always been equivalent to biblical Christianity. What follows is a brief reflection on the proper relation between faith and reason according to Scripture.

BIBLICAL REFLECTION ON THE FAITH-REASON RELATIONSHIP

Anselm's *fides quaerens intellectum* does agree with biblical Christianity's position. Remember Scripture teaches Christians must live by faith and cannot ignore reason. Numerous passages stress how individuals have to use their minds. The apostle Paul's apologetic ministry illustrates the reality (Acts 17:2-4, 17; 18:4, 19; 19:8-9; 20:7-9; 24:25). Paul's writings further support the position (1 Cor 2:16; 2 Cor 10:5; Rom 12:1-2; Eph 4:17-24; Col 2:8; 2 Tim 2:7).

Paul writes in 2 Timothy 2:7: "*Consider* what I say, for *the Lord will give you understanding* in everything" (emphasis added).[74] John Piper believes the verse unveils itself as perhaps the most beneficial concerning the proper faith-reason relationship, more specifically the role of reason and divine illumination.[75] One can easily distort Paul's words and intent here. Some individuals prefer to stress the first half of the verse ("Consider what I say"), which emphasizes the indispensable role of reason and minimizes the supernatural role of God's illuminating work. On the other hand, some people emphasize the futility of reason apart from God's divine illumination by

---

73. For further discussion on the expression *fides quaerens intellectum*, see Miller, "Faith in Search," 134-37.

74. Other modern translations will use either *think* or *reflect* instead of *consider* in this verse. It does not matter whether one uses think, reflect, or consider to translate Paul's imperative; each of these three words rightly conveys the Greek. See footnote 12 in this chapter for a list of articles related to this point.

75. Piper, "Faith and Reason," lines 91-100.

stressing the second half of the verse: "the Lord will give you understanding in everything."[76]

Piper correctly observes people cannot divide Paul's thoughts in this manner. It is not an issue of *either-or*, as some would like to think. Rather, it is an issue of *both-and*. "The willingness of God to give us understanding is the *ground* of our thinking, not the substitute for our thinking."[77] Hence, there is no reason to think God will grant us understanding if we do not reflect on the matter. Likewise, the opposite is true. There is no reason to believe God will grant understanding if we just think on the matter without prayerfully trusting that God provides illumination.[78]

Christians have a mandate to use their mental faculties. When believers encounter the Word of God, they need to engage their minds. Failure to do so can have eternal consequences. Christ makes this point in his parable of the sower:

> "Hear then the parable of the sower. *When anyone hears the word of the kingdom and does not understand it, the evil one comes and snatches away what has been sown in his heart.* This is the one on whom seed was sown beside the road. The one on whom seed was sown on the rocky places, this is the man who hears the word and immediately receives it with joy; yet he has no firm root in himself, but is only temporary, and when affliction or persecution arises because of the word, immediately he falls away. And the one on whom seed was sown among the thorns, this is the man who hears the word, and the worry of the world and the deceitfulness of wealth choke the word, and it becomes unfruitful. *And the one on whom seed was sown on the good soil, this is the man who hears the word and understands it*; who indeed bears fruit and brings forth, some a hundredfold, some sixty, and some thirty." (Matt 13:18–23, emphasis added)

It is, then, of vital importance that one understands with the mind. This is not optional.

Scripture supports the fact faith and reason are complementary. Furthermore, the Bible teaches that faith precedes all knowledge, reason, and understanding. Human reason, however, plays only an indispensable, *not the decisive*, role in establishing faith of any kind. God calls Christians to use reason when explaining and defending the gospel.

76. Ibid.
77. Ibid., lines 102–4.
78. Ibid., lines 104–7.

CONCLUSION

Tension will always continue between faith and reason. The philosophical problem will not be solved anytime soon. Philosophers and theologians have debated over the proper faith-reason relationship for centuries now. And philosophers and theologians will write more volumes on the topic in years to come. But certain truths will not change in the debate.

The doctrine of creation affirms God created human beings as intelligent and rational beings, since he created them in his image. Creation further reveals there are not only discoveries to be made about the world but a creator exists—who is knowable. But since the fall, our mental faculties have been flawed, though not totally destroyed.

The question ultimately is not if reason can be trusted or if faith can be trusted, for both can lead one astray if misunderstood or misapplied. The question is how faith and reason should be *properly* understood. Scripture encourages us to use our rationale. The Bible does not support the denial of the use of reason. Scripture discourages the improper use of reason. God's word also declares we must live by faith.

The question of the relationship between faith and reason is one that must be faced by every thoughtful Christian. Should philosophy have a role in the Christian's life? Philosophy presents a unique challenge for the Christian. The Christian needs to think critically, clearly, correctly, and comprehensively about God's creation. Christians, furthermore, have a unique philosophical burden because of our basic biblical beliefs. A follower of Christ must also think biblically. To accomplish this task, the Christian needs philosophy for the systemization of those beliefs into a coherent, consistent worldview, as well as communicating the perspective. Philosophy, throughout church history, is the tool by which Christianity formulated orthodox doctrine and defended the gospel of Christ against attacks from within and from without the church. Christ is the eternal Logos (John 1:1–14), the source of epistemology and the author and perfecter of faith (Heb 12:2). Philosophy assists the believer to proclaim faithfully this truth.

3

Christianity and Philosophy
Influence of Philosophy within Christianity

> "'Come now, let us reason together,'
> says the Lord."
>
> —Isaiah 1:18

"Beware that no one takes you captive through philosophy and empty deceit, according to the traditions of man, with the principles of the world, and not after Christ" (Col 2:8).[1] In the previous chapter, I showed how this verse must be read in its fuller context to be understood properly. The verse does not provide warrant for believers to ignore philosophy. Paul's exhortation, however, is as imperative for Christians today as when it was penned.

Individuals need to exercise discernment when studying any topic. As believers we would hope that everything we find on the shelves of Christian bookstores is edifying to the body of Christ. Being found in a Christian bookstore, however, does not mean its contents are biblical or it should be read. I cannot express the frustration I go through at times while at a Christian bookstore better than how Winfried Corduan phrased it: "In fact,

---

1. This rendering of Col 2:8 is the author's translation of the Greek text found in *Greek New Testament*.

sometimes one feels like a Diogenes with his lamp looking for one decent book in a so-called Christian bookstore."[2]

In my personal library, I have a wide range of books, including some titles that might shock people because of the intent of the authors and what they promote. For example, I have a four-foot section that focuses on atheistic arguments against religious belief. The best way to defend against opposing viewpoints and arguments is actually to know what those positions are through first-hand knowledge.

Paul's warning in Colossians 2:8 is clear. Inherent dangers exist for those without a solid foundation established in the word. It is vital one knows what one believes before examining opposing perspectives. Christ, himself, discusses this very point in Matthew 7:24–27:

> Everyone then who hears these words of mine and does them will be like a wise man who built his house on the rock. And the rain fell, and the floods came, and the winds blew and beat on that house, but it did not fall, because it had been founded on the rock. And everyone who hears these words of mine and does not do them will be like a foolish man who built his house on the sand. And the rain fell, and the floods came, and the winds blew and bet against the house, and it fell, and great was the fall of it.

At least one course in philosophy is now, and for generations has been, part of the education curriculum of those preparing for Christian ministry. Geisler notices Paul's warning is "not only true for Christians who call themselves philosophers but for those who do not, especially for biblical exegetes."[3] I would argue with Paul's warning in Colossians 2:8 applying to all those who claim Christ as Lord.

A survey of the history of philosophy reveals that no philosophical system is totally complete and perfect; therefore, it is dangerous for Christians to align their faith too closely with any single philosophical system. We can see the dangers of doing so throughout church history. In fact, there have been periods of time when Christianity lined up with nearly all philosophical systems—Aristotelianism, Existentialism, Idealism, Neo-Platonism, Platonism, Rationalism, and others. Colin Brown warns the danger of aligning Christianity too closely with a single philosophical

---

2. Winfried Corduan sent me this sentence in an email correspondence on November 28, 2015, as an illustration of how believers can feel as they glance over the shelves at a Christian bookstore.

3. Geisler, "Beware of Philosophy," 3–19.

system is twofold. The Christian faith has to be manipulated to fit into any single philosophical system. Moreover, when a fatal flaw is found within that philosophical system, it gives the impression Christianity likewise must collapse with it.[4] All this is not to say there is no value whatsoever in philosophy for the Christian. Brown goes on to note there is value in irreligious philosophy. This type of philosophy stimulates Christian thinkers to reexamine their position.[5]

A survey of church history exposes the crucial role philosophy plays in the formation and articulation of Christian doctrine, the proclamation and defense of the gospel, as well as the nurturing of believers. Practically, all of the first universities in Europe and the United States were centers for theological training. Within those institutions, "the study of philosophy was considered of central importance to the health and vitality of the university and the Christian life."[6] There are at least five functions of philosophy in the service of Christianity: an aid to the spiritual discipline of study, the handmaid of theology, the crux of apologetics, a defense against heresy, and an aid in communication.

PHILOSOPHY'S ROLE IN THE SPIRITUAL DISCIPLINE OF STUDY

The ultimate aim of the spiritual disciplines is to replace old, destructive behavior with new, life-giving habits. Total transformation of an individual is the sole purpose. How is a Christian to be transformed into Christ's likeness? Paul discloses the only manner in which this happens is through the renewing of the mind (Rom 12:2). For renewal of the mind to occur, one must set one's mind to ponder upon things leading to transformation. "Christians must realize that just as a fire cannot blaze without fuel, so burning hearts are not kindled by brainless minds. We must not be content to have zeal without knowledge."[7] Followers of Christ ought to be more; they should be life-long learners, which is at the heart of being a disciple of Christ.

---

4. Brown, C., *Philosophy and Christian Faith*, 268–71.
5. Ibid., 271.
6. Moreland and Craig, *Philosophical Foundations*, 14.
7. Whitney, *Spiritual Disciplines*, 224.

Philosophy can stimulate the spiritual discipline of study.[8] Since philosophy is one of the most rigorous fields to study and touches on so many aspects of life, it can encourage someone to seek truth from other areas of life. Christ in John 8:31–38 made it unmistakably clear that the knowledge of truth will set individuals free. Without a knowledge of the truth, Christians are not set free—for Christ is "the way, the truth, and the life" (John 14:6).

Solomon, the author of Proverbs, has many applicable things to say concerning our topic. Proverbs 1:5 declares a wise person will listen to instruction to gain new knowledge. "Give instruction to a wise man, and he will be still wiser; teach a righteous man, and he will increase in learning" (Prov 9:9). A wise and righteous man shows humility because he realizes there is much he does not know and needs to learn still. He never ceases to obtain new knowledge and understanding. The author of Proverbs says, "The mind of the discerning acquires knowledge, and the ear of the wise seeks it" (Prov 18:15, HCSB). A wise person desires to grow in knowledge and understanding. In fact, he stores up knowledge for future use (Prov 10:14). He knows he must apply the knowledge he learns to his daily affairs (Prov 23:12). Furthermore, the wise person knows "the fear of the Lord is the beginning of wisdom, and the knowledge of the Holy One is understanding" (Prov 9:10, HCSB).[9]

PHILOSOPHY'S INFLUENCE ON CHRISTIAN THEOLOGY

It is difficult to do systematic theology without the aid of philosophy. Scripture provides the basis for Christian theology. But its teachings are not grouped into categories. Rather, the biblical authors convey them throughout the Bible. Philosophy aids in the systematization of theology and plays both a positive and negative role in its development. The positive role assists in the construction of Christian doctrine, while the negative role promotes the elimination of contradictions. For example, philosophy helps theologians to bring clarity to numerous concepts of systematic theology, such as the attributes of God and the doctrine of the Trinity. Philosophy also makes clear there is no contradiction between the doctrines of the Trinity and the incarnation or between predestination and human freedom. Christian

---

8. Moreland and Craig, *Philosophical Foundations*, 16.

9. For more on the spiritual discipline of study, see Foster, "Study," 62–76; Hazelton, *Renewing the Mind*; Whitney, *Spiritual Disciplines*, 223–34.

theology would be impossible without the aid of logic and philosophy. It is for this reason philosophy serves as the handmaid of theology and permeates systematic theology.[10]

PHILOSOPHY'S IMPACT ON CHRISTIAN APOLOGETICS

Philosophy assists with the task of apologetics, which is the defense of the Christian faith from attacks outside the faith (1 Pet 3:15; Jude 1:3). Just as in theology, philosophy has both a negative and a positive role aiding the apologist. In fact, the negative task is twofold in apologetics. First, the use of philosophy and logic reveals how the attacks on Christianity are either contrary to fact or completely contradictory. Either way, the attacks are shown to be false. Secondly, philosophy assists further in revealing that the non-Christian worldview is not necessarily true. The unbeliever's perspective may be possible but not plausible. On the positive side, philosophy assists in the construction of clear, coherent, and consistent arguments, or justifications, for the basic tenets of Christianity. Most often this aspect involves arguments for the existence of God, as well as evidence for the historical truth of Christianity. Without philosophy, it would be extremely difficult, if not impossible, to accomplish the task of apologetics.[11]

PHILOSOPHY AIDS IN POLEMICS

Philosophy further aids the Christian in the task of polemics, which is the refutation of heresies within Christianity. It is crucial the Christian polemicist has a strong grasp of both theology and philosophy; for one cannot effectively argue against heresy without the aid of both. Heresies often arise

---

10. For more on this concept, see Allen, *Philosophy for Understanding*; Corduan, *Handmaid to Theology*; Erickson, "Theology and Philosophy," 39–61; Hodge, "Proper Office of Reason," 1:49–59.

11. For more on philosophy's role in apologetics and apologetics in general, see Augustine, *Civ.*; Frame, *Apologetics*; Frame, *Apologetics to Glory*; Geisler, *Christian Apologetics*; Geisler, *Reasons for Faith*; Geisler and Bocchino, *Unshakable Foundations*; Groothuis, *Christian Apologetics*; Groothuis, *Truth Decay*; Koukl, *Tactics*; McDowell, *Evidence that Demands*; McDowell and Wilson, *He Walked Among Us*; McDowell, *Ready Defense*; McGrath, *Mere Apologetics*; Moreland and Nielsen, *Does God Exist*; Sproul, *Defending Your Faith*, 29–69. These works are just a handful of the apologetics works revealing how essential philosophy is for apologetics.

from either fallacious conclusions or false presuppositions. The study of philosophy assists the Christian in recognizing both of these errors.[12]

PHILOSOPHY'S FUNCTION IN COMMUNICATION

Whether assisting in theology, apologetics, or polemics, the ultimate purpose of philosophy for believers is the establishment of a more effective means of communication of the Christian faith. In the end, the body of Christ needs to be able to communicate effectively biblical truth against opposing views both from within and without Christianity. Studying philosophy enhances one's reasoning and communication skills, both verbal and written. One's verbal and written communication are improved. One is capable of expressing and defending coherent views on complex issues through articulating well-constructed, systematic arguments. Furthermore, it helps to eliminate ambiguities and vagueness from one's speech and writing. As a result, one's ability to persuade others is also improved. One of the tasks of philosophy for the believer is to assist in revealing the inconsistency in opposing worldviews where the gospel of Christ is communicated effectively. Unless the intellectual ground is level, it is unlikely the Christian will be effective in presenting the biblical perspective. Through studying philosophy, believers learn to defend their faith, as well as to appreciate and anticipate opposing positions.

CONCLUSION

The function of philosophy in Christianity should not be seen primarily as theological, apologetical, or polemical. While it assists each of these areas, philosophy's primary function is to aid in the interpretation of life and reality as well as to discover what truth is. The chief aim is to proclaim truth so that it conforms to the Word of God, according to theologian Charles Hodge.[13]

---

12. For additional information on how philosophy aids Christianity with polemics, see Brown, H., *Heresies*; Chesterton, *Everlasting Man*; Chesterton, *Heretics/Orthodoxy*; Guinness, *Fool's Talk*; Nicole, "Polemic Theology"; Shedd, *Orthodoxy & Herterodoxy*. A slightly longer version of Nicole's article is found at Third Millennium Ministries (thirdmill.org) in a four part series under the title "How to Deal with Those Who Differ from Us: The Necessity of Godly Disputation."

13. Hodge, "Proper Office of Reason," 49–59.

Nevertheless, work within Christian philosophy may indirectly subserve as a theological, an apologetical, or a polemical purpose. Since Christian philosophy's primary concern is to establish what truth is, it is in a position to make contributions of unparalleled significance to the advancement of present-day philosophical reflection and instruction.[14] Philosophy also assists the theologian, apologist, and polemicist in their respective tasks. Thus, one participating in Christian philosophy is in a position to show how empty and deceptive worldly thought is while at the same time show the validity of the Christian faith to the irreligious world.[15]

---

14. Casserley, *Christian in Philosophy*, 255.
15. Ibid., 261–62.

PART TWO

How We Come to Know Things

4

Insights on the Operation of Revelation
Philosophy of Divine Revelation

"All Scripture is breathed out by God..."

—2 Timothy 3:16

A FUNDAMENTAL CASE FOR biblical revelation is laid out in Francis A. Schaeffer's short book *He is There and He is Not Silent*.[1] The title sums up the work well by making two claims. First, there is a God. Second, God speaks. What is the importance of the fact that God speaks?

Consider a god who does not speak or reveal himself, for example, the god of deism. First appearing in the seventeenth century, deism flourishes during the eighteenth century in both Europe and America. Deism is a loosely defined philosophical and religious movement advocating natural religion, emphasizes morality, and affirms the existence of God as the creator of the universe. Deists argue proper conclusions regarding religion—simple truths about creation, morality, and God—are attainable from the power of human reason and intellect.

Differing from traditional Christian thought, deism denounces the notion of the creator of the universe intervening in his creation. All notions of divine revelation, except for what is found in natural revelation

---

1. Schaeffer, F., *He is There*.

(also known as natural theology or general revelation), are rejected. Thus, concepts of the incarnation, miracles, or special revelation are rejected. As a result, the god of deism is nothing more than a clockmaker who after making a clock starts it up and lets it run on its own without interference.[2]

In stark contrast, Christians believe in a God who interacts with his creation throughout history. Under no obligation to do so, God chose to reveal himself. Nothing within us compels God to do so (Isa 64:6; Eph 2:1–5). Our response should be overwhelming gratitude.

According to Stephen T. Davis, "Christians should still—if they understand matters rightly—feel a sense of wonder when they grasp the fact that God has chosen to be revealed. There is no imperative or necessity that God do so. God could have remained silent."[3]

If God had remained silent, what consequences would follow? Some people believe humans would likely have found another method for answering religious queries if God had remained unrevealed.[4] It is plausible human beings would still have a curiosity in spiritual matters.[5] In Acts 16:30, the Philippian jailer asks, "Sirs, what must I do to be saved?" Posted with elegant simplicity, the question of the jailer is the most important religious question one can ask.

Left to our own devices in a quest to discover God, we might respond in four possible manners. One possibility is *legalism*. This option is nothing more than a set of rules human beings must obey. Obedience means reward, whereas disobedience means punishment. *Ritualism* is a second prospect. Similar in many respects to legalism, this system focuses on following prescribed ceremonies. Once again the end results are the same: do the ritual and appease the gods; if you do not, condemnation comes. *Relativism* is the third option, which affirms the only thing crucial is one being able to be sincere and live according to one's beliefs to the best of one's ability. What is correct for one person may or may not be for another. Hence, God is as humans define him and all views of God are highly subjective. A version of

---

2. For more on deism, see Geisler and Brooks, *When Skeptics Ask*, 39–40; Geisler and Watkins, *Worlds Apart*, 146–84; Hardwick, "Deism Defined"; Internet Encyclopedia of Philosophy, "English Deism"; Sire, *Universe Next Door*, 47–65; Taylor, *Secular Age*, 221–69; World Union of Deists, "Welcome to Deism."

3. Davis, S., "Revelation and Inspiration," 31.

4. Even when God speaks, human beings seek out ways on their own to appease their religious tendencies. For two biblical examples of this, see Genesis 11:1–9 and Exodus 32:1–10.

5. Anderson, *Natural Theology*, 3; Butler, "Idea of God," 3; Carus, *Idea of God*, 4.

nihilism is the fourth. There are no possible answers to any religious question (or to any question for that matter), according to this view. No such thing as definitive values exists. At death everything ceases to be. Trying one's best is all one can do along with hoping to make life more bearable.[6]

If God were silent, there would be no hope of salvation (Job 31:35). He is *not* silent and has graciously revealed himself in many ways.

THE RATIONALE OF REVELATION

> Long ago, at many times and in many ways, God spoke to our fathers by the prophets, but in these last days he has spoken to us by his Son, whom he appointed the heir of all things, through whom also he created the world. He is the radiance of the glory of God and the exact imprint of his nature, and he upholds the universe by the word of his power. After making purification for sins, he sat down at the right hand of the Majesty on high, having become as much superior to angels as the name he has inherited is more excellent than theirs. (Heb 1:1–4)

What is the rationale of this revelation? What is the necessity of this revelation? What is this revelation? What are the modes of this revelation? Each one of these questions is vital for the Christian. As such, they shall form the basic structure of what follows.

Before we can address the questions above, another question must be considered first: can God reveal himself? At the heart of this question is whether revelation is possible. Given God's omnipotence[7] and omniscience,[8] the answer must be presumed affirmatively. God would not be God if he lacked the ability and knowledge to unveil himself to humanity. Should humans presume they are the only beings capable of communication?

Revelation is possible. The question now is whether God *would* reveal himself. God revealing himself is probable. There are two intertwined

---

6. Davis, S., "Revelation and Inspiration," 31.

7. For the classical understanding of divine omnipotence, see Charnock, *Existence and Attributes*, 1:5–107; Erickson, *God the Father Almighty*, 165–83; Frame, *Doctrine of God*, 513–25; Geisler, *Systematic Theology*, 2:158–69; Grudem, *Systematic Theology*, 217–18; Pink, *Attributes of God*, 46–51; Tozer, *Attributes of God*, 2:71–87.

8. For the historical view of the doctrine of omniscience, see Charnock, *Existence and Attributes*, 1:406–97; Erickson, *God the Father Almighty*, 184–209; Frame, *Doctrine of God*, 483–505; Geisler, *Systematic Theology*, 2:180–210; Grudem, *Systematic Theology*, 190–93; Pink, *Attributes of God*, 17–21; Tozer, *Attributes of God*, 2:105–21.

reasons why this is the case. Foundationally, man is created in the *image of God* (Gen 1–2), which refers to the immaterial part of man. In both philosophical and theological discourse, thinkers argue humans are composed of two distinctly different parts—the material and immaterial. The material portion will eventually rot away while the immaterial part of a person will survive death in some way. The image of God is what sets man apart from the animal world, fits him to have dominion over the earth (Gen 1:28), and enables him to communicate with his Maker. Created as such, man is both rational and volitional. Furthermore, there is also a need for fellowship or social interaction associated with humanity since being created in the image of God (Gen 2:18; 3:8).[9] Secondly, human beings communicate to each other. Therefore, it is reasonable to expect God to communicate as well. Indeed, the creator of communication would very likely communicate. Theologian Carl F. H. Henry notes:

> The image of God in man nonetheless bears noetic implications that have constrained some of Christianity's profoundest theologians to insist that God is the source of all truth, that the human mind is an instrument for recognizing truth, and that the rational awareness of God is given a priori in correlation with man's self-awareness, so that man as a knower stands always in epistemic relationships with his Maker and Judge.[10]

Despite the fact revelation is not only possible but even probable, there remains a question that needs addressing. Why is revelation necessary?

THE NECESSITY OF REVELATION

One of the most crucial claims of the Christian faith is God reveals himself to human beings. May God be known? Does God reveal himself? If God may be known and does reveal himself, where does he do so? Those searching for answers to satisfy their pondering minds ask these questions. When this occurs the questions become personal queries. For example, "How can I know God?"

---

9. For more on the topic of the image of God, see Clines, "Image of God in Man," 53–103; Feinberg, "Image of God," 235–46; Henry, "Image of God in Man," 2:124–42; Hoekema, *Created in God's Image*; Machen, *Christian View of Man*, 125–48; Orr, *God's Image in Man*; Ryrie, *Basic Theology*, 195–200; Sherlock, *Doctrine of Humanity*, 29–91; Sproul, *Essential Truths*, 131–32.

10. Henry, *God, Revelation and Authority*, 1:78.

Insights on the Operation of Revelation

The question under consideration here is: Why must God reveal himself if he is to be known? In the scope of systematic theology, there are three primary reasons why revelation is necessary. The first reason is God is God. Second, human beings are created beings. The reality that humanity is corrupted is the third reason.

God is beyond unaided human knowing (Exod 33:20; Isa 55:8–9; John 1:18; 6:46; 1 John 4:12). As finite beings, humans can attempt to come to some knowledge of God through reason. While these attempts *may provide* evidence of the need of a god, they do not attain to the knowledge of the true God (1 Cor 1:21). The heavens declare God's glory, and creation speaks of God's handiwork (Ps 19:1–6). The created world around us gives testimony of God. But this witness is not enough to bring about saving knowledge of God. It is, however, enough to make all without excuse because God's "invisible attributes, namely, his eternal power and divine nature," are clearly visible around us (Rom 1:20; 2:1–15).

According to Scripture, God is only truly explicable through his self-revelation (1 Cor 2:10–11). Even though God discloses himself in creation and through his self-revelation, he continues to be unfathomable (Deut 29:29; Job 11:7; Ps 139:6; Matt 11:27; Rom 11:33; 1 Tim 3:16).[11] Job confesses that he does not fully understand the ways of God.

> "I know that you can do all things, and that no purpose of yours can be thwarted. 'Who is this that hides counsel without knowledge?' Therefore I have uttered what I did not understand, things too wonderful for me, which I do not know. 'Hear, and I will speak; I will question you, and you make it known to me.' I had heard of you by the hearing of the ear, but now my eye sees you; therefore I despise myself, and repent in dust and ashes." (Job 42:2–6)

The Lord declares that his thoughts and ways are not like ours (Isa 55:8–9). God is knowable despite the fact he is unfathomable because he makes himself known.

Theologically, the second reason God must divulge himself to us is an implication of the first. Human beings are created beings. John MacArthur notes:

> Men can imagine what God might be like, and people have plenty of ideas about Him. Almost everyone has an opinion as to what

---

11. For further discussion on the ineffability and incomprehensibility of God, see Boyce, *Abstract of Systematic*, 8–12; Charnock, *Existence and Attributes*, 1:394–95; Geisler, *Systematic Theology*, 2:245–51; Grudem, *Systematic Theology*, 149–51.

> God is or is not, or as to whether He even exists. But man's opinions are irrelevant because they can never be more than speculations. By his own resources, the creature cannot possibly comprehend his Creator.[12]

In theology this concept is expressed as *"finitum non capax infiniti,"* which translates, "the finite cannot comprehend or understand the infinite."[13] Human beings are created beings with a finite mind (Job 9:4, 10; 11:7; 23:3–9; 26:14; 36:26; 37:5, 23; Pss 139:6; 145:3; Eccl 3:11; Isa 40:13–14, 28). The apostle Paul avows the limitations of humanity in Romans 11:33 when he proclaims: "Oh, the depth of the riches and wisdom and knowledge of God! How unsearchable are his judgments and how inscrutable his ways!"

Our mind cannot discern God on its own accord in a salvific manner (John 1:5; Rom 1:18–32; 1 Cor 2:14; 2 Cor 3:14; 4:3–4; Eph 4:17–18). The failing and immorality of humanity are found in Isaiah 59:2 as the prophet proclaims, "But your iniquities have made a separation between you and your God, and your sins have hidden his face from you so that he does not hear." Recall from chapter 2 that sin affects our thinking as well. The apostle Paul writes, "None is righteous, no, not one; no one understands; no one seeks for God" (Rom 3:10–11).[14]

Hence, revelation is necessary because of humanity's finite knowledge and sinfulness. God in mercy makes himself known and knowable through revelation. "Revelation exists for the essential purpose of establishing a personal and loving relationship between God and human beings."[15] Thus, there is a redemptive quality within divine revelation. Without God taking the initiative, human beings would not seek God (Rom 1:18–32). What is revelation?

---

12. MacArthur, *1 Corinthians*, 60.

13. Muller, "*Finitum non capax infiniti*," 119.

14. For more on total depravity and the noetic effects of sin, see Berkhof, *Systematic Theology*, 246–48; Calvin, *Institutes of the Christian*, 1:255–89; Erickson, *Christian Theology*, 644–48; Geisler, *Baker Encyclopedia*, 540–43; Peels, "Effects of Sin," 42–69; Plantinga, *Warranted Christian Belief*, 199–240; Sproul, *Essentials Truths*, 147–49; Thiessen, H., *Lectures in Systematic Theology*, 191–92.

15. Davis, S., "Revelation and Inspiration," 32.

Insights on the Operation of Revelation

DEFINITION OF REVELATION

To establish what revelation is, one should observe two things. First, we need to examine the words used for the concept in the Bible. Second, we need to make a differentiation between revelation and discovery. The terms show there is a difference between knowledge gained through revelation and knowledge obtained through discovery. Distinguishing between them is necessary.

Several words in Scripture are used to express the notion. In the Old Testament, three primary words express the topic, and the writers of the New Testament use eight terms. While each word conveys slight nuances, the basic meaning of each is essentially the same. For the purposes here, it is sufficient to mention only the most significant of the Old Testament and the New Testament terms. *Galah* is the major Hebraic verb related to revelation. The basic and derivative meanings of this verb are "to uncover, to show, to reveal, to make known, or to disclose."[16] The most significant of the Greek is *apokalupto*. This word is a compound verb deriving from *apo*, "from," and *kalupto*, "to hide, cover," which means "to bring to light, to unveil, to uncover, etc."[17] Hence, revelation involves the uncovering of knowledge according to the meaning of these two terms.

There is a considerable difference between discovering something and having something revealed. When discovery of knowledge occurs, the recipient is *active*. He is the one seeking out what is unknown. This unknown knowledge is not being unveiled for him by someone else. Thus, the discovery of knowledge involves a single individual and a body of knowledge.[18]

By contrast, the recipient of knowledge is *passive* when revelation occurs. Someone unveils the knowledge to the receiver.[19] According to Albrecht Oepke, "In the strict sense revelation is always and everywhere the act of God. No one has a right to it simply because he is man."[20] In regards to divine revelation, God is always the revealer and humanity is always the receiver.

---

16. *BDB*, "glh," 162–63; Howard, "glh," 1:861–64.

17. Holtz, "apokaluptō, apokalypsis," 1:130–32; Mundle, "apokalyptō, apokalypsis," 3:310–16; Oepke, "apokaluptō, apokalypsis," 3:563–92.

18. Showers, "Foundations of Faith."

19. Ibid.

20. Oepke, "apokaluptō, apokalypsis," 3:574.

In religion and theology, revelation means the unveiling or disclosing of something previously hidden.[21] Henry Clarence Thiessen gives an amplified definition for revelation when he writes, "Revelation is that act of God whereby he discloses himself or communicates truth to the mind, whereby he makes manifest to his creatures that which could not be known in any other way."[22] Simply, revelation is the only means by which specific truths can be known.

Thiessen further remarks, "Revelation may occur in a single, instantaneous act, or it may extend over a long period of time."[23] For example, the redemptive story found in the Bible is told over an extended period; yet, when God reveals himself to Saul on the Damascus Road, he does so in a single event. When revelation does take place, those who receive it may do so in varying degrees. Nevertheless, revelation occurs. If God chose to remain silent, it would not be feasible to have accurate or propositional statements about God.[24] The crux here is that God discloses truth about who he is; and without God doing so, we would not otherwise know this information concerning God. How does God unveil himself?

THE MODES OF REVELATION

The question here is how God reveals himself. Scripture indicates God reveals himself in two broad categories—*general* revelation and *special* revelation. The first refers to the general truths that can be known regarding God through creation, whether it is through nature, providential history, or the human conscience. General revelation is knowable to all humans in any era whether or not they recognize it, hence the name. Special revelation refers to more specific truths, which are only knowable concerning God through supernatural means.

General Revelation

Throughout church history, Christian theologians have viewed general revelation as a necessary but insufficient means of providing a comprehensive

---

21. Enns, *Moody Handbook*, 155.
22. Thiessen, H., *Lectures in Systematic Theology*, 7.
23. Ibid.
24. Enns, *Moody Handbook*, 155; McArthur, *1 Corinthians*, 60.

knowledge regarding the Creator and his character.[25] While general revelation does provide certain truths about the existence of God and his character, it is incapable of imparting salvific truths such as the incarnation of Christ and the atonement.[26] Nevertheless, attention must be given to general revelation because Scripture testifies of it.

God is active in his creation. Elihu brings forth this point in his dialogue with Job (Job 36–37, especially 36:22ff.). Elihu proclaims the greatness of God and challenges Job to remember how great God is (Job 36:22–26). Then in Job 36:27—37:13, Elihu illustrates this point by describing God's activity in the storm; he tells how the rain waters the earth, the thunder and lightning strike terror in the heart, and the sun reappears afterward. In the thunderstorm, God's goodness, majesty, power, and severity are on display for all to see (see also Ps 18:7–15; Nah 1:2–8). Elihu ends his speech by challenging Job to reflect on God's greatness in nature (Job 37:14–22). In God's address to Job, he stresses the fact every natural phenomenon and how the animal kingdom operates attests to the existence and glory of God (Job 38–39).

According to Psalm 19:1–6, one can clearly see the existence and power of God by observing the universe: "the heavens declare the glory of God, and the sky above proclaims his handiwork" (Ps 19:1). The psalmist elaborates on the nature of the revelation of God's glory as well. According to Psalm 19:2, this revelation is perpetual or uninterrupted. In other words, it is continuous. It occurs "day to day" and "night to night." Everyone in every era is witness to it. The revelation of God's glory is not language specific: every tribe can understand it (Ps 19:3) although they may not acknowledge it (Acts 14:17; 17:27; Rom 1:20; 1 Cor 11:14).

After the miraculous healing of a lame man (Acts 14:8–13), Paul and Barnabas preach to the people of Lystra that they have a knowledge of God that is common with others as a result of general revelation. They appeal to God being the creator of all things (Acts 14:14–15). Further, God is

25. Of course, there are those who hold to other positions regarding general revelation. For example, revelation for Karl Barth means the incarnation of the Word. According to Barth, there is no such thing as general revelation after the fall. There are those of the more liberal persuasion, such as Otto, Rahner, Schleiermacher, and Tillich, who believe general revelation is sufficient for salvation.

26. For more on the inadequacy of general revelation, see Bavinck, *Reformed Dogmatics*, 1:312–14; Berkhof, *Systematic Theology: Combined*, 132–33; Frame, "Is Natural Revelation Sufficient"; Henry, "Rejection of Natural Theology," 2:104–23; Johnson, "Inadequacy of General Revelation"; Plantinga, "Reformed Objection," 187–98; Strange, "General Revelation," 40–77.

the providential provider of the necessities of life, according to Paul and Barnabas (Acts 14:16–17). Similarly, Paul makes the same point with the pagans in Athens (Acts 17:16–31). Observing the culture of his audience, Paul sets forth six truths they know from general revelation. God is the sovereign creator of the universe (Acts 17:24). God is self-sufficient (Acts 17:25a). God is the source of life and everything good in it (Acts 17:25b). God is an intelligent being who formulates actions and plans (Acts 17:26; compare Deut 30:1–10; Job 12:23; Pss 47:7–8; 66:7; Isa 10:5–13; Dan 2:21, 31–35; 7:1–28; 9:24–27; Hos 3:4–5; Matt 23:37—25:46; Acts 15:13–18; Rom 11:13–29; 2 Thess 2:1–12). God is immanent in his creation (Acts 17:27). God is the source and sustainer of human existence (Acts 17:28). Thus, God is visible in the workings of human history. He is seen in the preservation of the world (Col 1:13; Heb 1:3) and by his providence (Matt 5:45; Rom 8:28).

Like Psalm 19, Romans 1:18–21 teaches that creation gives evidence of God's existence. Bruce A. Demarest believes this passage is the "clearest teaching that all people possess a rudimentary knowledge of God as creator."[27] According to the universal revelation in nature, God is clearly seen and understood (Rom 1:20). Furthermore, God is known as well (Rom 1:19, 21). The Greek word for *know* in this passage implies knowledge is perceived with the senses and can be grasped with the mind.[28] This passage further teaches that there is no excuse for denying the evidence (Rom 1:20).

Additional evidence of general revelation is the implantation of moral law on the human conscience. Paul teaches this in Romans 2:14–15. All humanity is guilty of transgressing the law. Jews are guilty of violating the written law, and the Gentiles are guilty of failing to live by the moral law written on their hearts.

General revelation is limited in its extent. Nature contains enough evidence to bring responsibility to humanity to honor God as creator (Ps 19:1–6; Rom 1:20–21). Likewise, there is enough truth to bring guilt and condemnation upon humans if they fail to respond properly (Rom 1:18). Despite this evidence, general revelation does not provide enough truth to lead humanity to salvation (John 14:6; Acts 4:6; Rom 10:14). The purpose

---

27. Demarest, "Revelation, General," 945.

28. Bultmann, "ginōskō, gnōsis, epiginōskō, epignōsis," 1:689–719; Schmithals, "ginōskō," 1:248–51; Schmitz, "ginōskō," 2:392–406.

of general revelation is to persuade mankind to seek God (Acts 14:17; 17:24–27).[29]

Special Revelation

While general revelation has its place and purpose, there is a need for additional revelation if God is to be known. God delights in self-revelation, and because of this, he is not silent—further unveiling himself through special revelation. Francis Schaeffer writes, "There is no use having a silent God. We would not know anything about him. He has spoken and told us what he is and that he existed before all else, and so we have the answer to the existence of what is."[30]

Whereas general revelation is universal, special revelation is *direct* communication from God revealing specific truths to certain individuals at a particular time. When God speaks, he does so for an expressed reason and with a definite purpose. Although God reveals certain truths in this manner, it does not necessitate revelation is intended only for those to whom it was given.[31] In fact, the psalmist in Psalm 105:1 instructs those who have knowledge of God to "make known his deeds among the peoples."

Many people use the phrase *special revelation* to refer specifically to the Scriptures or the ministry of Christ. But God reveals himself through other methods as well throughout the ages. Certain modes are, however, primary: the self-revelation of God, miracles, the person and work of Jesus Christ, and the Scriptures.

God appears in tangible ways. God's self-revelation takes several forms. Theophanies—visible manifestations of God—hold a prominent place in Scripture. When God reveals himself in this manner, he does so in three forms. First, God appears as a human (Gen 18:1–2, 22; 32:24–30; Exod 3:1–6; 34:4–7; Num 11:25; 12:5; 14:10–12; Josh 5:13–15). Second, God appears in an angelic form (Gen 16:9–13; 18; 19; 28:12; 32:1–2; Exod 3:2–4; Deut 33:23; Judg 16:11–24; 13:3–23; Job 33:23). Third, God can also appear as a non-human (Gen 15:17; Exod 3:2; 33:18ff.; 19:9ff.; 24:16; Num 9:15–23; 11:17, 25; 12:5; 17:7; 20:16; Deut 31:15). Elsewhere God appears

---

29. For more on general revelation, see Bavinck, *Reformed Dogmatics*, 1:301–22; Berkouwer, *General Revelation*; Brunner, *Revelation and Reason*; Demarest, *General Revelation*.

30. Schaeffer, F., *He is There*, 16–17.

31. Thiessen, H., *Lectures in Systematic Theology*, 10.

in a dream or a vision (Gen 20:3; 28:12–16; 31:24; 37; 46:2; Num 12:6; 24:4; Deut 13:1; Judg 7:13–14; 1 Kgs 3:5; 9:2; Job 33:14–15; Ezek 1:1; 26–28; Matt 1:20; 2:13, 19; Acts 16). Another method God uses is direct communication (Exod 4:12; Num 12:6–8; 23:5; 1 Sam 3:4–14; Isa 50:4; 51:16; Jer 1:9; Acts 9:4). Furthermore, God appears without any circumstantial description at times (Gen 1:27; 17:1; 22; 26:24; 35:9; Exod 4:4; 6:2; 12:12, 23; 17:6; Num 23:4, 16; 1 Sam 3:21; 2 Sam 5:24). God also provides self-revelation in the form of prophecy, which is God's communication of his thoughts to humanity. This form of self-revelation can occur in various forms previously mentioned as well as through individuals; for examples, see the prophets of the Old Testament.[32]

God also makes himself known by his deeds; God's words and works are intimately connected. The psalmist declares God's Word is an act: "For he spoke, and it came to be; he commanded, and it stood firm" (Ps 33:9). God speaks, and creation responds. And elsewhere God's activity is described as speech (Pss 19:2; 29:3; Isa 28:26). Thus, God provides evidence of his presence by performing some deed.

Throughout Scripture, the words miracles, wonders, and signs are used interchangeably to express God's actions. For example, when Peter describes the miracles of Christ in Acts 2:22 as "miracles, wonders, and signs," he is not describing three separate types of acts. Peter is using the three words interchangeably to describe them from various viewpoints. According to Robert Saucy, God uses his deeds in revealing himself in two important ways—as a sign that revelation is occurring and to reveal his nature and purpose.[33] The full significance of this form of revelation is only knowable through Scripture.[34]

The writer of Hebrews declares, "in these last days he has spoken to us by his Son" (Heb 1:2). The person and work of Christ is the apex of God's unveiling himself to us because Christ is God incarnate (John 1:1–18). God in all his fullness dwells in Christ in bodily form (Col 2:9). Furthermore through Christ's teachings, God's revelation is revealed because God sends Christ as a teacher (John 3:2). The ultimate climax of God's revelation through Christ is in the cross and resurrection.

---

32. For more on the modes of God's self-revelation, see Bavinck, *Reformed Dogmatics*, 1:328–36; Kuntz, *Self-Revelation of God*; Saucy, *Scripture*, 47–50.

33. Saucy, *Scripture*, 51.

34. For more on this method of revelation, see Bavinck, *Reformed Dogmatics*, 336–39; Collins, *God of Miracles*; Lewis, *Miracles: Preliminary Study*; Lockyer, *All Miracles of the Bible*; Saucy, *Scripture*, 50–51.

Through these events, God reveals his infinite holiness, love, and righteousness. Christ is not simply the pinnacle of revelation; he is the theme of all revelation. All of Scripture testifies to Christ: "You search the Scriptures because you think that in them you have eternal life; and it is they that bear witness about me" (John 5:39).[35]

The written Word of God is the final form of special revelation. Within its pages is a written record of God's revealing himself to humanity. Through the Holy Spirit, God uses numerous human writers to convey his truth in written form (2 Pet 1:21). "All Scripture is inspired by God" (2 Tim 3:16). Since Scripture is God-breathed, it is living and active (Heb 4:12). The Bible accurately presents the revelation of God in Christ.[36]

> For behold, he who forms the mountains and creates the wind, and declares to man what is his thought, who makes the morning darkness, and treads on the height of the earth—the Lord, God of hosts, is his name. (Amos 4:13)

CONCLUSION

One of the vital elements of religion is the question of revelation, primarily whether God can be known, and if so how can he be. Within revelation itself, there are numerous other queries and concerns that arise, among them is the rationale and necessity of revelation.

God is there, and he is not silent. Because God is not silent, he is knowable. He wants to be known. Since this is the case, he provides the means whereby he can be known, in part due to his attributes and also in creating man in his image.

God's fingerprint is visible in creation (Ps 19:1–6; Rom 1:18–32). Even though evidence of God is visible in creation, it is not enough to restore us back into a proper relationship with him. God provides special revelation for the sole purpose of providing a means in which we can experience

---

35. For more on the person and work of Christ, see Bloesch, *Jesus Christ*; Bruce, F., *Jesus Past, Present & Future*; Bruce, F., *Jesus: Lord and Savior*; Letham, *Work of Christ*; MacLeod, *Person of Christ*; Morris, L., *Lord of Heaven*; Morris, T., *Logic of God Incarnate*; Walvoord, *Jesus Christ Our Lord*; Warfield, *Person and Work of Christ*.

36. For more on the various aspects involved with Scripture as a method of God's revelation, see Bavinck, *Philosophy of Revelation*; Bloesch, *Holy Scriptures*; Bruce, F., *Canon of Scripture*; Evans, T., *Transforming Word*; Frame, *Doctrine of Word*; Geisler, *Inerrancy*; Jensen, *Revelation of God*; Warfield, *Inspiration and Authority*.

restoration with him. The most important form of special revelation is the person and work of Christ. Through various methods of revelation, both general and special, man is brought into a fuller knowledge of God, thereby cementing the relationship between creation and creator.

5

What is Truth?
Developing a Biblical Perspective

"Pilate said to him, 'What is truth?'"

—John 18:38

Nearly two thousand years have passed since Pontius Pilate asked Christ: "What is truth?" You may recall the situation in which Pilate asked this question. Pilate interrogated Jesus during his last trial before being sentenced to death by crucifixion. Pilate asked this question in response to a reply Jesus gave earlier. In his reply Jesus said, "For this purpose I was born and for this purpose I have come into the world—to bear witness to the truth. Everyone who is of the truth listens to my voice" (John 18:37). Then Pilate questions Jesus one last time, "What is truth?" It is not known if Pilate truly desired to know its answer. Perhaps he is being cynical when he utters the question. If an answer were coveted, then one would expect Pilate to wait for Jesus to give a reply. Pilate, however, asked the question and then walked away.

Pilate was not the first person to pose the question, and he certainly was not the first individual to wonder what truth is. Philosophers have been seeking an answer to this question since philosophy's beginning. They also pondered related questions. Is truth absolute? If truth exists, is it knowable? If it is knowable, does it resemble reality?

Today many individuals argue truth does not exist. They also contend if truth were to exist, it would not be the same for everyone; what is true for me would not necessarily be true for you. In other words absolute truth ceases to exist, and everything becomes relative. N. T. Wright explains:

> Saying "It's true for you" sounds fine and tolerant. But it only works because it's twisting the word "true" to mean, not "a true revelation of the way things are in the real world," but "something that is genuinely happening inside of you." In fact, saying "It's true for you" in this sense is more or less equivalent to saying "It's *not* true for you," because the "it" in question—the spiritual sense or awareness or experience—is conveying, very powerfully, a message (that there is a loving God) which the challenger is reducing to something else (that you are having strong feeling which you misinterpret in that sense).[1]

If truth is based upon personal feelings, then all matters are up for debate and reinterpretation. Once truth becomes relative, an objective standard by which claims are to be judged is an illusion. Shifting away from an objective standard for truth-claims becomes more acceptable beginning in the second half of the nineteenth century, particularly with the use of the term *relative*. However, the concept dates back to Protagoras of Abdera (c. 490—420 BC).

For several decades now, Christian thinkers have been speaking out and writing against people adopting this mentality of rejecting an objective standard for determining truth. Accepting the prevailing way of thinking creates a slippery slope. We should not and cannot adopt this rationale as our method to evaluate issues. But why?

THE MAGNITUDE OF THE NATURE OF TRUTH

The nature of, essence of, and knowability of truth is immensely important to the Christian faith. Christianity claims an absolute, objective, and knowable truth exists. It further insists truth corresponds to reality exactly as things are. For example, a tenet of Christianity affirms the only way to God is through Jesus Christ, the Son of God, who "suffered under Pontius Pilate,

---

1. Wright, *Simply Christian*, 26–27. I am grateful for my colleague at Butler Community College, Christian Ramsey, reminding me of this quotation.

was crucified, died, and was buried . . . The third day he rose again from the dead."[2] This confessional statement claims Pontius Pilate and Jesus are historical figures. It acknowledges that Christ suffered under Pilate and was crucified. The Apostles' Creed testifies Christ died while on the cross and Christ's dead corpse was buried. It further proclaims Jesus supernaturally left the tomb alive on the third day. Norman L. Geisler proclaims, "If truth is not objective, real, and knowable, then the Christian faith is not only false but fraudulent."[3] The apostle Paul acknowledges this fact when he writes:

> And if Christ has not been raised, then our preaching is in vain and your faith is in vain. We are even found to be misrepresenting God, because we testified about God that he raised Christ, whom he did not raise if it is true that the dead are not raised. For if the dead are not raised, not even Christ has been raised. And if Christ has not been raised, your faith is futile and you are still in your sins. Then those also who have fallen asleep in Christ have perished. If in Christ we have hope in this life only, we are of all people most to be pitied. (1 Cor 15:14–19)

Other truth claims are made in the example. The exclusivity of Christianity is also proclaimed—Jesus Christ is the means by which one gets to God. Further, the claim affirms God's existence. Each of these Christian truth claims imply a specific hypothesis of truth: truth is equivalent to reality. Christianity affirms a correspondence view of truth.

Until the modern era, the vast majority of philosophers and theologians held this view of truth. The correspondence view of truth declares any statement is true *if and only if* it directly corresponds to or agrees with what is factually known about the world, which constitutes reality. The statement, "a Honda Accord is parked in my garage," is true only if there is a Honda Accord parked in my garage. As a result then, the declaration, "there is not a Honda Accord parked in my garage," must be deemed false based upon the previous one. Why? It fails to match with the state of affairs about what it claims as factual.

Three particular laws of logic are in play with the correspondence view of truth. First, it relies upon the law of bivalence, which declares any unambiguous, declarative announcement must be *either true or false*. Only one truth value can exist for such sentences. Then as a result, a proposition

---

2. Quotation is a portion of the Apostles' Creed, which is one of the earliest Christian confessions of faith.

3. Geisler, "Why I Believe Truth," 30.

cannot be neither true nor false, and it cannot be both true and false. "A Honda Accord is parked in my garage" is either true or false. No other options exist. Secondly, we have with this understanding of truth an acknowledgment of the law of the excluded middle, which is often confused for the first law because it is similar to it. The law of the excluded middle states a declaration is *either A or non-A*. Think of it as claiming there is no middle ground between being true and being false. It is one or the other. For example, either a Honda Accord is parked in my garage or a Honda Accord is not parked in my garage. No other possible answer is available. Last, we come to the final law of logic that the correspondence view of truth asserts, which provides further clarification—the law of non-contradiction. Here this law declares *A cannot be non-A in the same way and in the same sense or respect*. Look at the following claim: "A Honda Accord is parked in my garage." It is impossible for the proposition to be deemed true that there both is and is not a Honda Accord parked in my garage. If you find the notion of the laws of logic unnecessary, here is what theologian Carl F. H. Henry says about them:

> Language is a necessary tool of communication, but it cannot effectively serve this purpose unless it defers to the laws of logic. Logic is concerned not with the origin of ideas or with the origin of language, but with the formal validity of implications or inferences and not with the truth of their conceptual content. Human language must from the first have been connected with reason and logic. All significant speech presupposes a regard for the law of contradiction; the admission of contrary meanings to the same word at the same time and in the same sense would turn conversation into a madhouse.[4]

All propositional or declarative proclamations can be critiqued for its affirmation or its falsehood based upon the correspondence view of truth. If a propositional or declarative statement is shown to disagree with objective reality, then it is proven as false. This perspective of truth allows Christians to affirm basic truths of Christianity, such as the resurrection of Jesus of Nazareth occurring in space-time history.[5]

---

4. Henry, *God, Revelation and Authority*, 3:235–36.

5. For more on the use of logic and these laws, see Geisler and Brooks, *Come, Let Us Reason*; Nash, *Worldviews in Conflict*, 54–106; Moreland and Craig, *Philosophical Foundations*, 28–67.

What is Truth?

What is truth? Is it even possible to attempt to define the term? Even if a definition can be determined, can agreement be made on how individuals use it? These questions are only a sampling of the issues faced in our day when the idea of truth comes up in dialogue. But before one can reflect upon these questions, it must be determined whether truth actually exists. If truth is proven not to exist, then all else is futile. If truth is proven, in fact, to exist, then the conversation can move forward.

THE ENIGMA OF THE NATURE OF TRUTH

In philosophical discourse, truth seems an elusive, abstract notion. But is truth obscure? "Truth surely is the reason why intellectuals think passionately, read voraciously, pursue research tirelessly and argue about anything and everything interminably," as Os Guinness remarks.[6]

Hopefully, you recall from a previous chapter how it is vital to make sure terms are clearly defined when talking with others. If we are using a word differently than another person in a conversation, the ability to dialogue eventually will cease. What does a definition give us? First, it purports to describe how a given word has been used. An example of this is a dictionary definition. Second, a definition proposes to assert how a word ought to be defined. Historically, there are three different types of definitions that can be given—real, nominal, and stipulative. A real definition expresses what a word means in its common, every-day usage. In contrast a nominal definition refers to what a speaker wishes a word meant. Here the speaker feels the real definition is too ambiguous or undiscriminating, so clarity is required for a proper understanding. On the other hand, a stipulative definition seeks to remove all factors that are not crucial to understand the meaning of a given term or concept. Common usage of the word, however, may be irrelevant. Failure to understand how a term is being used or defined leads to confusion and misunderstandings.

Numerous views on the nature of truth exist. A majority of these views can be a result from people confusing the nature of truth with a defense for truth.[7] Thankfully, truth's nature aids in defining what truth is. By contrast, however, the defense for truth refers to how to test truth, not how to define it.

---

6. Guinness, *Fool's Talk*, 79.
7. Geisler, "Why I Believe Truth," 31.

What Truth is Not[8]

When we learn what something is, we are told what the item is through its essential characteristics and qualities for the thing in question. There is nothing wrong with this method. Occasionally, it is beneficial to approach things differently, such as examining it from what the thing is not. You may find this notion strange or even foreign, which is understandable and normal. But this is the case with the word *truth*. Approaching the discussion from what truth is not is extremely insightful and helpful.

- Truth is not simply whatever works.
- Truth is not simply what is coherent or understandable.
- Truth is not what makes people feel good.
- Truth is not what the majority says is true.
- Truth is not what is comprehensive.
- Truth is not defined by what is intended.
- Truth is not how we know.
- Truth is not simply what is believed.
- Truth is not what is publicly proved.[9]

You may be shaking your head about now and wondering: "What? Some of these statements appear to define what truth is." A reasonable thought to be having. Each of the statements does not provide a real definition for truth. I, however, need to explain each one of the points further to clear up any puzzlement.

Someone says to you, "truth is simply whatever works." Does anything come across as being odd or having you questioning its legitimacy? On the surface nothing may stand out as problematic with the assertion. After further consideration, though, problems should emerge. If something works, it does not mean or determine it is actually true. Philosophy has a term for this method of thinking—pragmatism. If you make up a lie to give to your boss on why a certain task was not complete by the deadline, the boss many accept the explanation. Since the fabricated story was accepted, the

---

8. The material following this footnote is an adaptation of the ideas expressed in Geisler, "Why I Believe Truth," 30–33; GotQuestions.org, "What is Truth?"

9. The exact wording of this list comes from the article from GotQuestions.org. But Norman Geisler in his chapter "Why I Believe Truth" addresses six of these statements in more of a philosophical language.

What is Truth?

lie appears to have worked. But you know good and well what was given as your reason is a lie. Telling an untruth is not equivalent to the real reason you did not finish the task on time; therefore, it is not possible for a lie to be the truth. A lie is simply that, nothing more than a fib.

By chance do you see any trouble with the second proposition? Here is a hint: similarity exists between this one and the previous assertion. Think about it for a moment. Imagine you are working on an extremely important presentation with some co-workers. As the group collaborates and analyzes the material over six months, several of you realize portions of the data does not support the intended conclusion. Those who see the problem present their findings with the rest of the group. A few options on what to do with the problematic material emerge during later meetings. If the decision is made to reveal the problematic data, all of you know the company will not get a much-needed contract. If this happens, some of you, if not all of you, will be terminated. None of you can risk this consequence. After some heated debates, the group disguises their game plan. Any and all problematic data will be altered so that the desired conclusion will be affirmed. After the contract is awarded, everyone will then figure out why certain test results revealed problems. All of you essentially form a coalition to tell a false narrative. By all practical purposes, the group develops a conspiracy based upon falsehoods. They lied by presenting their findings as supportive of the conclusion by altering problematic material where there is confusing or conflicting data that could raise questions. No matter what the group does to persuade themselves that their fabricated story is true, it does not make the findings presented completely truthful. At best part of the material is still inaccurate.

What makes me feel good must be true. Once again faulty thinking occurs. While we all may wish this were the case, in reality this notion does not work. Many things can make us feel good. Unfortunately, there are things that can make us feel good that are harmful to our wellbeing. All of us at various times in our lives have been given some bad news, whether a loved one or a dear friend has passed away or the job offer was given to someone else instead of you. If we think about it, the list can continue for a long time. It is never easy for me to have conservations with students who are receiving a failing grade for the class as a result of violating the Academic Integrity Policy. Likewise, it is never pleasant for the students to hear what I am saying. No matter how hard I try to make what I need to and must say in the private conversation, there is absolutely no way for it to be a joyous occasion for the individual. Despite how we try to alter the situation, bad news is bad news. We never feel good when we hear it. But bad news can be true, and often it is.

Next we come to the negation of if a majority says it is true, it must be true. Hopefully, this one sounds familiar. I purposefully set up my explanation for a previous avowal in a particular way for a reason. Even if a majority of people says something is true does not make whatever is in question automatically true. The same mindset exists here as in the first two claims. If the majority of the group agrees to change the harmful information, it does not change the fact it is a false narrative. It is possible for a majority, even if it is only 51 percent, to claim the findings as being supportive of the desired result and that majority reached the wrong conclusion. Bad data is still bad data.

Take a moment to see if you can determine why the fifth declaration is accurate. Here it is again: "Truth is *not* what is comprehensive." At this juncture, you are likely beginning to see a pattern. Yes, it is possible for an individual to give a lengthy, detailed lecture or presentation, and at the end of it, the conclusion stated is false. When a comprehensive lecture is given, an absolute guarantee does not exist its conclusion will be true. At times the conclusion can be shown as truthful, but it can also be determined the material does not purport its conclusion.

Instead of going into a long explanation on the next four statements, I am going to give a brief reason each cannot be a condition for determining if something is true. We can have all the best intentions actually to portray the truth. Good intentions, however, can be wrong; additionally, intentions are not affirmations of truth. How are we to know what someone's intentions are? Truth does not determine how we know a given issue; truth is what we actually know. Just because someone believes something, it does not guarantee it is true. I can believe unicorns are real. Does my belief prove their existence? By now you may be either laughing out loud or wondering if I have lost my mind. Either way I have accomplished my point. Because we believe something does not mean it is true. We can believe certain things are, in fact, true. But we cannot presume this is always the case. Recall earlier in this chapter when I said a lie is still a lie. We can believe in a lie, but do our actions make it true? No, it does not; it is still a lie despite the fact we believe it as truth. Certain concepts can be proven true in public. Once again this fact cannot guarantee its truthfulness. Are there things we know to be true that are not known by the masses? For example, my wife can know where she hid my Christmas gift, and this knowledge she knows is true. Others do not know where she hid the gift so it is not publicly proved unless she told the public, which is extremely doubtful she would. If truth is that which is only publicly known and proved, then what happens to information that is only privately known? Is privately known information then automatically deemed as false? We would say it is absurd to think the conclusion is correct. A truth can be known by a single individual or just by a small group of people.

Three simple methods to define truth emerge from a philosophical vantage point. First, truth corresponds to reality. For example, the sun rises in the east and sets in the west. Second, truth must match its object. When we are severely ill, we go to the doctor. The doctor is not going to prescribe anti-fungal ointment if what is needed is an antibiotic. You will get a script from the physician for the correct medication that is required to aid in making you better. Finally, the last perspective may seem a bit odd to some individuals—truth tells it like it is. In other words truth is what it is. For example, you are summoned to testify in court. A lawyer calls you to take the witness stand, and you are sworn in to tell the truth and nothing but the truth. As the lawyer questions you, the answers you give are what you witnessed during the specific situation in question. You are recounting the way it was at that given point in time. If you were to give an altered account of the happenings, it would not be the truth. Each one of your claims describes what truth is; they do not rely upon something else to determine whether they are true. To determine the truthfulness of them, they require there to be a correspondence view of truth being upheld.

We now should have a grasp on what truth is not. Are we, however, any closer to knowing what truth is? To this question I can answer, "yes and no." Several additional points of discussion are needed before a satisfactory conclusion can be made on what truth is. Since what is sought is a biblical perspective of truth, getting an idea of what the biblical words for truth would perhaps be helpful. After this examination we will be a step closer to answering our question. And at this juncture, we need to consider the positive side of truth since its negative perspective was considered.

Biblical Language and the Nature of Truth[10]

In both the Old and New Testaments, the concept of truth appears. The Old Testament does not hold the language of faith and belief that is prevalent and central throughout the New Testament in a similar fashion. We must remember the focus and purpose of the Old Testament and New Testament are different. R. W. L. Moberly suggests the reason for this difference "is perhaps more of one of terminology than of basic outlook, as the OT widely uses two verbs whose meaning closely approximates to that of 'have faith / believe' in the NT."[11] The authors of the Old Testament use the Hebraic words for *trust* and *fear* overwhelmingly in relation to moral obedience (e.g., Gen 22:12; Deut 5:29; Job 28:28).[12] A common scarlet thread does exist as we read through the Old and New Testaments.

Language for *belief* and *faith* can be found throughout the Old Testament. These two words appear in various forms of the same Hebraic root for *truth*, which is *'mn*. Some of the cognate forms express significant theological concepts. In fact, five forms of *'mn* have significant theological importance.[13] For our purposes here, however, I am only going to focus on the form that is the most common conjugation of the root *'mn*. The affiliated word is *'emet*.

> The major theological significance of *'emet* derives from its frequent usage in depicting the character of Yahweh. The most important OT passage in this regard is Exod 34:5–7, which is the most extensive statement about the name, i.e., character, of God in the whole Bible—a statement found, moreover, on the lips of

---

10. As I was working on this chapter, it occurred to me that I better go grab Douglas Groothuis's work *Truth Decay* from my library. It has been fourteen or fifteen years since I read the work. Opening the book and flipping to the chapter that came to mind, I discovered my outline for the remainder of the chapter and the next chapter are essentially the same as his in chapter 3: "The Biblical View of Truth." I do make some modifications, however, to the original layout. I am grateful for his impact in aiding in the shaping of my pursuit of a well-developed and trained Christian Mind. I am also grateful for his friendship and willingness to allow me to bounce around various thoughts with him. I am indebted to Steve Cowan as well for allowing me to think through some of the material that appears in this chapter with him.

11. Moberly, "'*mn*," 427.

12. Ibid.

13. Ibid., 428.

God himself—and thus representing the very heart of God's self-revelation within Israel.[14]

More than the notion that God, himself, is faithful exists in this form of the word. Often the biblical authors combine this word with other terms, such as justice, righteousness, steadfast love, and other moral terms to convey its broader scope.[15]

This family's root meaning may also connote *support* and *stability*, which implies concepts of faithfulness and truth. "Faithfulness is the quality that provides an appropriate ground for confidence, which gives support to trust on the part of those who depend on the faithful one. Truth is that firm conformity to reality that proves to be wholly reliable, so that those who accept a statement may depend on it that it will not turn out to be false or deceitful," observes theologian Roger Nicole.[16] These two ideas—faithfulness and conformity to fact—are not mutually exclusive or conflicting[17] "because truth is conformity to fact that confidence may be placed in it or in the one who asserts it, and it is because a person is faithful that he or she will be careful to make statements that are true."[18]

Despite the fact some scholars believe there is a significant difference between the Hebraic or Semitic mindset to the Greek vernacular, the concept of truth found in the New Testament is consistent with the Old Testament understanding.[19] The primary word for truth in the Greek New Testament is *alētheia*, the nearest equivalent for *'emet*. The Septuagint (the Greek translation of the Hebrew Bible, the Old Testament) frequently replaces the Hebrew word with this Greek term.[20] The Greek word for truth upholds the Old Testament understanding of conformity to fact. *Alētheia*'s most basic notion is to unhide or to uncover. Truth does not and by its nature cannot hide anything. Truth is always present and visible for everyone to see.

The idea of faithfulness, however, shifts to the Greek term *pistos* and its related words, which translate as faith, faithful, reliable, and trustworthy.[21]

14. Ibid.
15. Ibid., 429.
16. Nicole, "Biblical Concept of Truth," 288.
17. Ibid., 288, 291.
18. Ibid., 291.
19. Thiselton, "Truth," 874–83.
20. Ibid., 877.
21. See the discussion on the biblical understanding of faith in chapter 2 for a deeper

The biblical language of the New Testament affirms the Old Testament understanding. Throughout the biblical material, the words used for truth convey a constancy, duration, and firmness exists, especially as the terms are used in relation to the triune God. An implication emerges that truth is an everlasting entity or substance; furthermore, truth is something that can be relied upon. Truth is steadfast and is going to be what it is no matter what changes around it.

From a biblical perspective, truth extends beyond its veracity. Examining truth in the Old Testament reveals it is grounded in the very being of God; hence, truth embodies not only notions of faithfulness and reliability but also moral and ethical conduct. The concept of truth further develops in New Testament to embrace completeness and all of reality.

What Truth Is

Since the negative side of and the biblical language of the nature of truth has been discussed, I can turn our attention to examining the positive side of truth. In the opening pages of the chapter, I eluded to what truth is. To find truth one needs to look no further than what corresponds to its referent: truth is simply telling the way it truly is. Truth is what corresponds directly to reality. Truth agrees with the facts. By contrast falsehood alters or misleads the state of affairs from how they are. Falsehood strives to deceive and distort the facts, which disagrees with what the reality is. It is not telling it like it is. This understanding of truth is its most simplistic form.

CONCLUSION

When we describe something to someone, we begin with listing characteristics of the thing in question. But we could do the opposite, and at times doing so is beneficial. This method, however, seems strange to approach the process in this manner. Certain topics lend themselves to being approached from different viewpoints. Learning about the nature of truth is one of those topics we can tackle from a variety of angles, including examining truth by what it is not.

Based upon truth being equivocal to the correspondence view of reality, certain distinctive features of biblical truth are determinable. Further

---

explanation.

distinctions can be made regarding the biblical nature of truth. Remember, Christianity rests upon some specific truth claims. With this being the case, the content in the following chapter should not be a complete surprise.

6

Truth Leads to Freedom
Distinctions of Biblical Truth

> "...and you will know the truth,
> and the truth will set you free."
>
> —John 8:32

WHILE IT MAY SEEM as if truth is an abstract and elusive concept, thinking such would be inaccurate and unwise. Circumstances arise that make one's search for truth more difficult and challenging, however. When one seeks truth, one does not stop until one finds it. And when truth is found, the person desires to learn as much as possible about it. The search, however, only ends at one's death.

After determining what truth is, certain biblical distinctions emerge to the forefront. Despite this a challenge exists as well. Do we want to know them? For if we know them, we are held accountable for the information. While having more knowledge is seen as a good thing, responsibility comes with it as well. "For in much wisdom is much vexation," says King Solomon, and continues with, "and he who increases knowledge increases sorrow" (Eccl 1:18). Responsibility is not the only thing that increases with gaining more knowledge. With knowledge comes responsibility and accountability. Paul makes this added point in Colossians 2:1–3. As an individual learns more, an implied expectation exists in which the person will act morally based upon the knowledge obtained. Arthur Holmes points to Colossians 2:3 as being the pinnacle reference point "in thinking about truth and evaluating knowledge claims."[1] He further elaborates upon this by saying, "the God-creation distinction implies that all truth is God's truth, like everything else is his."[2] Because of the transcendent, unchanging, and omniscient God, we can know, discover, and evaluate truth.

ATTRIBUTES OF THE BIBLICAL PERSPECTIVE OF TRUTH

Augustine is the first theologian to focus on establishing a Christian philosophy and theology on what truth is. Between 391 and 395 AD, Augustine writes the second and third books of his treatise, *On Freedom of the Will*. Augustine in Book II presents an argument for the existence of God based upon the notion of truth and its nature. One can summarize Augustine's argument in six short statements. Truth exists. Truth is unchangeable. Truth is eternal. Truth is spiritual. Truth is superior to the human mind. And finally, truth is God.[3]

Since the formulation of Augustine's argument from truth for the existence of God, two twentieth-century Christian philosophers have provided slight alternations to its original formulation. Alvin Plantinga modifies Augustine's argument in a less technical format in his Presidential Address he delivered to the Western Division of the American Philosophical Association on April 29, 1982.[4] While Plantinga's version is well done, it does not help us here since a more philosophical layout works best for discussing the features of the biblical understanding of truth. However, the other philosopher's adaptation of the argument is quite helpful. In his work *A Christian View of Men and Things*, Gordon H. Clark provides a slight modification to Augustine's original position.[5] Clark's structure can be summarized in six statements as Augustine's. Truth exists. Truth is immutable. Truth is eternal. Truth is mental. Truth is superior to the human mind. And truth is God.[6]

1. Holmes, *Contours of a World*, 129.
2. Ibid.
3. Augustine, *Lib.*, 134–69.
4. Plantinga, "How to be an Anti-Realist," 47–70.
5. Clark, *Christian View of Men*, 222–27.
6. I am grateful for Justin Wishart, one of my Columbia Evangelical Seminary

Douglas Groothuis, in his thought-provoking *Truth Decay*, lists eight key features of what truth is when approached from a biblical worldview. One finds some of these features in the thoughts of Augustine, Clark, and Plantinga. While these three Christian thinkers use their premises about truth to establish an argument for the existence of God, my variation of the argument is intended to establish the key attributes of truth, not to put forth a philosophical argument to prove God's existence. Each of these distinctions, however, follows this rich tradition that begun with Augustine, the premier theologian of the church until the Protestant Reformation. Naturally my list may, likewise, overlap with some of these other Christian philosophers and theologians. Regardless of how one labels and describes them, Carl F. H. Henry's words remain true, "Theological laws of correct thinking are principles to which all one's thinking must conform if truth is an object. Without these normative constraints, any and all arguments would lack validity and all propositions would lack meaning."[7]

Truth Exists

No matter how one responds to this statement, it stands as being true. Truth exists either way regardless if one proclaims it as being false or if one declares it is true. To deny the existence of truth is self-defeating. If someone claims "truth does not exist," simply asking the individual if the statement is true or false proves the very existence of truth. If the person claims the statement is false, then truth does exist. If the individual claims it is true, then truth, in fact, exists. Ronald H. Nash notes, "It is impossible to even conceive [sic] of the non-existence of truth."[8] If truth does not exist, then how can particular aspects of society function? For example, a country's justice system relies upon the existence of truth and can only function if a standard exists based upon truth's existence.

---

students, for assisting me on tracking down some material in Gordon H. Clark's work in the Trinity Foundation's edition of *A Christian View of Men and Things*.

7. Henry, *God, Revelation and Authority*, 3:234.
8. Nash, "Gordon Clark's Theory," 158.

Truth is Immutable—Absolute in Its Nature

It is impossible for truth to change. Gordon Clark states "truth must be unchangeable. What is true today always has been and always will be true."[9] If a proposition is deemed as true, it must be so because it is based upon immutable truth. If truth changes, it causes problems for those who define truth as that which works because what is true today will be deemed as false at some point in the future. Pragmatists have a serious problem if truth changes. "To speak of truth as changing is a misuse of language and a violation of logic."[10]

If truth is immutable, it must also be absolute in its nature. By definition, if something is labeled as an absolute, it is both consistent and agreeable. If it is both consistent and a constant, it is also immutable. For if an absolute changes, it is no longer consistent nor a constant. If it is no longer consistent and constant, truth is mutable. But truth is not changeable.

Earlier in the previous chapter, I mentioned there is a mindset that what is true for one person is not necessarily true for another. This type of thinking is known as *relativism*.[11] It argues absolute truth does not exist. But if truth is relative, it shifts and morphs into whatever the person wishes it to be who is arguing for this position. If truth can shift and morph into various meanings, then it cannot be absolute and immutable. Relativism is self-defeating. The person arguing for this perspective insists what is being argued for not only applies to the individual speaking but also applies to the person being spoken to. If what is true for the person speaking for relativism applies to another person, then how can it be? It cannot be. The relativist insists forcing his views onto another person as being an absolute. But the person does not believe truth is absolute when it disagrees with his beliefs; this is the position, however, that he is now attempting to uphold and apply to someone else. Truth cannot be both relative and absolute in its nature. If truth is immutable, it cannot be relative. If truth is immutable, it must also be absolute in its nature.

---

9. Clark, *Christian View of Men*, 223.

10. Ibid.

11. For a detailed discussion on relativism, see Beckwith and Koukl, *Relativism*. Another aspect appears in this method of thinking will be mentioned later in this chapter. It is the notion of the person's statement being objectively true while arguing truth is relative and completely subjective in its nature.

Truth is Eternal and Universal

As a result of truth being immutable and absolute in its nature, truth must also be eternal and universal. This is by extension of its immutableness and its absoluteness. As soon as someone attempts to deny the fact truth is eternal and universal, the person ends up affirming that which was sought to deny. For a moment assume a tornado destroyed your house and everything is lost. Now if you were asked if everything in your house was destroyed, the truth remains you did, in fact, loose everything. This fact is eternally and universally true. Nothing can change the fact of what happened to your possessions. Even if truth, itself, ceases to exist, the fact that truth no longer exists would still exist eternally and universally. Thus, the affirmation of truth's eternity and universality has been established.[12] Additionally for truth to be universal, it must apply everywhere and to everyone.

Truth is Knowable

The mere fact truth exists presupposes that it is knowable. Augustine argues truth is spiritual, and Gordon Clark argues truth is mental. These two Christian thinkers believe the existence of truth presupposes the existence of minds—that which is capable of rational and critical thinking. If minds do not exist, truth could not exist. Consider the words of Clark on the matter: "Without a mind truth could not exist. The object of knowledge is a proposition, a meaning, a significance; it is a thought."[13]

If truth is not knowable, then how can we determine what is true and what is false? Determining truth from falsehood is possible. People do so all the time. To say truth is unknowable is problematic. How can it be known? The statement ultimately is self-refuting.

Truth is Objective

Many individuals want to dispute the notion truth is objective and advocate the opposite—that is, truth is subjective. What is true for me may not be true for you. Once again the idea of truth being relative enters the conversation. But internal problems with relativism causes it to self-destruct. Despite this being the case, Douglas Groothuis makes a crucial point that

---

12. Clark, *Christian View of Men*, 223–24.
13. Ibid., 223.

needs mentioning here: "The biblical emphasis on objective truth does not minimize the imperative to make God's truth subjectively or existentially one's own."[14] There are certain issues and matters people need to accept on a personal level. But this does not establish truth is not objective at its essence. This will make more sense when we get to the last distinctive of what truth is from a biblical perspective. Truth is objective because it "is not dependent on any creature's subjective feelings, desires or beliefs."[15] Objective truth exists independently from what we may think and wish.

Truth is Exclusive

In Eastern thought, it is not uncommon for people to merge or morph elements of various religions into their religious beliefs. For example, both Hinduism and Buddhism have their origins in India. The founder of Buddhism, Siddhartha Gautama, sought to fix the inconsistencies he found within Hinduism. Over time, Confucianism emerged in China. When Buddhism moved into China, practices within Buddhism morphed into where they became Chinese. But the people accepted various aspects of Buddhism and Confucianism to shape their religious beliefs. This is even more evident in Shinto, which the Occupation forces required Japan to abolish State Shinto as part of the peace agreements at the end of World War II with the Shinto Directive.[16] When the Chinese moved into Japan, they named the religion that was practiced by the natives. As the natives of the islands learned the customs and religious beliefs of the Chinese, they accepted and adopted aspects of both Buddhism and Confucianism into their religious practices. Buddhism influences the Shinto teachings on death and the afterlife; Shinto accepted the ethical teachings of Confucianism as their standard on how to live honorably. How is this possible for a single religion to accept the teachings and practices of another religion? If a religion does not see itself as being exclusive and declares itself as being inclusive, it happens.

When we look at Judaism, Christianity, and Islam, each religion declares itself as being the only true religion. These religions teach they are exclusive in their nature. Being exclusive prevents other religious teachings and practices from being accepted into the religion.

14. Groothuis, *Truth Decay*, 68.
15. Ibid., 67. See also Kreeft and Tacelli, *Handbook of Christian Apologetics*, 362–83.
16. Molloy, *Experiencing the World's Religions*, 262–63.

Truth is the same way. It is exclusive. Because truth is exclusive, certain characteristics must be omitted. By definition of being exclusive, truth must exclude all that opposes it.

Truth is God and Originates from God

An ontological basis for truth must exist. However, the ontological foundation cannot be perishable or contingent—dependent upon something else for its existence. Augustine's, Clark's, and Plantinga's version of the argument from truth for the existence of God all conclude truth is God because he is the only Being who possesses the previous attributes. "God is both the locus of truth and the one who makes knowledge possible," according to Arthur Holmes, and he continues with, "Confidence about human reason is confidence in God."[17] If we replace the word *truth* with *God*, this is what we would get:

- God exists.
- God is immutable—absolute in his nature.
- God is eternal and universal.
- God is knowable.
- God is objective.
- God is exclusive.
- God is truth.

The arguments from these Christian thinkers declare these attributes apply equally to truth and to God. Additionally, they can only apply to these two equally. In other words, truth and God are identical. Therefore, God is truth, and truth originates from God. As a result then, the only true propositions are about God; hence, knowing truth is knowing God.

This rests completely upon what the word *is* means. The English verb *to be* drives people crazy when learning the language, especially those who are learning English as a second language. A clear reason why this is the case emerges; we use the verb in a variety of ways. The verb can be quite ambiguous because the verb's function often relies upon what one's definition of *is* actually is.

---

17. Holmes, *Contours of a World*, 130.

There are four common usages of the verb. *Is* can imply existence, such as the statement God is. Here we can replace the verb *to be* with the verb *exists*. By swapping out the verbs, the sentence's meaning remains unchanged. *Is* can be a predication. Terry is smart. Here the verb serves as a predication because smart is an attribute, quality, or characteristic of Terry. *Is* can infer a class-inclusion. Justin is a student. While you may think this structure is the same as the previous one, it is different. Yes, being a student can be a characteristic of Justin. But a better option is available. Being a student places Justin into a group of people—a class inclusion. And *is* can mean identity. Mark Twain is Samuel Clemens. The verb in the last sentence means *is the same as*. The material after the verb can replace the material before the verb. Samuel Clemens is Mark Twain. Since the subject of the sentence and its identification are the same, they can be interchanged with each other without altering the meaning of the sentence.[18]

Only one option emerges as the way in which the verb should be understood in our original statement, *truth is God*. If we consider the first option, truth is God would mean *truth exists*. While truth does exist, this does not make sense with this use of the verb in question. Consider *truth is God* as a predication for a moment. God is *not* an attribute, characteristic, or quality of truth; therefore, we can rule this meaning out. What about the third option? *Truth is God* as a class-inclusion also does not work. Does truth belong to a class of things or beings called God? No, it does not. Our only possibility left is *truth is God* means truth and God are identities. Thus, *truth* and *God* are two different names for the same entity. In other words we could rephrase the sentence as *truth is the same as God*. By doing so we do not damage the meaning of the original expression. Transposing the two nouns so it reads *God is truth* still produces a logical and meaningful statement.

BIBLICAL SUPPORT FOR THE DISTINCTIONS OF TRUTH FROM A CHRISTIAN PERSPECTIVE

Up until this point, I have refrained from providing scriptural support for the seven distinctions of truth from a biblical perspective. Before now, it

---

18. Gottlob Frege is considered as the founder of modern logic and at times heralded the father of the analytic philosophy. He is the one who worked on the semantics of the ambiguity of the verb *to be* by completing what Plato and Aristotle began. However, there is not a single work in which all of this is worked out in Frege's writings.

was important to put forth the distinctions and the justification for each so that I could establish the rationale. I can now begin providing the scriptural support for each, moving from the last distinctive to the first.

Scriptural Warrant for Truth is God and Originates from God

The Bible does not give an explanation for or a defense for God's existence. Frankly, we do not need one. While the Bible contains no formal argument for the existence of God, it presumes the reader has inherent knowledge of God's existence. The Bible opens with, "In the beginning God . . . let us make man in our image" (Gen 1:1, 26), which indicates God gave humans instinctive knowledge of himself. Job 32:8 further supports this notion when it claims the "breath of the Almighty" gives humanity understanding since it refers to Genesis 1:26. We can find additional support in Ecclesiastes 3:11–22, where King Solomon proclaims God set eternity in the heart of man (cf. Rev 1:8, 11). The apostle Paul gives the fullest account concerning the knowledge of God being innate in Romans 1:18–32, even if it is suppressed. In this passage, Paul repeatedly states humanity possesses knowledge of God (cf. Acts 14:16–17; 17:24–28). Paul continues giving support for this belief in the next chapter (Rom 2:14–15).[19] This is all we need to know—God was in existence before he created all things into existence out of nothing (*ex nihilo*).

The Bible does, however, provide more than enough information on who God is. Looking at the entirety of the Bible, we discover God has a unique integrity, which he displays in the perfection of his attributes and character. The truth of God begins with that he alone is God. The servants of God who recorded his divine thoughts and messages for us speak of this fact repeatedly throughout the pages of the Bible. The weeping prophet, Jeremiah, proclaims, "The LORD is the true God; he is the living God and the everlasting King" (Jer 10:10). For he alone is the true God; for he alone is the living God, and for he alone is the everlasting King. Jeremiah is not the only person who proclaims God alone is God. This testimony concerning God is established early in the beginnings of Judaism (cf. Deut 4:39; 2 Chr 15:3; Isa 43:10–11; 45:5–6, 14, 21; Zech 14:9). And it continues in the teachings of the New Testament (John 1:18; 17:3; 1 Thess 1:9; Rev 6:10).

---

19. For additional information on Paul's treatment on how the knowledge of God is innate, see Hodge, *Epistle to the Romans*, 21–36, 46–48; Schreiner, *Romans*, 85–87.

To call God *the one and only true God* means he alone contains complete divinity and is worthy to be praised and worshiped as God.

The Bible frequently refers to God as being the God of truth (Pss 31:5; 40:10–11; 43:3; Isa 65:16; John 3:33; 7:28; 8:26; 1 John 5:20; Rev 15:3). Truth is also seen as an aspect of God's character (Ps 51:4; Rom 3:3–4, 7; 15:8; Rev 16:7; 19:2, 11), which is demonstrated by God's faithfulness and reliability (Num 23:19; 1 Sam 15:29; Pss 12:6; 33:4; 119:151, 160; Isa 45:19; Jer 42:5; Dan 10:21; Mic 7:20; Rom 3:4; Titus 1:2; Heb 6:18; Jas 1:7) and by his justice and mercy (Pss 96:13; 119:30, 43–44, 142, 151). Because God's essence is truth, the truthfulness of God undergirds everything he does, which is supremely shown in the person of Jesus of Nazareth who is the Christ.

God reveals his truth in the revelation of himself in his Son. The apostle John opens his Gospel with an account of how the Word became flesh (John 1:1–18). In this passage there are two verses pertinent to our discussion. "And the Word became flesh and dwelt among us, and we have seen his glory, glory as of the only Son from the Father, full of grace and truth. . . . For the law was given through Moses; grace and truth came through Jesus Christ" (John 1:14, 17). Here we have the first pronouncement that the Son of God was "full of grace and truth." Later in the Gospel of John, Jesus proclaims he is "the way, and the truth, and the life" (John 14:6). We can with this pronouncement conclude truth is defined by Jesus Christ's person and work. In light of the entirety of the New Testament, we can see the truthfulness of God undergirds the teachings of Jesus as well (Matt 5:18; 22:16; Mark 3:28; 12:14; Luke 4:24; 20:21; John 1:17, 51; 8:31–32; 18:37–38). Additionally, God's truth is revealed through the Holy Spirit who speaks truth (John 1:14; 14:17; 15:26; 16:13; Rom 15:8; 1 John 4:6; 5:6).

As a result of who God is and what he does, all truth originates with God and from God. New Testament scholar Stanley Porter notes:

> I find that God is seen as the origin of truth; the Son is seen to be the embodiment of the truth, mediating between God and humanity and the Spirit, also known as the Paraclete, is the one sent to continue the work of the Son after his departure. . . . Each of these—Father, Son, and Spirit—is a representative of, or bearer of witness to, the truth. Truth originates with God but is found in Jesus and the Spirit—who is known as the Spirit of truth. . . . As a whole, the Gospel [of John] indicates that truth originates in the tripartite relationship of the Father-Son-Spirit, and it is realized in truthful relations between the Son and human beings.[20]

---

20. Porter, *John, His Gospel*, 9, 175.

The Gospel of John is not the only place in Scripture where discussion can be found concerning the origins of truth. The psalmists declare in four different Psalms that truth originates with God (Pss 25:5; 26:3; 43:3; 86:11). The prophets Isaiah and Daniel both infer truth originates with and from God (Isa 65:16; Dan 9:13).

God is truth. Truth originates with and from God because he is the source of all truth as being truth itself. Another way of saying this is with the phrase—*all truth is God's truth*. The church fathers assert *all truth is God's truth* because truth's ontological foundation is rooted in God and his omniscience. But they also understand truth is unified due to its relation to God and his divine purposes found within his creation.[21] Thus, truth is exclusive, objective, knowable, eternal and universal, immutable and absolute, and exists and corresponds to reality.

Scriptural Warrant for Truth is Exclusive

Truth is, by its very definition, exclusive. If something is true, it naturally excludes itself from falsehood. Scripture attests to this fact (1 Kgs 17:24; 22:16; 2 Chr 18:15; Neh 6:6; Prov 8:7; 12:17; 16:13; Isa 45:19; Zech 8:16). God's nature further prevents him from doing anything that is untrue to himself, which means God cannot tell a lie (Num 23:19; Rom 3:4; 2 Tim 2:13; Titus 1:12; Heb 6:18).

We need to relook at what Jesus says in John 14:6 further: "I am the way, and the truth, and the life. No one comes to the Father except through me." Christ's statement makes Christianity exclusive. The promised Messiah clearly declares he is the only way anyone gets to the God the Father. By implication Christianity and another religion cannot both be true. It is possible both can be false, however. But it is impossible for both of them to be true. Remember the laws of logic I briefly mentioned towards the opening of the previous chapter. This is where the law of non-contradiction once again comes into play. Unfortunately, this is where many people want to disagree with this law of logic. It is okay to be true for all matters, except when it comes to religious truth claims. The laws of logic do not work that way. They are either always valid or always invalid. Being a law means it is always valid and applies to this type of situation.

---

21. Holmes, *Contours of a World*, 133.

Scriptural Warrant for Truth is Objective

If truth is exclusive, it presupposes objective truth. Jesus' truth claim in John 14:6 establishes the objective nature of truth. Truth deals with matters of fact. It does not dwell on matters of feelings, which are subjective. Since God is truth and he exists outside of someone's feelings, truth is objective. "But truth is also objective because God is the final court of appeal, the source of all truth, by virtue of his nature and his will."[22] Theologian R. Albert Mohler Jr. states, "Christianity is predicated upon a claim to absolute, objective *truth* . . . To surrender this ground is to surrender the faith itself."[23] There are certain claims Christianity makes about itself that will be forsaken if an absolute, objective truth ceases to exist in reality. Here is what Mohler says is at stake:

> If Scripture is not objectively true, independent of our acknowledgment, and if God is not objectively real, independent of our knowledge of Him, then we are without hope. If Jesus Christ did not die on the cross as our substitute and if He was not resurrected on the third day, if we have not been justified by faith and if His righteousness has not been imputed to us, then we are dead in our sins.[24]

Scriptural Warrant for Truth is Knowable

The apostle John records Jesus told to the Jews who believed him to be the promised Messiah of the Old Testament these words: "If you abide in my word, you are truly my disciples, and you will know the truth, and the truth will set you free" (John 8:31–32). The very fact Jesus states people can know the truth means truth is knowable. There is no way around the words of Christ here. Because truth is knowable and we have the ability to learn, obtaining knowledge is possible, which implies the knowledge of truth is cognitive and intellectual.

The psalmist in Psalm 19:1–6 and the apostle to the Gentiles, Paul, in Romans 1:18–32 declare that certain truths are knowable through natural theology. Paul even proclaims the unrighteousness of humanity causes truth to be suppressed (Rom 1:18). However, this is not the only way to

---

22. Groothuis, *Truth Decay*, 67.
23. Mohler, "'Evangelical'," 39.
24. Ibid.

gain knowledge of the truth. God reveals the truth about himself through special revelation.[25]

Furthermore, remember God is truth. Because truth is exclusive, objective, and absolute, it is knowable. Since truth is knowable, God—himself—is knowable. It would be great if we could have an exhaustive understanding and knowledge of God and truth. But we will not have this capability. Because God has particular attributes and is knowable, they cannot be applied to us.

Scriptural Warrant for Truth is Eternal and Universal

God's eternal being is the cornerstone for the eternality of his truth. David in Psalm 119:89 mentions God's Word is eternal. And the prophet Isaiah declares that God's Word will stand forever (Isa 40:8). So whatever is true at any given point in time-space history is still true today. Think about it this way—truth statements are true for all people, cultures, and under all conditions regardless of the historical setting. Truth is truth. It is eternal and universal.

Scriptural Warrant for Truth is Immutable—Absolute in Its Nature

Jesus' statement declaring he is "the way, and the truth, and the life" is an absolute truth claim (John 14:6). Jesus does not say he is "a way, and a truth, and a life." He uses the definite article to make sure there is no confusion in the minds of his disciples. I can only speculate here, but I would not be surprised if he wanted to drive this point to his listeners. Jesus' remarks that he is the only way to the Father in the second half of the verse is another absolute claim. There is only one method by which to get in a right relationship with God, according to Jesus. And he is the means by which it occurs.

Truth is static. It does not change or morph into something else. It is a constant. We would never argue $2 + 2 = 5$. We all know $2 + 2 = 4$. As long as the context does not change, then truth will never become error. If we are to

---

25. If this point is not completely understood, please revisit the previous chapter where I discussed the philosophy of divine revelation. Do not get frustrated if it takes some time to grasp these concepts. The Christian life is a life-long journey. We do not learn everything God desires us to know immediately after coming to him in faith through Christ's atoning work. Paul addresses this fact throughout his letters on how believers are to gradually move from milk to solid food.

add something else to the mathematical equation—such as 2 + 2 + 1 = ?—then our context has changed. Now, we would agree the answer is five. This example is fairly easy to see truth as being immutable and absolute. What about the following example? "It is snowing on Pike's Peak, and it is in the middle of the summer." If someone witnessed the event, it is considered truthful. The statement, however, would no longer be true when it stops snowing. So does this change the truthfulness of the original statement? No, it does not. The event is locked into an unchangeable reality that relates to the exact time when the statement was true. If it did snow at the specific time it was recorded to be snowing, the fact goes unscathed for eternity.

Truth is God and originates from God. Truth is exclusive. Truth is objective. Truth is knowable. Truth is eternal and universal. And truth is immutable—absolute in its nature. God is immutable. We find this attribute of God taught throughout the Bible. For example, God affirms that "I the Lord do not change" in Malachi 3:6 (cf. Num 23:19; 1 Sam 15:29; Isa 46:9–11; Ezek 24:14; Jas 1:17). Despite what people may wish and think, God does not change his mind, his will, or his nature.

Unlike us—who are consistently changing our minds, changing our attitudes, and changing our moods—God is consistently constant in who he is. He does not fly off the handle when he is angry as we may think. Theologically and philosophically there are some logical reasons why God is immutable. First, God exists outside of the constraints of time and space as an eternal being (Pss 33:11; 41:13; 90:2–4; John 17:5; 2 Tim 1:9). For something to change, it must be done so in some form of chronological order within the constraints of time and space. Second, God is completely perfect as he is. For something to change, it either must add something that is needed or lose something. If something is gained, the change makes it better. If something is lost, then the change makes it worse. Think about this for a moment: If God were to gain something, he would not have been completely perfect to begin with. If God were to lose something, he would no longer possess perfection. As a result of losing something, he would have changed for the worse. Third, God's immutability is closely intertwined with his omniscience. If he were to change, he would not have been omniscient from the start. God cannot gain new knowledge he does not already know about by definition of being omniscient. But there are a few passages of Scripture where the biblical authors speak about God changing his mind (Exod 32:14; 1 Sam 15:11–29). When we consider the full context and think through the material, we should notice God does not change his mind. Something within the contextual account indicates something about the situation changed, which describes how God interacts with humans.

While truth is absolute in its nature, it does not mean our understanding of it is. At times it would be wonderful if our grasp of truth was absolute. But as finite beings, we cannot grasp truth completely in a totality manner. Our understanding of truth does increase as we learn more.

Scriptural Warrant for Truth Exists

We are now back to the place where our discussion on the biblical distinctions of truth began. Because of the fact truth exists, we can make the other declarations about the nature of truth from a biblical perspective. We can also claim truth exists because God is truth; truth originates from him. If it were not for the transcendence and immanence of God's workings in time and space with his creation, we would not know about truth. But God has been active with his creation so we know about the concept of truth.

"And we know that the Son of God has come and has given us understanding so that we may know him who is true; and we are in him who is true, in his Son Jesus Christ. He is the true God and eternal life" (1 John 5:20). Hopefully, you recall I previously mentioned truth corresponds to reality. The Bible affirms this (John 1:9; 4:23; 17:3; Eph 4:24; 1 Thess 1:9; 1 Tim 1:2; 6:19; Titus 1:2; 3:2; Heb 8:2; 9:24; 12:8; 1 Pet 5:12; 1 John 2:5, 8; Rev 19:9).

The reality is truth exists. Truth is immutable—absolute in its nature. Truth is eternal and universal. Truth is knowable. Truth is objective. Truth is exclusive. And truth is God and originates from God. The reality is God is a God of truth. The reality is Jesus is truth. The reality is the Spirit of God is truth. And the reality is the gospel message and the Christian faith is truth (John 8:31–32; Acts 20:30; 2 Cor 4:2; Eph 1:13; Gal 2:5; Col 1:5; 1 Tim 2:3–4; 4:6; 2 Tim 2:18; 4:4; Titus 1:1; Jas 5:19; 2 Pet 2:2; 1 John 3:19). This is reality.

CONCLUSION

In today's world a large group prevails in which individuals are not concerned with what truth is. Not only are these individuals unconcerned about truth, they question if there is even such a thing as truth. If truth exists, it is relative and applies to each individual differently. What is true for person X does not have to be true for person Y or even for person Z. Truth is determined by each individual separately.

By its definition, truth must apply across the spectrum to *all* people, in *all* places, and in *all* times if it is, in fact, truth. Despite what we may like to be the case—especially when we are faced with the uncomfortable hardships and facts of reality—we cannot change what truth is to fit our specific needs and desires. Yes, being able to do so would be nice at times. I have no issue admitting this. For example, back in high school, I got pulled over for speeding by a state trooper. I would have loved for the truth to be that the state trooper's radar gun was incorrect and for his reality of the matter not to match with authentic reality. But it did. No matter what I could have tried to say it was not the truth would not be able to change reality, especially when the summons to appear in court arrived in the mail. Truth corresponds with reality. There is no successful means around this fact.

When we look at the nature of truth from a biblical perspective, several features of truth emerge to the forefront. Truth exists as immutable—absolute in its nature—as eternal and universal, as knowable, as objective, as exclusive, and is God and originates from God. As creator of all things that are in existence (Gen 1:1—2:25; Col 1:15-19), truth has its foundation in the very being of God.

7

Truth and Falsehood
How Do We Know What is True?

"Lead me in your truth and teach me..."
—Psalm 25:5a

In the previous two chapters, we looked at the definition of and the nature of truth. And because of that information, certain biblical distinctions of truth were determined. Those key attributes have a rich theological history tracing back to the writings of Augustine of Hippo. If truth is as described—as existing, immutable and absolute, eternal and universal, knowable, objective, exclusive, originating from God because of its relationship with God, and corresponding to reality—then additional philosophical implications must also be true.

Since truth exists and is immutable and absolute, eternal and universal, knowable, objective, exclusive, originates from God, then learning is possible. If learning is possible, then one can be mistaken or deceived. If one can be mistaken or deceived, then truth claims may be made and believed. If truth claims may be made and believed, then a proposition can be true only if it affirms or denies something. If a proposition can be true only if it affirms or denies something, then truth can be verified. If we can verify truth, then truth can be tested. If we can test truth, then the laws of logic are applicable. If the laws of logic are applicable, then truth can relate to other truths so that reality is interpreted.

If truth is as described in the last two chapters, then how can one be mistaken or deceived? On the face of it, one would think if the truth is all I said, then it should not be possible to be mistaken nor deceived. If truth is absolute, immutable, universal, objective, derived from God, and even knowable, how could anyone possibly miss it?[1] We must consider this question here: does biblical warrant exist for truth to be these things and yet unattainable?

Yes, there is. You may recall the discussion from chapter 2 on how sin affects people's ability of cognitive reasoning.[2] Then in chapter 4, I discussed how this makes one incapable of discerning certain truths of God on our own accord, particularly the truths of salvation. Both of these issues come into play here. People suppress the truth because of their unrighteousness, according to the apostle Paul in Romans 1:18. Those who are still in their natural state of depravity are incapable of discerning certain information without divine assistance (1 Cor 2:14). Paul further declares in 2 Corinthians 4:4 the god of this world blinds the minds of unbelievers. Then, we must take into consideration Paul's teaching that there are individuals who have "futility of their minds" because "they are darkened in their understanding" as a result of the hardness in their heart (Eph 4:17–18). So is it possible for truth to be declared as it was in this section of the book and someone be clueless on its knowability? According to the teachings of Paul in the New Testament, it can be the case. We, however, may not want to admit that our quests for knowledge are limited and problem-laden. Regardless how hard we try, we are incapable of fully transcending beyond conditions and situations that strap us to dependency as finite beings.[3]

When determining whether a statement is true or false, logic is extremely helpful. This philosophical tool aids in uncovering either the error or truthfulness of a claim. The heart of critical thinking is logic. In this area of philosophy, three laws of thought and logic are essential. These are the law of bivalence, the law of the excluded middle, and the law of non-contradiction. Some logic textbooks will not list the law of bivalence. They

---

1. Winfried Corduan raises this question in an exchange of messages he and I had on October 19, 2015.

2. In addition to the sources found in chapter 2, see Sproul et al., *Classical Apologetics*, 241–52.

3. Holmes, *Contours of a World*, 130.

instead list the law of identity. This law simply affirms something is what it claims to be. A German chocolate cake is a German chocolate cake. It cannot be anything else. If it were something else, then it is not what it identifies itself as. Remember that the law of bivalence affirms any unambiguous, declarative announcement is either true or false. But when we look into the truthfulness and falsehood of a proclamation, two of these laws are of greater importance.

CONSTRAINTS ON TRUTH AND FALSEHOOD

Philosophers commonly accept two constraints on truth and falsehood. They require that all propositions can only have a single truth-value. The first constraint is the *law of the excluded middle*. This restriction affirms every proposition is true or false. The second constraint is the *law of noncontradiction*. Here the affirmation is a proposition cannot be both true and false. Most philosophers take the second restriction a step further by stating the proposition's truth-value never changes in space or time. Another way of saying this is the statement cannot be both true and false in the same way, manner, and at the same time.

These two laws of thought have a rich history in philosophy. We can see both of these laws in Aristotle's teachings. Here is what Aristotle says:

> For a principle which every one must have who knows anything about being, is not a hypothesis; and that which every one must know who knows anything, he must already have when he comes to a special study. Evidently then such a principle is the most certain of all; which principle this is, we proceed to say. It is, that the same attribute cannot at the same time belong and not belong to the same subject in the same respect; we must presuppose, in face of dialectical objections, any further qualification which might be added. This, then, is the most certain of all principles, since it answers to the definition given above. For it is impossible for any one to believe the same thing to be and not to be, as some think Heraclitus says; for what a man says he does not necessarily believe. If it is impossible that contrary attributes should belong at the same time to the same subject (the usual qualifications must be presupposed in this proposition too), and if an opinion which contradicts another is contrary to it, obviously it is impossible for the same man at the same time to believe the same thing to be and not to be; for if a man were mistaken in this point he would have contrary opinions at the same time. It is for this reason that

all who are carrying out a demonstration refer it to this as an ultimate belief; for this is naturally the starting-point even for all other axioms.[4]

The Law of the Excluded Middle

This law affirms a statement is either true or false. No other option exists. For example, I am a married male. It is either true or false that I am a married male. Here is another example: During one of the Spring Breaks while in college, I spent ten days in Nicaragua with several classmates, a professor, and with a group of Christians from a local church near the University of Mobile. Once again the statement is either true or false. In this case the statement is true because I did spend ten days in Nicaragua during Spring Break of 1997. But what about the other conditions mentioned in the original declaration? For the statement to be true, all parts of it must be true. One of my religion professors supervised the trip, and some classmates and a group from a local church were there with me. The original statement is true. Hopefully, you understand how the law of the excluded middle works. Here is another example to see if it is making sense: I am pregnant. What do you think? Remember the statement is either true or false. This one should come to you more quickly than the previous example. I am a male; therefore, the proposition must be false. As a male it is not possible for me to be pregnant. But if the author of this book were a female, the statement would require more thinking before you can determine your answer. For a female under normal bodily conditions, it is possible for her to get pregnant. The answer to the statement under these considerations is either true or false. A condition does not exist for a female to be *kind-of* or *sort-of* pregnant. She either is pregnant or not pregnant. The law of the excluded middle ought to be viewed as there is no middle ground between a statement being true or false.

The law of the excluded middle is significant. This law of logic allows us to work with and establish absolutes. Remember from the last two chapters that today people question the existence of absolute truth, but one of the features of truth is it is absolute in its nature based upon the fact it is immutable. Many people want to argue truth does not exist, particularly absolute truth. Instead of truth being absolute, these individuals advocate

---

4. Aristotle, *Metaph.*, 4.3.1005b14–33.

its relativity. Truth cannot be relative as many may wish it to be. The law of the excluded middle demands that every proposition must be one or the other—true or false. No other options are possible.

The Law of Non-Contradiction

Most of us are familiar with the concept of the law of non-contradiction; some sources see this law as a subcategory of the law of contradiction. In fact, many of us use it on a regular basis—if not on a daily basis. If I told you that I am a single male as I write this book, a number of you (if not all of you) will be shaking your head side-to-side. If you read the dedication page in the first pages of the book, you would know I cannot be a single male as I was working on this book. On the dedication page, you will find I dedicated this book to my parents and my dear wife, along with a former professor. An evident contradiction emerges with the two declarations. If I have a dear wife, can I be single when I wrote this book? It is impossible for me to be single and married by the legal definition at the same time and in the same way.

Here is another example. We are at work and having small talk during a break. You ask me what my wife cooked for dinner last night. I tell you that she cooked these amazing stuffed pork chops with all the fixings. Later in the day, you ask me how I enjoyed the stuffed pork chops. I look at you and tell you that my wife did not cook stuffed pork chops. Your facial expressions change to a look of confusion because I gave you two statements during the same day that are contradictory. Which one is it? Either my wife cooked stuffed pork chops or she did not cook stuffed pork chops. It cannot be both. It is impossible for it to be both.

With the law of non-contradiction, we know a true statement is not self-contradictory. We can rely on this law when determining truth. This is why it is a law. "Strictly speaking, the law of noncontradiction cannot be proved. The reason is simple. Any argument offered as proof for the law of noncontradiction would of necessity have to assume the law as part of the proof. Hence, any direct proof of the law would end up being circular. It would beg the question."[5]

One of the bumper stickers that drives me crazy happens to be the *Coexist* where the word is spelled out with the various religious symbols of a

---

5. Nash, *Worldviews in Conflict*, 82.

handful of the world's religions. Despite what many people want to believe and do believe, all religions cannot coexist with an equal claim to truth.

The world's religions fall into several categories on how they perceive the existence or non-existence of a divine Supreme Being—God. Several religions have no problem with the existence of other religions. In fact, a number of them adopt and adapt aspects of other religions and morph them into their own beliefs and practices. But three religions make explicit truth claims they are the *only true* religion. Is it possible for all three of these religions to be individually the only true religion? If so, how can it be? Simply said, it is impossible for all three to be the only true religion because of the law of non-contradiction. Remember truth is not self-contradictory.

The Christian philosopher Gordon H. Clark comments on what would happen if contradictory statements were both true:

> If contradictory statements are true of the same subject at the same time, evidently all things will be the same thing. Socrates will be a ship, a house, as well as a man; but then Crito too will be a ship, a house, and a man. But if precisely the same attributes attach to Crito that attach to Socrates, it follows that Socrates is Crito. Not only so, but the ship in the harbor, since it has the same list of attributes too, will be identified with this Socrates-Crito person. In fact, everything will be everything. Therefore everything will be the same thing. All differences among things will vanish and all will be one.[6]

Clark is correct in his assessment of the implications of denying the law of non-contradiction. Ronald H. Nash illustrates Clark's reflections to show the severity of what is at risk here.

> There is no quicker way to become swallowed up in nonsense than to deny the distinction between *B* and non-*B*. I once heard a young man who was called into his local office of the Internal Revenue Service for an audit. The reason for his trouble was his failure over several years to file a tax return. When asked by the IRS agent why he had failed to file, the youth replied that in college he had learned that the law of noncontradiction is an optional, nonnecessary principle. Once he had learned that there is no difference between *B* and non-*B*, it was only a matter of time before he realized that no difference exists between filing a tax return and not filing a tax return. "That's very interesting," said the tax agent. "I've never heard that one before. Since you believe that no difference

---

6. Clark, *Thales to Dewey*, 103.

exists between *B* and non-*B*, I'm sure you also believe that there is no difference between being in jail and not being in jail!"[7]

I am quite confident every one of us would agree there is clearly a difference between being behind bars and not being behind bars. When I have a student wishing to deny the law of non-contradiction, I have asked if the individual would mind getting an *F* in the course. Naturally, the student quickly protests. If there is no difference between getting an *F* and not getting an *F* in the course, then you should not have a problem with the *F* being your final grade. Of course, I cannot give that grade to a student solely on the basis of the denial of the law of non-contradiction. But playing devil's advocate with the student does cause more consideration into the law applying to all areas of life by the student.[8]

LOGICAL CONSISTENCY AND THEORIES OF TRUTH

In the two previous chapters, I intentionally upheld the correspondence theory of truth without presenting any alternative theories. Other hypotheses do exist to describe the relationship between truth and reality.[9] Unfortunately, I am unable to examine every possible option with the numerous variations. For our purposes here, however, it is critical to have an overview of the three most popular views—the coherence theory of truth, the pragmatic theory of truth, and the correspondence theory of truth.

The Coherence Theory of Truth

For a statement to be true, according to the coherence theory of truth, it must *cohere*—be consistent—with all of the declarations within the given system. Truth only exists *if and only if* coherence is found between all the various statements that are entailed with what is desired to be affirmed as truth. Each statement relies upon all the others by implication.

There is no reason to want to pull your hair out. Trust me. I have been right where you are at this moment trying to make sense of this madness.

---

7. Nash, *Life's Ultimate Questions*, 195.

8. For more on the law of non-contradiction, see Ciocchi, "Contradiction," 176–79; Clark, *Thales to Dewey*, 97–107; Nash, *Life's Ultimate Questions*, 193–208.

9. For a critical introduction to the various theories of truth, see Glanzberg, "Truth"; Geisler and Feinberg, *Introduction to Philosophy*, 235–51; Kirkham, *Theories of Truth*.

Think of the coherence theory of truth like you would of a section of chain. Each individual link represents a statement within the system that is being checked for its truthfulness. How are the links connected in the chain? Another way of thinking about this question is to ask: How are the links related to the one before and after it? Each of the links depends upon the one before and after it to function as it is meant to and to stay intact. If we get a pair of bolt cutters and cut out a link from the chain, it gets shorter. Now think of the removal of the link as you found a problem with one of the premises of the system. The problem does not have to be a complete falsehood being found with the statement. Even if it is a smaller impurity, it causes the strength of the overall statement to be weakened.

Unfortunately, two consequential implications emerge with this theory of truth almost immediately. First, each statement depends on its relationship with the rest of the statements. The relationships determine meaning and truth, which requires for "all knowledge to become necessary within the system"[10] because of the doctrine of internal relations. Secondly, a byproduct of this doctrine is truth can come in various degrees. The truthfulness of the entire system is intimately connected to the truthfulness of each link, and the reverse is true as well.

Once a portion of the system is deemed questionable or only partially true, it means it is also partially false, which puts the entire system into jeopardy. "Saying that there are degrees of truth, as the coherentist does, and that all truths are dependent is just another way of saying that all truth is relative. If all statements are dependent (contingent) on the system, then no truth can be absolute," according to Norman Geisler and Ronald Brooks.[11] The truthfulness of the entire system must not be absolute. Remember each part of the system depends on all its contingent parts being coherent.[12]

More significant problems exist with this theory of truth. One problem is the coherence theory makes truth contingent on the logical fallacy of infinite regress. Regardless of the number of cascading propositions, the validity of each one depends upon the validity of the statement that directly comes before and after it. The process never ceases to arrive at any truth. While the theory may be logically consistent among a set of statements, another coherent system can also exist. The problem emerges when the two contradict each other. Both positions cannot be true. An additional

10. Geisler and Feinberg, *Introduction to Philosophy*, 236.
11. Geisler and Brooks, *When Skeptics Ask*, 260.
12. Ibid.

problem occurs for the coherence theory when the propositions are consistent but do not match with what we know and see happening in the world around us. Imagine you are back in high school, your normal teacher is out for a week due to illness. The class is the typical one that misbehaves when a substitute is in charge. Mid-week, a football gets thrown across the room and hits the substitute's back. The substitute turns around fuming and demands who threw the football. All of the students know who threw the football, but everyone blames the wrong student. The substitute knows the class is blaming the wrong student, but she cannot prove who did it. Everyone's testimony is unified, implicating this one student is responsible. But all of the students know person who is being blamed is innocent.[13]

The Pragmatic Theory of Truth

During the first half of the twentieth century, American philosophy was heavily influenced by the theory of pragmatism. In the fifth chapter, I briefly introduced the basic tenet of this theory of truth. Pragmatism has three dominant variations.[14] But the basic premise of each one is the same. For truth to be what it is, it must work.

But the question remains if something works, does this make it true? If pragmatism's central thesis claims truth is the byproduct of an experimental method, could someone name a more simplistic explanation what has occurred than it being a mere byproduct? According to Ockham's Razor, when two or more reasons can be given to explain why something has happened or for why it is what it is, the explanation that is the simplest option is always preferred.

We can also ask, "What does *work* mean?" The term work is ambiguous as some philosophers have pointed out. This can be seen with how different professional athletes hold certain superstitions and ritual practices. For example, a baseball pitcher may have eaten a meal before pitching his best game ever. The only thing the pitcher did new from other games was to have this one meal before the game. He has eaten meals previously before playing a game. But he has not previously eaten this exact meal. So before the next game, he eats the *magical* meal. And he has another spectacular game. Twice now this meal has been the secret to the pitcher's success. Should we consider this meal as being the real cause for the pitcher's

---

13. Geisler and Feinberg, *Introduction to Philosophy*, 237–39.
14. Ibid., 239–44.

outstanding games? Could another explanation account for the success? What if those two games the opposing teams were forced to bench their best players due to illness?

With the pragmatic theory of truth, it is possible for something to work in a particular situation that we know will not work if it were tried independently. A man goes to his family physician after his wife hounds him until he breaks down to go. The wife found a mole on his neck, which was drastically changing in color, size, and shape. His doctor has enough concern of its appearance that a referral is made to a specialist. By the time the husband gets into the specialist, his wife has searched WebMD and other websites trying to determine if the changing mole is skin cancer. The wife joins the husband for the appointment, and she is extremely nervous as they walk into the specialist's office. The specialist completes the examination. And the doctor has his concerns after seeing it. But the dermatologist informs the couple nothing serious is wrong in hopes to comfort the wife's nerves. The specialist, however, knows the situation is much more severe than the wife thinks. The wife lets out a huge sigh of relief. The dermatologist tells them he needs to remove the mole along with some of the extra skin around it to send off for testing. Telling the couple nothing serious is wrong to calm the nerves of the frightful wife *worked*. But was it true? On the basis of pragmatism, it was; but is it true on independent grounds? We have to admit that it is not.[15]

The Correspondence Theory of Truth

Throughout the annals of history, the correspondence theory of truth has a long and rich history. At its core, the theory holds that truth must match with what actually takes place in reality. The truthfulness or falsehood of a statement is determined based upon whether it corresponds with what we know is fact. The United States Postal Service only delivers on days that are not Sunday or a national holiday.[16] It is Saturday. Mail will be delivered today. Since we know it is not a Sunday or a holiday, the United States

---

15. Ibid., 242–43. The idea for the illustration of the nervous wife is an adaption of one given by Geisler and Feinberg on the pages referenced.

16. A week after writing this point, I received a package from the United States Postal Service on a Sunday afternoon for an item I ordered off of Amazon. I was shocked when the delivery came. I did not request for Sunday delivery. Apparently, there are some exceptions where the United States Postal Service will make a Sunday delivery. So there is no confusion here, I do mean the United States Postal Service.

Postal Service will, in fact, be delivering mail. If you do not get any mail on Saturday, the statement is still true. Mail was delivered to other people's mailboxes. It matches what you knew to be the facts.

The previous example is rather easy to determine its truthfulness or falsehood. But this theory should always be fairly simple to figure out what is true and false. Dirty snow is no longer completely white is true if and only if dirty snow is indeed not completely white. Those who have ever seen a fresh snowfall know it is white in color. It is then safe to say dirty snow is not completely white. This once again shows the truthfulness of a property within a statement has a relationship with external reality.

Because of the truth-claims Christians affirm, the correspondence view of truth is the only theory for truth that can be held as truthful by followers of Christ. "It is the only biblically and logically grounded view of truth available and allowable. We neglect or deny it to our peril and disgrace," according to Christian philosopher and jazz enthusiast Douglas Groothuis.[17] Paul's argument for the resurrection of Christ in 1 Corinthians 15 demands the events to match what occurred in time-space history. If someone can prove successfully that the resurrection of Christ did not happen, then Christianity fails as a religion and as a worldview.[18]

CONCLUSION

There are times when it is very obvious someone is lying to you. On the other hand, someone may be lying to you, and you do not recognize the lie. Depending on the situation, the false information can have major implications or very little impact. Either way the fact remains a lie still conveys false information. In fact, even if someone is straightforward and honest with the majority of the information but leaves out certain details so that you are misled into drawing a conclusion based upon the information given, a problem arises on the truth worthiness of the conclusion. If the left out information was known, you may have drawn a different conclusion completely. By leaving out key details, the person essentially shared falsehoods.

17. Groothuis, *Truth Decay*, 110.

18. For more on the resurrection of Christ and its defense, see Beasley-Murray, *Message of Resurrection*; Geisler, *Battle for the Resurrection*; Habermas and Licona, *Case for the Resurrection*; Habermas et al., *Did the Resurrection Happen*; Hanegraaff, *Resurrection*; Harris, *From Grave to Glory*; McDowell, *Resurrection Factor*; McDowell and McDowell, *Evidence for Resurrection*.

Truth and Falsehood

The Bible declares truth is knowable. And the Bible affirms that individuals will be held accountable for their knowledge or the lack of it (Rom 14:2; Jas 4:17). Here is what the prophet Hosea has to say about people being held accountable for the lack of knowledge: "My people are destroyed for lack of knowledge; because you have rejected knowledge, I reject you from being a priest to me. And since you have forgotten the law of your God, I also will forget your children." By the context of this passage, we know the phrase lack of knowledge refers to the opening verses of the chapter. The phrase connects specifically with the fact the Israelites have no knowledge of God and have forgotten his law (Hos 4:1–3). God's chosen people knew better. But they chose to be disobedient.

This same notion appears in the New Testament in one of Jesus' parables found in Luke 12:35–48. In the parable, Jesus distinguishes between faithful and evil servants. The parable reveals those who know the master's will and do not follow it are held to greater punishment than someone who is ignorant of the master's will. Having knowledge and doing something otherwise is equivalent to sinning arrogantly and presumptuously (Ps 19:12–13); more responsibility awaits those who have knowledge and privilege (Num 15:27–31). The servant who does not know the master's desire is still responsible for any disobedience. This individual while guilty of misbehaving, however, will suffer a lesser penalty because he did not have the same extent of knowledge as the other person who knew the master's will (Luke 12:47–48).

We cannot accept theories of truth that lead to problems. The internal issues with the coherence theory of truth give way to relativism. And the pragmatic theory of truth has its own internal complications, which are seen as not being upheld when examined independently. Because something works or appears to work, it does not make it true.

Recently my car broke down when I was waiting on my wife to get off from work on a Friday evening. I knew at least one of the three possibilities caused the issue: a bad battery, a bad alternator, or a bad starter. That night we ended up getting the car towed to the repair shop I use and trust. The next morning my wife drove me to the shop where I could talk with the reception staff, letting them know what occurred the night before. The ladies noticed my car in the parking lot when they arrived so they were glad when I arrived and told them the issue. In all honesty, the two of them were relieved when they learned the events because earlier in the day I had gotten my oil changed there. They were slightly worried the mechanic had not tightened the plug, and it worked its way out of the oil. I requested the mechanics look at all three possible causes for the problem. It did not take long before I got a phone call informing me the cause of the problem. It was a dead battery cell. While I trust the mechanics at the repair shop, I insisted they check the other two options to make sure. I have had experiences in college where I was told it was a dead battery, but it turned out to be a dead battery and alternator. And other time in college, I had car issues where it was a dead battery, a bad alternator, and a defective starter. I wanted to be reassured that the only issue as a dead battery cell, even though the mechanic was sure no another issue was involved.

What would have happened if I had picked up the car later on Saturday after replacing the battery, and the car broke down again? I believed them when they told me it was only a dead battery cell. But now I am stranded somewhere with the car broke down again. I would have not been in a good mood. I definitely would rather be certain there were no additional issues in the horizon than assume everything was fine. I wanted to make sure what I was being told completely matched the facts and reality. If I had not had specific experiences while in college, I likely would not have been insistent on having the alternator and starter checked.

8

Truth or Truths?
Confronting Truth-Claims

> "Whoever speaks the truth gives honest evidence,
> but a false witness utters deceit."
>
> —Proverbs 12:17

Up to this point, I have discussed the operations of general and special revelation, the nature of truth, the truth's relationship with freedom, and distinguishing truth from falsehood. But the summit still awaits us. What is the point of knowing this material if we cannot use it? There are features in the previous chapters in this section of the book that are applicable. If it were not the case, then a handful of the issues would be problematic to discuss.

As a Presbyterian minister, maverick theologian, prolific author, and profound thinker, Francis A. Schaeffer provided the intellectual framework and encouragement for evangelical Christians to counter society in ways that have not been since the Reformers. He freely expressed his concerns about what the body of Christ were and would be facing in decades to come. At the center of his convictions was how the world needed to hear and see the truths of Christianity. But he knew it comes with a price: *"Truth carries with it confrontation.* Truth *demands* confrontation; loving confrontation, but confrontation nevertheless."[1]

Everyone does not like being confronted with the truth all the time. Knowing the truth can cause someone to be extremely uncomfortable. The apostle Paul is well aware of this fact, according to Romans 1:20–23, where people ignore and reject the truth revealed through natural theology concerning God. Additionally, Paul understands the effects of what happens when individuals are confronted with the gospel of Christ. This is apparent when he writes, "the word of the cross is folly to those who are perishing, but to us who are being saved it is the power of God" (1 Cor 1:18). Being faced with the truth of the message of Christ can be unpleasant for people. Being confronted with the truth can hurt.

When students come to the realization that some religions make exclusive truth-claims, their first reaction is to say immediately the laws of logic cannot and do not apply to religious claims. They have grown up in a politically correct society where it is frowned upon to affirm what is deemed being close-minded or intolerant. The reality, however, is we cannot choose to apply the laws of logic only when we want them to support or favor our position and turn the laws off when we like. Truthfully, it would be wonderful if this were possible. But it is an impossibility. This would be like us having a means to turn on and off Isaac Newton's law of gravity at will.

Students are not the only ones who have an issue with the laws of logic in this particular situation. Many people do. It is as if they do not want to risk the possibility of offending someone else's beliefs even though they may be utterly clueless on what those beliefs are. Yes, this is the world in which we live. It is sad when people will not take a stand against a position just because of the concern of possibly offending someone by doing so. Unfortunately, political correctness has gone amuck. Personally, I would rather be told that something is offensive than have an individual side-stepping all around the issue to avoid confrontation.

IS THERE TRUTH IN NON-CHRISTIAN RELIGIONS?

Previous to the last century, the relevancy of this question was remote. The vast majority of Christians had very little knowledge of non-Christian religions, except perhaps for an occasional missionary presentation focused

---

1. Schaeffer, F., *"Church at the End,"* 110. Emphasis belongs to the original author.

upon the strange people groups from *over there*. Even in the 1980s, I recall listening to Christian missionaries share their experiences as if the groups they were proclaiming the gospel message to where savages living in the jungles.[2] Not every missionary presentation portrayed the unreached parts of the world in this manner. Before the past century when other religions were largely unknown, ministers and missionaries could easily answer this question simply by saying, "No." Today, however, we cannot get away with such an answer. Much more is known about the various religions around the world. Further, many of those once unknown religions are around us daily, whether at work or in our neighborhoods. This question is much more relevant to us now than a few generations back. People, in general, have a greater knowledge of the non-Christian religions, but it is safe to say most Christians' knowledge of these religions has also increased significantly in the past century, even more so within the last twenty to thirty years. Simply saying, "No" is no longer an acceptable answer.

Trust me when I say it would be much easier if this answer were still an option at times. Even if this former answer were still an option today, it would not be a satisfactory one to anyone, including Christians. The world in which we live seems smaller today than other generations because of the advancements in transportation and especially the ease of access to nearly all of the news and information we what to know with a few clicks on the internet.

To be faithful to the goals of this book, we desire a biblical answer to the question on whether if truth can be found in non-Christian religions. Here is what Terry C. Muck and Frances S. Adeney have to say in response to the question:

> Those who argue that the Bible teaches that there may be truth in other religions argue from the classical texts used in defense of natural revelation: Genesis 1:27, which tells us we are all made

---

2. I recall in the early 1980s my parents hosting two missionaries in our apartment for a week or two while we were living in West Germany. I was fascinated with the stories of the missionaries but do not recall any specifics of them today. But I do recall the two missionaries had a profound impact on my coming to Christ. It was not long after they stayed with us that I became a Christian at a very young age. I do recall the events of that Sunday night very clearly, though my parents do not remember the details. After walking down to speak to the pastor during the end of the service, the pastor and his wife invited us to visit with them longer at their home, which was either above or next door to the church. The pastor wanted to truly make sure I understood what I was doing since I was so young. During the visit with the pastor, he realized I actually understood the gospel message and the decision I was making and proclaiming.

in the image of God; Psalm 22:27, which finds the glory of God everywhere in the created world; Romans 1:19–20, which assures us that no one anywhere has been left without a knowledge of God; Romans 2:15, which tells us that even our flawed human consciences remind us of God's law; Acts 17:22–34, in which Paul sermonizes about the unknown god the Athenians seemed to be aware existed; and Revelation 21:24–26, which indicates that representatives from every culture will worship God around the throne. Those who argue that there is no truth in other religions usually define truth in a much more limited way, as knowledge that leads to salvation only, and use passages such as John 14:6, where Jesus says no one comes to the Father except through him; Acts 4:12, which says that salvation comes by no other name; Ephesians 2:8, which locates salvation in grace, not works; 1 Timothy 2:5, which talks of only one God and one mediator; and 1 John 5:11, which reminds us that life is found in the Son only.[3]

Interpreting the thoughts of Muck and Adeney can go a few different ways. There are two extremes of the pendulum. On the one hand, one possible reading is that non-Christian religions contain absolutely no truth within them. On the other hand, one can argue these non-Christian religions contain significant amounts of truth within them. Depending on one's theological convictions on the restrictiveness of the word *truth* will impact how one understands how much truth can be found in non-Christian religions. If a person affirms Christ is not the only way to obtain salvation and there are multiple paths to God, the individual will see much more truth in other religions than a person who believes Christ is the only means of salvation. For the purposes here, however, time does not permit for us to get into these debates. While they are worthy of discussion and need serious contemplation, the issues require additional training in systematic theology and more advanced knowledge of philosophy than a layman's introduction can provide.[4]

---

3. Muck and Adeney, *Christianity Encountering*, 46.

4. Muck and Adeney consider a handful of the questions related to the issues involved here on pages 46–49. But the material presented is not by any means exhaustive in this source. In the past thirty years, a number of books have been written on the topic and generally focus upon the question—what happens to those who do not hear the gospel of Christ? For more on this topic, see Erickson, *How Shall They Be Saved*; Fackre et al., *What About Those*; Kreeft and Tacelli, *Handbook of Christian Apologetics*, 342–60; Pinnock, *Wideness in God's Mercy*; Sanders, *No Other Name*; Tiessen, *Who Can Be Saved*.

Truth or Truths?

Truth can be found in *all* non-Christian religions. Dean C. Halverson acknowledges all non-Christian religions contain some truth within them. What he says next is even more crucial: "Christians should be encouraged to recognize and appreciate that truth."[5] And he is correct in saying Christians can learn something related to their walk from other world religions. This proclamation does not mean these various religions contain truth leading an individual to the salvific knowledge of the God of the Abraham, Isaac, and Jacob (Matt 22:32; Acts 3:13). And he does admit this aspect of truth is missing in other religions.[6]

What truths can be found in other religions? Confucianism encourages one to respect others from family members to governmental authorities; this issue is addressed by Jesus in the Sermon on the Mount in Matthew 5–7 and by Paul in Romans 13. Buddhism acknowledges the existence of suffering and the torments it can cause; while many passages of Scripture can be mentioned here, the book of Job and Luke 13:1–9 immediately come to mind. Hinduism emphasizes the immanence of God; in Acts 17:27 Paul proclaims God is "not far from each one of us." Islam stresses the greatness of Allah. Even though Allah is not the God recorded in the Bible,[7] the biblical authors repeatedly emphasize the magnitude of God's greatness (1 Chr 16:25; Ps 96:4; Jer 10:6; Luke 1:49; Eph 1:19–20; 1 John 3:1). Here is what the prophet Nahum has to say about God's greatness:

> The Lord is a jealous and avenging God; the Lord is avenging and wrathful; the Lord takes vengeance on his adversaries and keeps wrath for his enemies. The Lord is slow to anger and great in power, and the Lord will by no means clear the guilty. His way is in whirlwind and storm, and the clouds are the dust of his feet. He rebukes the sea and makes it dry; he dries up all the rivers; Bashan and Carmel wither; the bloom of Lebanon withers. The mountains quake before him; the hills melt; the earth heaves before him, the world and all who dwell in it. Who can stand before his indignation? Who can endure the heat of his anger? His wrath is poured out like fire, and the rocks are broken into pieces by him. The Lord is good, a stronghold in the day of trouble; he knows those who take refuge in him. (Nah 1:2–7)

---

5. Halverson, D., "World Religions Overview," 25.

6. Ibid., 26.

7. See George, *Is the Father of Jesus*, for a detailed study examining the issue on the relation between the God of the Bible and Allah, the god of Islam.

Other points of truth can be listed here. Even some of the basic tenets of atheism can benefit Christians. Atheists hope for and strive for answers to questions through rational thinking and the use of logic. This behavior should encourage believers "to be clear in our thinking and consistent in our living."[8]

CRITERIA FOR EVALUATING RELIGIOUS TRUTH-CLAIMS

In the previous section, I gave attention to discussing whether truth can be found in non-Christian religions. Since truth can be found in them, the question we need to be asking ourselves deals with how to go about evaluating religious truth-claims. But in our politically correct society, we cannot make judgments about anything—especially about religious truth-claims. Those who object making judgments often cite Jesus' statement "Do not judge, or you too will be judged" (Matt 7:1, NIV). Taking this statement of Christ as an absolute principle to follow is interesting. In fact, it is more than interesting; it is ironic. Every single day those individuals, along with everyone else end up, make countless judgments. And many of those judgments are justifiable. If we are not to make judgments, then how do we respond to Jesus' words that are found later in Matthew 7:15–23, where we learn we will know people by their fruit? And how do we handle John 15, the entire book of 1 John, and not to mention numerous other passages within the New Testament?

Arguing Christians are not to make judgments is absurd.[9] Even if a person says this only applies to religious judgments, the argument does not hold up. If we are not to make religious judgments, why not? Simply stating this applies only to religious judgments is itself a religious judgment. Further, if we contend people are not to do this, are any religious judgments legitimate? Jesus' words in the opening verses of Matthew 7 are not a declaration to avoid making all judgments.

8. Halverson, D., "World Religions Overview," 26.

9. For more on the absurdity of this stance, see Lutzer, *Who Are You to Judge?* Closely connected with the issue of Christians' being judgmental is the issue of Christians are intorelant. Many Christians are open to listening to varying viewpoints and can even consider them. But then when they begin to share opposing views, they are often times prevented from getting to far into the discussion by those who disagree with the Christian perspective. So is the issue in Christianity being intolerant, or is the issue that others fit the definition better?

Jesus gives a guideline on how we are to go about critiquing others and issues. "To pretend that religions do not make truth-claims is demeaning and fails to take religions seriously on their own terms."[10] All religions make truth-claims. Therefore, those truth-claims must be examined and evaluated. Because truth-claims are made and must be analyzed, criteria must exist to assist us with this process. Evaluating religious truth-claims is by no means an easy task. But being able to do so assures us that it can be done: it is possible. For a religion or a worldview to hold up, the position needs to withstand certain criteria: logical consistency and internal coherence, external correspondence, and existential viability.[11]

A Religion's Beliefs Must Be Logically Consistent and Internally Coherent

Take heed to Douglas Groothuis's words here: "The logical consistency of the biblical worldview is a *necessary* condition of its truth, but it is not a *sufficient* condition" (emphasis added).[12] I added emphasis to two words because they need to be discussed further where everyone understands what the difference is between them.

We can think of these two words in relation to cause and effect. In fact, philosophers analyze the relationship of cause and effect in terms of necessary and sufficient conditions. Philosophers enjoy lively debates. And it does not always take much to spark these debates. Many debates center upon the notion of causation, according to Daniel Bonevac.[13]

What is meant by something being a necessary condition? Once again remember it is essential that we are clear on what we mean by words; therefore, definitions are needed. "A condition is *necessary* for an event if and only if the event cannot occur when the condition does not hold."[14] At the moment this definition is likely confusing, which is okay.

---

10. Netland and Johnson, "Why is Religious Pluralism Fun," 62.

11. It is possible to find other authors list four or five criteria tests for evaluating truth. The issue rests in how the author understands how each test relates to the other and whether the author wants to emphasize something further. Originally, I debated having four criteria tests. But I see one of the tests I originally listed as being a sub-point in one of the other tests.

12. Groothuis, *Truth Decay*, 97.

13. Bonevac, *Simple Logic*, 422.

14. Ibid.

Let me illustrate a necessary condition: for a student to get an A in my Comparative Religions course, it is necessary for a student to submit a research paper. If a student fails to do this submission, the student will not get an A. This is equivalent to the following statement: if a student gets an A in my Comparative Religions class, then the student submitted the required research paper. Submitting a paper for the course is a necessary condition for earning an A in the class.

Here is a definition for a sufficient condition: "A condition is *sufficient* for an event if and only if that event occurs when the condition holds."[15] If a student earns an A on all of the coursework for Comparative Religions, then the student will receive an A at the end of the semester. A sufficient condition for receiving an A in Comparative Religions is to earn an A on all graded coursework for the class.

Simply handing in the research paper is not, however, a sufficient condition for earning an A in Comparative Religions. The reason is that a student can submit the research paper and not receive an A in the class. Additionally, because a student earns an A on all coursework is not a necessary condition for receiving an A in Comparative Religions. A possibility exists that a student may receive an A at the end of the semester for Comparative Religions despite the fact the student failed to earn an A on every assignment.

For a religion to be logically consistent, the religion's beliefs must be consistent with one another, logically, and be free from any internal problems according to the laws of the excluded middle and non-contradiction.[16] This factor also draws upon a religion's beliefs and must have internal coherence. Rick Rood makes a crucial point about using reason to examine religious beliefs. He states, "To put religions under the scrutiny of reason is not to say, however, that all religious beliefs can by fully explained by reason."[17] Rood is correct.

A specific Christian doctrine comes to my mind, and it happens to be the same one Rick Rood mentions as his example. During my undergraduate studies, I took six courses with James W. Bryant. He is one of the key individuals who God used to shape and develop my philosophical and theological passion and encouraged me to love the development of my Christian mind. In his classes, particularly in the two courses of History of

---

15. Ibid.
16. Groothuis, *Truth Decay*, 97; Rood, "Is Jesus the Only Way," 248.
17. Rood, "Is Jesus the Only Way," 248.

Christian Thought and in Christian Theology, Bryant would make sure his students understood that despite how hard we try to illustrate the concept of the Trinity that any and all analogies eventually fail. When teaching the doctrine of the Trinity to others, a common objection to the doctrine is that it contradicts itself. Christian theology affirms God is one. If God is one, then how can God be three? Another way of stating this question is: how can God be both three and one?

Honestly, I can understand people seeing the doctrine of the Trinity as being a contradiction when they are first introduced to it or when people first begin studying the doctrine in-depth. Throughout most of Christianity's history, the doctrine of the Trinity is among the most controversial doctrines. And part of the reason for this is due to this very issue on how God can be one yet three. Here is the scriptural support for the doctrine: First, John 1:1 reveals Jesus Christ was with God in the beginning and was God. Later in John, the second point is made on the relation between God the Father and Christ; we learn God the Father and Christ are unified (John 10:30). And a third biblical text is used to support the doctrine is Matthew 28:19. Here Jesus tells his disciples to baptize new believers in the name of the Father, Son, and Holy Spirit. As the doctrine of the Trinity developed in the early church, a decisive distinction was made in creedal statements and theological treatises. The theologians insisted God is one in his *Essence* but three in *Person*. In philosophy and theology, the terms essence and person are not the same thing. Since they are not the same thing, the doctrine of the Trinity does not affirm and deny the same thing in the same respect. Therefore, no contradiction exists with the doctrine. Our finite minds, however, have difficulty grasping the doctrine of the Trinity.[18]

A Religion's Beliefs Must Exhibit External Correspondence

The premise behind this point is straightforward. William James is an original thinker of sorts across three disciplines of study—physiology, psychology, and philosophy. While his writings date back to the late 1870s, many scholars agree James's most significant philosophical contributions occur in the last decade and a half of his life. Those writings include *The Varieties of Religious Experience* (1902), a burst of essays written during 1904–1905 that were eventually collected and published together in *Essays in Radical*

---

18. For more information on the doctrine of the Trinity, see Erickson, *Making Sense*; Morey, *Trinity*; White, J. R., *Forgotten Trinity*.

Empiricism (1912), and his influential work *Pragmatism* (1907). William James layouts a systematic discussion on several themes that permeate his writings beginning in the late 1870s up to the publication of *Pragmatism*. Those themes include the nature of knowledge, of philosophy, of reality, of religion, and of truth.

While I do not agree with many of the conclusions made by William James, he is worth mentioning here. A few of his contributions are beneficial to this discussion. We need to acknowledge that William James is not a trained theologian or even versed in the study of religion. He admits this fact in his *Varieties of Religious Experience*.[19] This publication is the byproduct of a series of twenty lectures he gave at the University of Edinburgh in 1901. This work is unique because it has remained in print for over a century. The book examines the relation between religious experiences with what he knew about human nature. There are, however, two cautions regarding James that need mentioning before I go much further in our discussion. First, James utterly disdains any and all forms of organized religion. This fact feeds the second caution. Because of his distaste for religion, James is very skeptical towards the notion of religious experience.

The primary issue for James's focus centers around whether one's religious experience is capable of matching what is known about reality and along with any and all facts that can be seen as relating to it, including known facts about humanity. James essentially wants to have either a pragmatic or empirical test to prove people's religious experiences. Does external evidence support the claims, events, and experiences of the religion and her followers?

Earlier in this section of the book, I set forth an argument originating with Augustine of Hippo. The argument establishes God is truth. Since the Christian God is the God of truth, he is not going to have his worshipers believe things that contradict known facts about reality and humanity. The Hebrew Bible—the Christian Old Testament—and the New Testament are regularly read and interpreted as historical documents that record actual historical events. As a result of this method of understanding many passages found in the religious texts, skeptics have sought out to disprove their historical reliability. While no evidence has been discovered to disprove any of the biblical accounts of historical events, a few cases exist, however, where the archeological findings could not confirm the biblical record. But

---

19. James, *Varieties of Religious Experience*, 16.

the exact opposite has repeatedly happened. Archeologists continually find historical evidence confirming the stories of the Bible.[20]

Our desire here is to make sure a religious belief fits the facts of reality. Beliefs of a religion need to be able to explain or be capable of giving an account of our experience in the world. It must have answers to the various issues that surround us all the time regardless if it relates to anthropology, civil government, history, psychology, science, or something else. For a religion's truth-claims to withstand its challenges, it ought to have explanations for the origin of the world, the standard for morality, and how to understand evil and suffering. These are only a few of the issues a religion or a worldview must consider and address. It must have relevance for people. Once a religion or a worldview is seen as being irrelevant, people will eventual forsake it.

A Religion's Beliefs Ought to have Existential Viability

This criteria tests whether a religious belief system or a worldview can function in the real world. I hate clichés, but one seems appropriate here: this is where the rubber meets the road. Can a person live consistency in the world while holding to those beliefs? Do you recall the issues that were pointed out with the pragmatic theory for truth? This position goes too far in making whether something works as its sole criterion for determining the truthfulness of a truth-claim. Stating the question as I did three statements back is not the proper question to ask. "At this point it is best to think more in terms of a negative criterion: if one cannot live according to the precepts of a worldview, it fails an important test."[21]

Is it impossible for a Christian to live according to the beliefs and truth-claims of Christianity? According to Corduan, distinguishing between *do not* and *cannot* is vital here.[22] And I completely agree with him on this point. Take an honest examination of your life as a Christian. Do you always live in complete accordance with your religious beliefs and convictions all the time? I do not have to know you personally to know the answer. I know myself and of many generations that have gone before me. Nobody

---

20. For specific details on archaelogy discoveries and their relation to biblical narratives, see Holden and Geisler, *Handbook of Archaeology*; Geisler and Brooks, *When Skeptics Ask*, 179–209.

21. Corduan, *Reasonable Faith*, 76.

22. Ibid.

is capable of living in complete accordance to the teachings of Christianity. If a belief system could be deemed as false based upon this fact, Christianity would fail. But the same goes for all other worldviews and religions. No one is capable of living every moment of one's life in complete accordance to the teachings and beliefs of whatever position is held. Because someone is unable to live by the individual's beliefs, it may not be the fault of the position held. Therefore, we cannot deem it false solely on this basis if we wanted to do so. However, if it is determined the position is intrinsically impossible for anyone to live according to the beliefs, it becomes an entirely different issue. When this is the case, only one conclusion is available about the viewpoint. We must deem it as being false.

If the religious belief system can work in real life, then we can conclude the perspective is true. For example, there are Eastern religions that teach life and the physical universe are illusions in our minds. In other words, everything is an extended dream lasting one's entire life, and it will continue when one is reincarnated after one's death. Yes, I realize this strikes people as unusual when they hear it. This issue catches many of my students off guard when they begin reading about Eastern religions in Comparative Religions. If you were to travel to Asia where one of these religions is widely practiced, you would surely witness people who hold to life is an illusion looking both directions before attempting to walk across a heavily trafficked road. And it is possible that once the person journeys out into the street, the individual may make several stops during the process to avoid being hit by an oncoming vehicle. If life is solely an illusion, would not the numerous vehicles traveling in both directions simply be a mirage? I would venture to say if the individual is hit by a fast approaching bus, the person is going to experience severe pain for a while afterward, that is, if the individual survives.[23]

There are those individuals who insist on being naysayers against all viewpoints that disagree with their own, especially from those who deemed others to be politically correct. It is this mindset that currently launches many of the present-day objections to the exclusiveness of Christianity. Unfortunately, the list of common objections can be quite extensive if one

---

23. For additional information on evaluating truth-claims, see Corduan, *Reasonable Faith*, 65–79; Holmes, *Contours of a World*; Holmes, *Faith Seeks Understanding*, 51–60; Mitchell, B., *Justification of Religious Belief*; Nash, *Worldviews in Conflict*; Netland, *Dissonant Voices*, 151–95; Rood, "Is Jesus the Only Way," 248–49. For those who would like to get into a more in-depth reading on how issues here can be seen in a broader scope, see Pearcey, *Total Truth*; Pearcey, *Finding Truth*.

looks back through the annals of history. Thankfully, we do not need to rehash every point of contention. Many of the objections simply rephrase previous issues, which were raised by skeptics.[24]

OVERCOMING THREE COMMON OBJECTIONS RAISED AGAINST CHRISTIANITY

Today when I hear someone raise an objection to Christianity, I am typically unphased by it, because I have either heard it before or a variation of the skepticism. Many of those comments cannot be defended by those who raise the issue. It seems as if they have heard or read someone else making the objection against Christianity and cannot recall anything else about the objection.

In my religion courses, I truly am unconcerned with what my students' personal religious beliefs are. My job is not to proselytize for a single religion over another at the community college. I am to inform them of the material with its evidence, point out objections to the various religions or interpretations, and to explain how one may respond to the objections. The students need to know the different perspectives so that they can make a well-informed decision at some point in their life about what religion best explains and corresponds to the world. I am, however, concerned that my students can defend their objections they raise against a position and to be able to defend their current beliefs they hold.

All Religions Lead to the Same Place. They are All Equal

A common objection I hear on a regular basis is all religions are equal: no single religion is better than another. If all religions are the same, then they continue with something like the following. Since there are many different religions, this fact alone proves that no single religion contains the only way to heaven and God if either exists.

When we think about this objection, immediately the laws of logic should come to mind—particularly the law of non-contradiction. What

---

24. Here I am using the term *skeptics* in its broadest sense to include everyone who objects to any part of the claims of Christianity. Traditionally, this term refers to a set group who questions religion for a variety of reasons. But there are individuals who are not skeptical about all religious viewpoints. While they can be acceptable of other perspectives, they, however, despise Christianity.

happens when two or more religions claim to be the only means to obtaining some form of salvation or eternal bliss? Now when this happens according to the law of non-contradiction, all of them cannot be right.

Another objection that occasionally comes up, as a response to the reply based upon the law of non-contradiction is claiming religious beliefs are relative. But this response desires to side-step the issue and the conservation. Well that is good for you and glad it works for you, but it does not apply to me. We have previously dealt with this objection a few chapters back when we looked at what truth is and its distinctions from a biblical worldview.

Both of these objections are irrational when the laws of logic are applied to them. Further, it is not unheard of for the person raising the objection to have a hidden presumption of truth and knowledge, which may or may not be spoken to those who support the view that is being objected. The skeptic essentially affirms knowing how God thinks, acts, and behaves.[25] Ironically the individual can know this information, but another person cannot. A double-standard emerges in the dialogue. However, it is okay for the skeptic to hold this perspective while it is not for others.

Christians are Nothing More than Hypocrites

John Wesley leveraged the claim that more people would be Christians if it were not for the Christians.[26] Sadly, the words of John Wesley still ring true all these years later. A common complaint raised by many people is the church is filled with nothing other than hypocrites—people living one way Monday through Saturday and completely different on Sunday.

I would be the first to admit this objection is problematic. Through the years, I have witnessed this first-hand. And I still see it today. In the Bible Belt, it is still socially expected for families to attend church on Sundays for the sole purpose of seeing who showed up and who did not. The church is the country club where they are not required to pay membership fees to show up.

It is shameful that people see the church being full of two-faced people. But if we look at the situation through a biblical lens, this is where these individuals need to be. No one is perfect, including those who raise this objection against Christianity. Even if the individuals living one way

---

25. Kreeft and Tacelli, *Handbook of Christian Apologetics*, 371.
26. Jones, G., *1000 Illustrations*, 189.

during the week and another way on Sundays are Christians, they may be new, young followers. If this is the cause, I would expect for this behavior to change as they grow in maturity in the faith. If the opposite is true and they claimed to be Christians for decades, other possible issues come to my mind. And regardless to what the case is, being in the church on Sundays is exactly where they need to be. Hopefully, the gospel message takes hold whether it is they need to experience God's grace and forgiveness for the first time or if it needs to be they put away childish behaviors and move to solid food away from infant's milk (1 Cor 3:1–3; Heb 5:11–14; 1 Pet 2:1–2).

The issue we truly need to consider and be concerned with is not whether or not those who claim to be Christians are hypocrites. It does not matter one way or another to be honest. Even after an individual surrenders to Christ, the person's sin nature does not automatically disappear. The apostle Paul reveals he struggled with the desires of the flesh and doing things he did not want to do after his conversion (Rom 8:1–17). What objectors need to be concerned with is this question, is Jesus a hypocrite? If someone can successfully show Jesus, himself, is a hypocrite, then Christianity has a serious flaw and a devastating one at that. The trustworthiness of Christianity should not rest on the shoulders of its followers since they are still sinners. But they are sinners saved by grace. Christianity's trustworthiness rests on the truth of Jesus being who he claimed to be, the truth of his deeds, and the truth of his actions.

An All-Loving God Would Not Send Anyone to Hell

This objection is perhaps the biggest objection raised against Christianity. The issue at hand here is part of a larger one—the problem of evil and suffering. Those who raise this objection have two hidden premises that shed light on philosophical and theological biases. First, this position overestimates the basic nature of humanity at its core as being good. Secondly, the position thinks too lightly of God by underestimating a number of his attributes. Another way of wording these two points is that a particular worldview is the starting point of this objection. Humanity is good, and certain attributes of God are more important than others, such as his love and forgiveness are superior to his holiness, justice, and wrath.

The Bible only portrays humanity as good one time in their history (Gen 1:31), which occurs right after God created Adam in the image and likeness of God (Gen 1:27). After the Fall of Adam and Eve in Genesis 3, depravity characterizes humanity (Gen 6:5; 8:21). We find this fact about humanity recorded throughout the Bible. The psalmist points out the problem plaguing people while they are in their mother's womb (Pss 51:5; 58:3). The prophet Isaiah states even our righteous acts are filthy rags to God because of our unclean nature (Isa 64:6). The prophets Jeremiah and Ezekiel proclaim the same thing about humanity being depraved (Jer 17:9; Ezek 36:25–27). The theme is carried over into the New Testament and first appears in the Gospels (Mark 7:20–23; John 3:19; 8:34). Then Paul continues this teaching (Rom 3:9–18; 7; 8:7–8; 1 Cor 2:14; 2 Cor 4:4; Eph 2:1–5; 4:18). And humanity's depravity is seen in 1 John 1:8 as well. Since humanity's current condition is of depravity, we can do absolutely nothing to earn merit and favor with a holy, just, and loving God.[27] Additionally, humanity is responsible and accountable for their thoughts, deeds, and speech.

Because of Christ's atoning work upon the cross, humanity can be restored to a forgiven status through repentance and faith in him (Rom 3:21–26; Eph 2:1–10).[28] And it is only because of God's doing that salvation is even possible. Denying it or disliking the notion of hell does not make it unreal. Originally, God created hell for Satan and his angels. But in the future, those who reject God's means of restoration will face their final, eternal fate with Satan and his angels in hell.

Despite what people may think about a loving God sending people to hell, the fact remains God is loving even in this act. He allowed his only son to be sacrificed so that he was a propitiation for God's wrath, which we all deserve. Christ's death is seen as being penal substitutionary. He took our rightful place, and he took our punishment. So to raise this objection indicates the person does not recognize the all-loving God did an extremely loving act so that hell could be avoided. The same all-loving God who sends people to hell also died for them, which is the ultimate act of love.

And trying to insist that the God of the Old Testament is not the same God of the New Testament does not support the objection. Jesus speaks of his Father's wrath, righteous anger, justice, and holy indication more than

---

27. For more on the attributes of God, see Charnock, *Existence and Attributes*; Morey, *Exploring the Attributes*; Nash, *Concept of God*; Packer, *Concise Theology*; Packer, *Knowing God*; Pink, *Attributes of God*; Tozer, *Attributes of God*, vols. 1 and 2; Tozer, *Knowledge of the Holy*; Trevethan, *Beauty of God's Holiness*.

28. For more on the atoning work of Christ, see Morris, L., *Apostolic Preaching*; Morris, L., *Atonement: Meaning*; Morris, L., *Biblical Doctrine of Judgment*; Morris, L., *Cross of Jesus*; Stott, *Cross of Christ*; Tidball, *Message of the Cross*.

double of his teachings speaking of God's love, mercy, and forgiveness.[29] To say it is not fair for an all-loving God to send people to hell implies it is unjust for God to do so, which means the objector is accusing God of injustice. For all sin to go unpunished is unjust for those who accept God's gift of salvation in Christ. If God is to ignore transgressions against him (Rom 3:23; 6:23), what else do the objectors wish for him to do? God's holiness and righteousness demands sin is dealt with through a just and fair means.

CONCLUSION: SPEAKING THE TRUTH IN LOVE

With Peter being filled with the Holy Spirit, he proclaims, "This Jesus is the stone that was rejected by you, the builders, which has become the cornerstone. And there is salvation in no one else, for there is no other name under heaven given among men by which we must be saved" (Acts 4:11–12). This is the message of the gospel of truth, Jesus Christ. The author of Hebrews continues this same message by describing Christ's sacrifice as being once for all (Heb 10:1–18).

For those who are perishing, they despise hearing the message of the cross—to these individuals the message is folly. But to those who are being saved, it is the power of God (1 Cor 1:18). But we must remember that it is a terrifying thing for a person to fall into the hands of the living God (Heb 10:31). Paul writes in Romans 1:16 that he is not ashamed of the gospel. These verses ought to shape our mindset and be our driving force to speak the truth in love. The focus of the next chapter is on this very point—how should believers engage culture with the gospel message?

When we confront individuals with the message of Christ, it often takes someone hearing the message multiple times before it takes hold. For those who have certain objections, it will likely take even longer before coming to grips with Christianity. When sharing the good news, we need to meet individuals on three levels: intellectual, needs, and emotional. To meet a person's intellectual level, we need to be able to address objections or concerns an individual has against the message and Christianity. The needs level addresses issues of if the message is relevant in today's society. But

---

29. My senior thesis project at the University of Mobile was examining the biblical teaching of God's wrath in both the Old and New Testaments. This material will serve as the cornerstone for a future research project, which has been approved for another research doctorate in dogmatics. For this reason I do not wish to elaborate on this discussion any further.

it also takes into consideration whether it has functional adequacy. And the third level we need to address when sharing Christ with someone is the emotional level. No one makes a decision solely based upon either the intellectual or the needs levels. We generally will make a decision based upon our emotions after we have the factual information we need to be able to make a choice.

PART THREE

Philosophy and the Gospel

9

How Shall We Live?
Living in and Engaging a Pagan Culture

> "Surely our transgressions and our sins are upon us,
> and we rot away because of them. How then can we live?"
>
> —Ezekiel 33:10

THINGS THAT WERE TABOO a few years ago are now acceptable. What the prophet Isaiah observed in his lifetime is clearly occurring today: evil is called good, and good is called evil (Isa 5:20). Each generation thinks this is the case.

Growing up in the late 1970s through the 1990s, I can see drastic changes in society. But those who grew up during the Great Depression through the mid-1970s can tell us of many more shifts in our culture. Our society in many ways is very similar the first century. Immorality is as rampant today as it was during the New Testament era. Sin is still sin in God's eyes. And people still need Christ as their savior if they want to escape God's holy, righteous wrath.

How shall we live? This question has been asked by believers throughout the ages in one form or another ever since Old Testament times. The first time this question was asked in this format can be found in Ezekiel 33:10: "And you, son of man, say to the house of Israel, Thus have you said:

'Surely our transgressions and our sins are upon us, and we rot away because of them. How then can we live?'"

In more recent years, the late Francis A. Schaeffer asked the question, *How Should We Then Live?*[1] Charles Colson and Nancy Pearcey asked the same question in their book, *How Now Shall We Live?*[2] The need for a Christian witness and testimony is at the heart of this question, along with the need for apologetics—both non-verbal and verbal. How are believers to live their lives so that those around them can see the difference Christ has made in their lives?

I shall pose this question neither as Schaeffer did nor as Colson and Pearcey did for a distinct, yet crucial reason. *How shall we live* is stated in this manner because there is a distinct way Christians should live their lives from the moment of conversion to ultimate glorification. It is not merely, how shall we *then* live because posing the question this way appears to imply a conditional state that one may choose not to live according to God's design. Posing the question as Colson and Pearcey did suggests believers can ignore how they live until they make the decision to live differently, though this is not their intention.

There are, in fact, numerous passages of Scripture that answer the question at hand. But I want to draw your attention to two passages: 1 Peter 2:11–25 and 1 Peter 3:13–17. To understand the selected passages, it is crucial to have an understanding of their context. The theme and purpose of 1 Peter is found in 5:12. Peter wants to encourage his readers to stand firm in the grace of God in the face of suffering and persecution. Furthermore, Peter desires his readers to live "triumphantly in the midst of hostility without abandoning hope, becoming bitter, losing faith in Christ, or forgetting his second coming."[3] The following is an outline for the book of 1 Peter:

> Opening (1:1–2)
>
> > I. Called to Salvation as Exiles: Suffering Christians Should Remember Their Great Salvation (1:3—2:10)
> > > A. The Certainty of Their Salvation (1:3–12)
> > > B. The Consequences of Their Salvation (1:13—2:10)
> > II. Living as Aliens to Bring Glory to God in a Hostile World: Suffering Christians Should Remember Their Example Before Men (2:11—4:6)

1. Schaeffer, F., *How Should We Then Live?*
2. Colson and Pearcey, *How Now Shall We Live?*
3. MacArthur, *1 Peter*, 10.

A. Living Honorably Before Unbelievers (2:11—3:7)
B. Living Honorably Before Believers (3:8-12)
C. Living Honorably in the Midst of Suffering (3:13—4:6)
III. Persevering in Suffering: Suffering Christians Should Remember Their Lord Will Return—Coming to Grips with Christian Suffering (4:7—5:11)
A. The Responsibilities of Christian Living (4:7-11)
B. The Reality of Christian Suffering (4:12-19)
C. The Requirements of Christian Leadership (5:1-4)
D. The Realization of Christian Victory (5:5-11)

Conclusion (5:12-14)[4]

From the outline one will notice in 1 Peter 2:11—3:12 the apostle Peter describes the attitudes and actions that God's children should exhibit toward both unbelievers and believers. Then in 1 Peter 3:13—4:6, Peter elaborates upon how God's children should live in an evil and hostile world in the face of persecution and suffering. Does it really matter how believers live their lives? It absolutely does matter. The apostle Paul discusses this in Titus 3:1-8 and elsewhere in his writings (particularly in 1 Corinthians and the second half of Romans). James, the brother of Jesus, addresses this very issue throughout his letter. These are not the only people who talk about how God's children are to live in the Bible. Example after example can be given from the opening chapters of Genesis to the closing chapters of Revelation.

Some of us may not think it matters how we live our lives, despite the fact numerous authors of the Bible tell us otherwise. Listen to what one Anglican theologian and evangelist said in the eighteenth century: "John Wesley declared that the world would be Christian were it not for the *Christians!*"[5] This is coming from one of the founders of Methodism that later developed into the Methodist Church, the Holiness Movement, and Pentecostalism.

I want to focus specifically on 1 Peter 2:11-25:

> Dear friends, I urge you, as aliens and strangers in the world, to abstain from sinful desires, which war against your soul. Live such good lives among the pagans that, though they accuse you of

---

4. This particular outline of 1 Peter is an adaptation of three different outlines found in the following sources: Davids, *First Epistle of Peter*; MacArthur, *1 Peter*; Schreiner, *1, 2 Peter, Jude*.

5. Jones, G., *1000 Illustrations*, 189.

Part Three: Philosophy and the Gospel

> doing wrong, they may see your good deeds and glorify God on the day he visits us.
>
> Submit yourselves for the Lord's sake to every authority instituted among men: whether to the king, as the supreme authority, or to governors, who are sent by him to punish those who do wrong and to commend those who do right. For it is God's will that by doing good you should silence the ignorant talk of foolish men. Live as free men, but do not use your freedom as a cover-up for evil; live as servants of God. Show proper respect to everyone: Love the brotherhood of believers, fear God, honor the king.
>
> Slaves, submit yourselves to your masters with all respect, not only to those who are good and considerate, but also to those who are harsh. For it is commendable if a man bears up under the pain of unjust suffering because he is conscious of God. But how is it to your credit if you receive a beating for doing wrong and endure it? But if you suffer for doing good and you endure it, this is commendable before God. To this you were called, because Christ suffered for you, leaving you an example, that you should follow in his steps.
>
> "He committed no sin, and no deceit was found in his mouth."
>
> When they hurled their insults at him, he did not retaliate; when he suffered, he made no threats. Instead, he entrusted himself to him who judges justly. He himself bore our sins in his body on the tree, so that we might die to sins and live for righteousness; by his wounds you have been healed. For you were like sheep going astray, but now you have returned to the Shepherd and Overseer of your souls. (1 Pet 2:11–25, NIV)

Peter just finished reminding his readers who they are (1 Pet 1:13—2:10). From time-to-time, believers need to be reminded who they are in Christ. For a brief summary, look at 1 Peter 2:9–10. In this section of Scripture, Peter shifts his focus to practical matters on how we are to live our lives in a hostile environment. But as he does so, he once again reminds us who we are in a passionate and urgent plea: "Dear friends, I urge you, as aliens and strangers in the world" (1 Pet 2:11a). We are God's dearly beloved children. We are, however, more than that. We are also "aliens and strangers." This is not our country or home; rather, "our citizenship is in heaven, from which we also eagerly wait for a Savior, the Lord Jesus Christ" (Phil 3:20).

Since this is not our home, we are called to live a certain way. Even today when a United States' citizen travels to a foreign land, the individual is expected to obey the laws of the country. When I was in Singapore, I was expected to follow their laws. For example, if I accidently dropped a piece of paper from my pocket, I had to pick it immediately up. Otherwise, I could be punished and receive twenty lashes across the back with a sugar cane stick.

Because of our relationship with Christ, we should want to live godly lives in a godless culture. Jesus says, "If you love me, you will keep my commandments" (John 14:15) and, "If anyone loves me, he will keep my word" (John 14:23). We ought to want to live distinctly different from those around us out of duty to be obedient to Christ. How is it that we are to live in this hostile world? This is what Peter exactly addresses.

Peter, in fact, gives us three commands to follow. First, we must abstain from sinful desires (2:11b). Second, we must live honorable lives among the pagans (2:12–20). And third, we must remember who our example is (2:21–25).

ABSTAIN FROM SINFUL DESIRES (1 PET 2:11b)

As children of God, we have an obligation to abstain from certain behaviors. Peter tells us that we are to abstain from sinful desires that are at war with our soul. Not all desires are wrong or sinful. Those desires become wrong and sinful if we try to satisfy them contrary to what God tells us in his word. Other desires are sinful from the very beginning (1 Pet 4:13; Gal 5:19–21).

The Christian walk is a battlefield. This is why the apostle Paul speaks of his struggles with the desires of the flesh in Romans 7:13–25. And then in Ephesians 6:13–20, Paul tells believers how to prepare for this spiritual battle. Just because Peter does not mention what type of sins he is referring to specifically, we cannot presume that he had any particular sins in mind here. Each of us are tempted differently to do various things.

The point is not to figure out what sin Peter has in mind here. The crux of the verse is that we know what things cause us to be tempted. And we are to avoid those things because these desires can hinder one's spiritual growth. Furthermore, they can destroy one's public witness and testimony with others. Nobody sins in a vacuum. Our sins affect others around us. They may not do so immediately. But they will eventually.

Part Three: Philosophy and the Gospel

LIVE HONORABLE LIVES AMONG THE PAGANS (1 PET 2:12)

This verse makes it clear that the early church was under scrutiny and criticism. Unbelievers spread rumors and made false accusations about Christians. Early believers were said to hurt businesses, and they were called atheists because they did not own idols and participate in the religious practices of the Roman Empire. As Rome burned in 64 AD, Nero blamed the Christians for starting the fires. We should not be surprised by this behavior, because Christ told us that the world will hate us since it hates him (Matt 10:22; John 15:18).

Peter advises his readers not to attempt to defend themselves or to debate with their accusers. Actions can speak louder than our words; therefore, we are to conduct ourselves in an honorable manner, living as a witness for Christ to the unbelievers around us.

The goal for living godly lives is so that unbelievers will eventually glorify God by becoming followers of Christ. Living good lives is like walking around wearing a billboard advertisement. Someone is always watching you. It may be your children, grandchildren, neighbor, co-worker, and so on. For me, it is primarily my students in my courses and my co-workers. Our desire should be seeing the lost saved.

The question that naturally arises is—how are believers to live so that their lives are a positive witness and testimony? Peter illustrates this for us in his letter. He gives three examples in the following verses starting with 2:13 through 3:7. But we are going to look only at two of them. Peter begins by focusing on how Christians are to respond to our leaders in local government and those who are in greater power above our local leaders.

Be an Example by Submitting to Every Authority (1 Pet 2:13-17)

Despite what we may think or how we often feel, we are to submit to the people who are placed in positions of authority over us. We are to *submit* to their leadership. In other words, we are to place ourselves under those individuals. This is not always an easy thing to do. But we must remember that God put those individuals in power for a reason, according to Paul in Romans 13:1-2:

> Everyone must submit to the governing authorities, for there is no authority except from God, and those that exist are instituted

by God. So then, the one who resists the authority is opposing God's command, and those who oppose it will bring judgment on themselves.

Submission to authority, however, does not involve actions that are contrary to what God tells us to do elsewhere in Scripture. God is not going to make us sin or tempt us to sin (Jas 1:13). We can look at the opening chapter of the book of Daniel to see how Daniel and his friends were able to be faithful to God while being submissive to the king. As children of God, we must obey those in authority except when it causes us to sin against God.

"The apostle Peter wanted believers to submit willingly, but his words are not presented as an option, but as a command. We are to submit because that is God's desire for his people. He wants us to trust him because all governments and authorities are ultimately appointed and controlled by him."[6] Remember even Christ when asked about taxes said, "Give to Caesar what belongs to Caesar" (Matt 22:15–22; Mark 12:17).

Thomas Schreiner notes:

> Modern people are not familiar with governments praising those who do what is right. The Romans, however, would erect statues, grant privileges, or commend in other ways those who helped the community. Still, evidence is lacking that Peter encouraged wealthy readers to engage in public benefaction. He addressed all believers and did not particularly focus on the well-to-do. All believers should do what is right and strengthen the social fabric. Rulers help maintain order in society by commending good citizens.[7]

Look at verse 15 in our text: "For it is God's will that by doing good you should silence the ignorant talk of foolish people." Peter recounts "doing good" in this verse with living "good lives" in verse 12. We are always to do what is right in the eyes of God. If we do this, then what results is a powerful witness and testimony for who God is. Furthermore, there is a silent argument against the false accusations that unbelievers raise against us. Our actions speak volumes to those around us.

By submitting to governmental authority, we do not give up our freedom as followers of Christ. David Walls and Max Anders make this observation about Christian freedom:

---

6. Walls and Anders, *I & II Peter*, 33.
7. Schreiner, *1, 2 Peter, Jude*, 129–30.

The Bible emphasizes that in those areas where the Word of God gives no command or primary principle, we are free and responsible to choose our own course of action. This is a freedom to choose what is right. Christian freedom does not allow us to do wrong. It does not permit us to disobey human laws unless these are in direct conflict with God's ways. Nor does our freedom permit us to disobey God, because we are servants of God.[8]

In other words, we are not free to do what we want. But we are free to do as we ought. Paul in 1 Corinthians 9:19–23 tells us how we are to use our freedom properly. We are to become all things to all people for the sake of the gospel so that others may become children of God.

Peter ends the first illustration on how we are to live by telling us that we are to "show proper respect to everyone." We are to "love the family of believers." We are to "fear God." And we are to "honor the emperor" (1 Pet 2:17). Submitting to governmental authority is not always very visible. So Peter takes his illustration to a more practical example.

Be an Example by Submitting to Your Boss (1 Pet 2:18–20)

Slaves are to submit to their masters, even if they are abusive and completely unreasonable. This is perhaps a more powerful testimony than the first illustration because this is visible day in and day out, challenging one's faith continually.

Slavery in biblical times does not equate with slavery that was experienced in modern times. During the New Testament era, many of the slaves were well-educated and held high positions of leadership; for example, slaves included medical doctors, teachers, and musicians to name a few groups that we would not typically think of being enslaved.

Today in our society, the slave master would be equivalent to a person's boss at work. A person agrees to work for the entity that the individual works for. All of us who have jobs place ourselves voluntarily under the authority of those who are in charge. As a result of that, we are to respect those whom are in authority above us despite how they treat us.

Our motivation, however, does not earn the respect of our bosses. As children of God, we are to do our work unto the Lord (Col 3:23–24). We are to work out of respect and reverence for God.

---

8. Walls and Anders, *I & II Peter*, 34.

All bosses are not the same. Some of them are great to work for. And some of them are extremely difficult to work under. Through the years, I have worked for both types of people. It is much easier and more pleasurable to work for a boss who is not harsh. But that is not always possible in life. When we work for a difficult person, we are to remember who our example is.

REMEMBER WHO OUR EXAMPLE IS (1 PET 2:21-25)

Unfortunately, there are times when God calls a believer to endure suffering that is unjust and painful. How we respond to that situation is a powerful witness and testimony to the unbelievers around us.

Peter reminds us that our suffering is nothing when compared to the suffering that Christ endured. Throughout Jesus' life and ministry, he experienced suffering. According to 1 Peter 1:11, Peter considers that suffering dominated Jesus' life. Christ's life is our ultimate example on how we should respond to difficult and harsh situations. This is much easier said than done.

But remember this:

> To this you were called, because Christ suffered for you, leaving you an example, that you should follow in his steps.
> "He committed no sin, and no deceit was found in his mouth."
> When they hurled their insults at him, he did not retaliate; when he suffered, he made no threats. Instead, he entrusted himself to him who judges justly. He himself bore our sins in his body on the tree, so that we might die to sins and live for righteousness; by his wounds you have been healed. For you were like sheep going astray, but now you have returned to the Shepherd and Overseer of your souls. (1 Pet 2:11-25, NIV)

Someone is always watching how Christians respond to situations that they face. Living our lives according to how God has commanded us is a silent witness and testimony to those around us. What we do has an impact whether it is positive or negative. How are you going to live in a pagan culture?

Our non-verbal communication affects what others think of us, especially if it does not agree with what we say. If we say one thing and do something else, people will consider us to be hypocrites. And they would be correct in doing so. Believers must be consistent in their actions and speech. It is time to shift our focus to the verbal witness and testimony.

Part Three: Philosophy and the Gospel

Now I would like shift our focus to 1 Peter 3:13-17. There are three primary points that need to be made about this particular passage, which I am quoting in full below:

> Now who is there to harm you if you are zealous for what is good? But even if you should suffer for righteousness' sake, you will be blessed. Have no fear of them, nor be troubled, but in your hearts honor Christ the Lord as holy, always being prepared to make a defense to anyone who ask you for the a reason for the hope that is in you; yet do it with gentleness and respect, having a good conscience, so that, when you are slandered, those who revile your good behavior in Christ may be put to shame. For it is better to suffer for doing good, if that should be God's will, than for doing evil. (1 Pet 3:13-17)

The points are: First, know that you are blessed (3:13-14a). Second, trust in Christ (3:14b-15a). And finally, be ready to give an account (3:15b-17).

KNOW THAT YOU ARE BLESSED (1 PET 3:13-14a)

Common sense seems to tell individuals that, if they obey the law, they will be protected from punishment. However, this is not always the case. Peter is not telling his readers that if they do *right in the eyes of humans,* they will escape from unfair and unjust treatment. Later on in his letter (3:20), Peter will make this point: believers can do right and expect to suffer.

The phrase *even if you should suffer* is worded in such a way in the original language that Peter is thinking of an event that could be considered highly unlikely to happen but still possible. Peter wants God's people to be prepared for the possibility of persecution; and furthermore, he tells believers how they should react if they find themselves in the midst of suffering and persecution.[9] How shall Christians live when in the midst of suffering? What follows is the answer to this question.

TRUST IN CHRIST (1 PET 3:14b-15a)

In 1 Peter 3:14b, Peter alludes to Isaiah 8:12-13. He is counseling God's children not to fear persecution. Rather than fearing our enemies, we are told to trust in Christ as our sovereign Lord, who is in absolute control of

---

9. See 1 Peter 4:12-15 and Matthew 5:11. In 1 Peter 4:12-15, Peter warns believers more directly of the forthcoming suffering and persecution they will face in the future.

all things. Furthermore, Peter recalls Christ's words: "And do not fear those who kill the body but cannot kill the soul. Rather fear him who can destroy both soul and body in hell" (Matt 10:28).

Peter tells God's children in 1 Peter 3:15a to replace fear with faith and reverence. When Christians acknowledge Christ as their Lord and Savior, they recognize his holiness and sovereignty. And as a result, they can rest and find refuge in him. When we set apart Christ as Lord, we acknowledge he is in control of all events and that all powers and authorities ultimately must answer to him. Christ is the sovereign King of kings and Lord of lords.[10]

BE READY TO GIVE AN ACCOUNT (1 PET 3:15b–17)

When believers have Christ set apart in their hearts, the courage Christ gives them ought to make them always ready to testify about him. Christians are to live out the hope that is in them in such a manner where others can see it. Our lives should be distinctly different from those of the world. This is the only way unbelievers can see that there is something different about us. If we live our lives as the world does, how are they going to see the hope we have in us?

Always be ready to make a defense to anyone who asks why you have hope. In other words, every Christian should be able to explain clearly his reasons for being a Christian. The believer's response should be both reasonable *and* rational.

What does a reasonable and rational response mean? Christianity is a logical and coherent worldview; therefore, a believer's explanation for why he holds the view should be presented as such. As followers of Christ, we are called to be different from the world. This means not only living a lifestyle different from the world but also *thinking* differently than the world. Hence, Christians need to develop a distinctly Christian philosophical worldview. Christians are to take every thought captive to Christ (2 Cor 10:5), and obedience requires a proper Christian philosophy.

An unbeliever's mind is distinctly different from a believer's. The mind of the unbeliever is at enmity with Christ. Furthermore, the unbeliever's mind is foolish and deceived (Rom 1:18–32). In Colossians 1:21, Paul describes the unbeliever as being "alienated and hostile in mind." The unbeliever is not capable of upholding God's greatest commandment, which is:

10. Osborne, *1 & 2 Peter and Jude*, 96.

"you shall love the Lord your God with all your heart and with all your soul and with all your mind and with all your strength" (Mark 12:30). The unbeliever despises both the wisdom and instruction of God (Prov 1:7; Rom 3:18). Hence, the unbeliever is incapable of realizing any of the treasures of wisdom and knowledge found in Christ (Col 2:3).

The philosophy of this world is not only deceptive but also hopeless. The apostle Paul writes in Ephesians 4:17–18 that the unbelievers walk "in the futility of their mind . . . darkened in their understanding, alienated from the life of God because of the ignorance that is in them, due to their hardness of heart."

The wisdom of God is nothing like the wisdom of this world. Paul makes this point clear in 1 Corinthians 1:18–31. Naturally, the question comes up: since the wisdom of God is nothing like the wisdom of this world, can Christians use philosophy to articulate and account for their worldview? Depending on to whom this question is addressed, the answer can be no or yes. Because this question has already been addressed in chapter 2, there is no reason to rehash it here.

The primary distinction between Christian philosophy and worldly philosophy is its foundation for epistemology. Christian philosophy is rooted in the knowledge of Christ—faith in Christ is the starting point. Christ himself is the only source of truth and knowledge. John 14:6 states Christ is "the way, the truth, and the light." All knowledge begins with Christ, the standard of true philosophy.

Furthermore, Christians cannot be naive in their reasons for being a Christian. Christians have the responsibility to clearly and comprehensively respond to critics of the faith. To be effective in refuting other viewpoints, the believer must be able to critique other worldviews and philosophies. And studying philosophy is the best way for individuals to prepare themselves to know how to raise objections in other worldviews to show the inconsistencies within them. Apart from faith in Christ and recognizing Christ as the source of truth, all other philosophies are flawed.

In what manner shall Christians respond when questioned about the hope they have? First Peter 3:8 tells believers to be sympathetic, brotherly, kindhearted, and humble in spirit. First Peter 3:9 declares Christians are not to return evil for evil. In 1 Peter 3:15c, Peter tells believers they are to respond with gentleness and reverence. In 1 Peter 3:16, he goes on to tell Christians to stay humble; therefore, they should not be prideful with their responses. Their conscience should be filled with God's desires.

How can believers follow Peter's advice to keep a clear conscience? First, Christians can treasure their faith in Christ more than anything else and do what they know is right. Second, believers can avoid willful disobedience. Third, if Christians do disobey, they should stay in consistent communication with God, repenting and asking for forgiveness.

Why is there all this concern about right living and clear conscience? The reason for this concern is because believers live in a hostile world. Christians should not give their accusers ammunition to bring more charges against them by breaking the law or acting and speaking in an ungodly manner.

If Christians are to suffer, it should never be for wrong doing (1 Pet 3:17). Why would it be better to suffer for doing good than for doing evil? Because Christ suffered unjustly so that people might be saved, therefore, believers ought to patiently endure unjust suffering because such an attitude is a powerful witness that could lead unbelievers to Christ (1 Pet 3:18). *How shall we live?* Christians are to live distinctly different than the world. Christians are to be ready at all times to give an account for their faith in Christ. Their response should be reasonable *and* rational. Peter's words in 1 Peter 3:15 regarding *be ready to give a defense* is not exclusive to only some Christians. *Every* believer should be ready to defend the faith.

10

God's Mandate and the Christian Thinker

The Solution to the Madness

"Go therefore and make disciples of all nations..."

—Matthew 28:19a

BEGINNING IN THE 1980s, a renewed interest in Christian scholarship and the integration of faith in academia emerged. What resulted was an increase in the number of books published on the nature of Christian higher education. This renewed interest began to flourish during the 1990s and still continues today. Many of these works encouraged Christian institutions to rediscover, maintain, and cultivate the distinctive features that distinguish them as Christian.

These works address important themes such as the development of a Christian worldview, the life of the mind, the vocation of the Christian scholar, and various methods of integrating faith and learning.[1] To varying

---

1. The following are some of the more insightful and thought provoking authors and their works on the topics: Colson and Pearcey, *How Now Shall We Live*; Dockery and Thornbury, *Shaping Christian Worldview*; Guinness, *Fit Bodies, Fat Minds*; Holmes, *Making of Christian Mind*; Holmes, *Idea of Christian College*; Hughes, *Vocation of Christian Scholar*; Marsden, *Soul of American University*; Marsden, *Outrageous Idea*; Moreland,

God's Mandate and the Christian Thinker

degrees, they also discuss the kinds of people Christian institutions should strive to graduate. The graduates should be prepared to engage, transform, and serve their communities. As insightful and provocative as these works are, perhaps one of the more *beneficial* works, yet not widely known, is an address presented by Charles Malik at the inauguration of the Billy Graham Center at Wheaton College on September 13, 1980.

Malik challenged thousands of evangelical Christians to engage in what he considered the two *principle* tasks of responsible Christians, "that of saving the soul and that of saving the mind."[2] He warned further: "the problem is not only to win souls but to save minds. If you win the whole world and lose the mind of the world, you will soon discover you have not won the world. Indeed, it may turn out that you have actually lost the world."[3] Charles Malik understood the heart can only accept what the mind can entertain. For this reason, it is vital to present Christianity as being real to reach the world for Christ.

For those in academia, Malik had a special challenge. Malik considered the university "one of the greatest creations of Western civilization."[4] He realized the university dominates the world more than any other institution and what is taught by professors in the classroom ultimately becomes the philosophy of the world.[5] He noted:

> All the preaching in the world, and the loving care of even the best parents between whom there are no problems whatever, will amount to little, if not to nothing, so long as what the children are exposed to day in and day out for fifteen to twenty years in school and university virtually cancels out, morally and spiritually, what they hear and see and learn at home and in the church. Therefore the problem of the school and university is the most critical problem afflicting Western civilization.[6]

Love the Lord; Noll, *Scandal of the Evangelical*; Sire, *Discipleship of the Mind*; Sire, *Habits of the Mind*; Williams, *Life of the Mind*.

2. Malik, *Two Tasks*. This work was originally Charles Habib Malik's address to the Dedication of the Billy Graham Center at Wheaton College in Wheaton, Illinois on September 13, 1980. Malik's address is the motivation behind Craig and Gould, *Two Tasks of the Christian Scholar*.

3. Malik, *Two Tasks*, 42.

4. Malik, *Christian Critique*, 15.

5. Ibid., 19–20.

6. Malik, *Two Tasks*, 37.

Malik knew ideas have consequences, and "the university in general and the professors in particular are the gate-keepers of ideas—influencing directly and indirectly all aspects of thought and life in our world."[7] Hence, Christian scholars and professors were likely in the forefront of Malik's mind when he delivered the address, despite his encouragement that *all* Christians are to engage in the two tasks. Malik realized the profound influence educators could have on their students' minds; furthermore, he knew certain students would potentially become protégés of charismatic professors.

Malik's challenge to participate in the two tasks of responsible Christians is the very heart of the Great Commission:

> All authority in heaven and on earth has been given to me. *Go therefore and make disciples of all the nations*, baptizing them in the name of the Father and of the Son and of the Holy Spirit, *teaching them to observe all that I commanded you*. And behold, I am with you always, to the end of the age. (Matt 28:18–20, emphasis added)

Discipleship is no longer a condition for being a Christian in churches of the Western hemisphere, according to Dallas Willard, and this has been the current trend for at least several decades. "One is not required to be, or to intend to be, a disciple to become a Christian, and one may remain a Christian without any signs of progress toward or in discipleship."[8] Despite these contemporary ideas, the biblical mandate to make disciples still stands.

When Jesus' public ministry started, his top priority was to recruit and train twelve disciples. When Christ called the first disciples, he said, "Follow me and I will make you fishers of men" (Matthew 4:19). Jesus invested roughly three and a half years training these twelve men. Before Christ ascended to heaven, he told his disciples to make more disciples.

The Christian's worldview should impact daily affairs. In reality, however, this may or may not be the case. Dallas Willard, while leading a faculty retreat at a Christian college in the United States, opened his presentation with what Christ might say if he were the guest speaker. Willard continued to say Christ would likely ask the faculty members two simple questions: "Why don't you respect me in your various fields of study and expertise? Why don't you recognize me as master of research and knowledge in your fields?"[9] Willard was astonished at the various reactions of the Christian

---

7. Gould, "Two Tasks Introduced," 19.
8. Willard, *Great Omission*, 4.
9. Ibid., 18–19.

professionals. Many were shocked Willard suggested Jesus would ask such questions.[10]

There is more to being a disciple of Christ than just having mere faith in Christ. In Luke 9:23, Christ said, "If anyone would come after me, let him deny himself and take up his cross daily and follow me." The task of this chapter is to apply the mandate of the Great Commission to the role of the Christian thinker. Part of the aim, therefore, is to establish that the Christian thinker is in a unique situation.

All of us have influence on others around us. A percentage of us are in a position of authority over others. For example, I am in my tenth year being a Faculty Mentor with Columbia Evangelical Seminary. As a professor with this institution, I have the responsibility to help shape and challenge the minds of my theological students. In this role I, as the professor, must understand that I am in some regards and aspects God's undershepherd. I also teach for a state community college. My role with the community college is different than my role with the theological seminary. While I am still God's servant, my primary focus at the community college is to introduce students to various world religions, the Old Testament, and the New Testament. Additionally, I am to give students the tools to analyze critically the information where they can make an informed decision in the future on what they believe about the topics discussed.

The same is true for others in education; the Christian educator has a high calling in life. With this higher calling, there comes great responsibility and accountability. We are obligated to assist in the mental and spiritual development of our students.

But do not think just because you are not a Christian educator you are off the hook and what is being said here does not apply to you.[11] Having this mindset is the furthest from being the case or the truth. All of us think. And God places each one of us in areas of influence and to some degree in positions of authority for a reason. God gifts us each with different strengths and weaknesses for the tasks he has planned for us. We need to see our vocation is a divine calling and as an opportunity to carry out the Great Commission. Here is something else that we need to realize about the Great Commission: "Christian communication is a communication of the gospel

---

10. Ibid.

11. Since my primary profession is working in higher education for two institutions, I am using the education profession as my example to convey my thoughts. Everyone can replace the educator illustration with one's own profession. The same principles apply.

that is shaped by our understanding of God's communication in Christ, just as God's communication in Christ is shaped by God's understanding of the condition of our hearts that God addresses in the gospel," as Os Guinness points out.[12]

THE CALL OF THE CHRISTIAN THINKER

It has often been said teachers are born and not made. A teacher's experiences throughout his life contribute to who the teacher is.[13] For the Christian, teaching is considered a divine calling. The Lord summons individuals to himself so that they belong to him and serve him in his world. The Lord does not just call his people to salvation. He calls his children to carry out his will in various ways. Throughout history God has called the faithful for specific tasks. When the Lord calls, he bestows the gifts needed to equip the person for his mission in life.

Our vocation fits within the scope of God's calling. According to Eavey, "the divine call of the teacher needs to be put on the same plane as the call of the evangelist and the call of the pastor."[14] God gives certain individuals the spiritual gift of teaching. The apostle Paul writes:

> And he gave the apostles, the prophets, the evangelists, the shepherds and *teachers*, to equip the saints for the work of ministry, for building up of the body of Christ, until we all attain to the unity of the faith and of the knowledge of the Son of God, to mature manhood, to the measure of the stature of the fullness of Christ. (Eph 4:11–13, emphasis added)

The educator, at times, functions as an evangelist; and moreover, the person is to see himself as one of God's undershepherds. When God calls and equips an individual for the teaching vocation, the individual takes on a great responsibility. James warns that many should not desire to be teachers because those who teach will be judged at a higher standard (Jas 3:1).

It is important that all of us take our calling seriously, and that we see our vocation as a higher calling. This divine calling is intimately connected with the Great Commission. The Christian thinker understands that Christ demands the individual is an ambassador for him to others (2 Cor

---

12. Guinness, *Fool's Talk*, 27.
13. Eavey, *Principles of Teaching*, 18.
14. Ibid., 31.

5:16—6:10). Likewise, we must understand Christ's commission to make disciples. Thus, the thinker sees that included among the many job responsibilities is making disciples, caring for the soul and the mind of those God allows us to mentor.[15]

THE CHRISTIAN THINKER AS A DISCIPLER

The New Testament teaches it is the responsibility of every Christian to make disciples. The task of discipleship encompasses both evangelism and equipping. Scripture exhorts for all Christians to share their faith (1 Thess 1:8; 1 Pet 2:9–10; 3:15). Christians, likewise, are called to assist other believers in growing in their faith (Rom 14:19; Col 3:16). Robert Coleman states it well when he writes:

> The Great Commission is not a special calling or a gift of the Spirit; it is a command—an obligation incumbent upon the whole community of faith. There are no exceptions. Bank presidents and automobile mechanics, physicians and schoolteachers, theologians and homemakers—everyone who believes on Christ has a part in His work (John 14:12).[16]

James R. Slaughter notes teachers perhaps have the most promising opportunity for discipleship.[17] The educator has a captive audience. Those in the class look at the teacher as an authority on the subject matter and want to know how the topic relates to the real world. Those who teach subjects directly related to Scripture may clearly see the relationship between their subject matter and discipleship. Those who teach secular subjects, however, may not see the relationship as clearly. The following principles on discipleship will assist in showing the relationship between making disciples and teaching.

---

15. For more on the divine calling of the Christian educator, see Evans, C., "Calling of the Christian," 26–49. For a look into the divine calling God has on all Christians, see Badcock, *Way of Life*; Guinness, *Call: Finding and Fulfilling*; Smith, G., *Courage and Calling*.

16. Coleman, *Master Plan*, 10.

17. Slaughter, "Teacher as Discipler," 258.

Part Three: Philosophy and the Gospel

THE ULTIMATE GOAL OF A DISCIPLE-MAKING THINKER[18]

The ultimate goal of a disciple-making thinker is to lead the pupil to mirror the image of Christ in his thinking and behavior (Luke 6:40). When the disciple-making process is complete, the disciple should be capable of renewing his mind and shaping his behavior by studying the Word of God. The pupil should also have a working knowledge of God's principles as they apply to life so that he can fight temptation, take every thought captive, and defend the faith against those who attack (2 Cor 10:3–5; 2 Tim 3:16–17; 1 Pet 3:15). The student should also be capable of effectively articulating a philosophy of disciple-making that is biblically grounded. The pupil should be comfortable with personal evangelism and the mentoring process. Thus, the individual should be capable of motivating others to be discipled.

To achieve the ultimate goal of discipleship, it is vital for disciple-making thinkers to have a proper perspective of their role in carrying out the Great Commission. The individual needs to be committed to Scripture. This commitment to the Word of God allows the person to develop the mindset required to be a disciple maker. One commits oneself to studying and knowing God's Word. One's ambition is to be an approved workman who is not ashamed of the gospel message (2 Tim 2:15).[19]

The thinker's commitment to the Word of God prepares the individual to teach the Word (2 Tim 4:2), proclaiming it in and out of season. The person reproves and rebukes those who need correction. The thinker also exhorts and encourages those who need a word of encouragement. The discipler effectively communicates the Word of God. Bill Hull states, "Effective communication of Scripture means that the trained disciple maker knows systematic theology. . . . a framework into which he can put additional information and has a grid work to defend against false teaching."[20] Furthermore, since the disciple-making thinker is committed to Scripture, the Word of God directs the person's priorities and the entire discipling process "that the man of God may be complete, equipped for every good work" (2 Tim 3:17).

---

18. For additional insights into the ultimate goal of teaching, see Eavey, "Aims in Christian Teaching," 42–68.

19. Hull, *Disciple-Making Church*, 170–86. Though Hull talks specifically to the church as a whole, the principles he gives are to be applied to all Christians who follow the mandate of the Great Commission.

20. Hull, *Disciple-Making Pastor*, 242.

God's Mandate and the Christian Thinker

The thinker counts the cost required before beginning the discipling process. We must decide whether or not we are willing to mentor others God's way no matter what the cost may be. The disciple-making thinker realizes the Great Commission is not primarily about evangelism—it is about discipleship.[21] Thus, the mentor desires every Christian to be a witness who is equipped to engage the world for Christ. The thinker must accept biblical discipleship is a lifelong commitment. It is not a program or ministry.[22] Disciple-making is a lifestyle.

The disciple-maker knows there are obstacles that must be tackled. Part of counting the cost of discipleship is realizing this fact. Since the importance of discipleship is seldom stressed, encouraging others to rethink its importance is one of the challenges an individual will encounter. We must desire to see a paradigm shift in how others view discipleship. George Barna suggests the following transitions will assist in creating the needed paradigm shift for anyone interested in trying to change the present mindset on discipleship:

> Shift from program-driven ministry to people-driven ministry.
> Change from emphasis on building consensus to building character.
> Deemphasize recalling Bible stories; emphasize applying biblical principles.
> Move from concern about quantity to concern about quality.[23]

One of the goals of the process is to get others passionate for disciple making so that they share their convictions and passion for discipleship with additional people. Furthermore, by sharing our thoughts with others, we hope our excitement will encourage others to become passionate for discipleship.

Unfortunately, there will be resistance from people in and out of the church. This resistance should be no surprise to us because we know when we follow Christ's mandate in the Great Commission we actively engage in spiritual warfare (2 Cor 10:3–6).[24] Not only will individuals attack us for

---

21. Morris, L., *Gospel According to Matthew*, 746. See also Hendriksen, *Matthew*, 999–1000.

22. Barna, *Growing True Disciples*, 19. See also Arn and Arn, *Master's Plan*; Eims, *Lost Art*. The basic thesis of each of these books is disciple-making is a lifestyle.

23. Barna, *Growing True Disciples*, 8–9.

24. For more on this notion, see Lawless, *Discipled Warriors*; Lawless and Franklin, *Spiritual Warfare*. For more information on how Christians are to prepare themselves for spiritual battles, see Gurnall, *Christian in Complete Armour*; Lloyd-Jones, *Christian Warfare*; Lloyd-Jones, *Christian Solider*.

obeying God's command to make disciples, those who we mentor are likely to be attacked as well. It is crucial we prepare ourselves for spiritual warfare and teach our students how to prepare themselves for it also (Eph 6:10–20). Acknowledging that our students in many respects will reflect our actions, it is vital we safeguard our integrity: "a disciple is not above his teacher, but everyone when he is fully trained will be like his teacher" (Luke 6:40). Just as our students sit under us, we ought to continue to be students who sits under the teaching of the Lord.

The disciple-making thinker is committed to following Christ's call to make disciples and models it no matter what obstacles may arise. Mere verbal decisions for Christ do not satisfy the thinker; the individual does not seek or desire this behavior because the person desires for individuals to be *true* disciples. Thus, the disciple-maker is committed to investing time into others with the end goal being they can grow towards maturity and reproduce what they were taught. In other words, the process of making disciples is at the heart of the disciple-making thinker's calling and vocation.[25]

The disciple-maker has a clear theology of discipleship. As a result, one is capable of viewing one's mission through a discerning, scriptural lens. There is no way possible for a single person to do everything that is needed in making disciples. The individual also knows the church can accomplish more when believers are taught and equipped to be ministers, for he has a biblical view of the priesthood of all believers: "you yourselves . . . a holy priesthood, to offer spiritual sacrifices acceptable to God through Jesus Christ" (1 Pet 2:5). Therefore, the disciple-maker exercises discernment and wisdom.

Disciple-makers are selective in whom they decide to mentor one-on-one. When Jesus began his public ministry he invested himself more intimately with twelve men, and within the group Christ spent more time with three of them—Peter, James, and John. Christ ministered to the masses, but he was more focused on twelve. Likewise, the disciple-maker is not able to personally disciple every believer. It is crucial we seek out individuals whom God wants us to disciple.

Since the disciple-making thinker can only invest in a limited in the number of people at any given amount of time, there are several characteristics we should look for in an individual we are considering. These

---

25. Hull, *Disciple-Making Pastor*, 32. Though Hull is dealing with how disciple-making pastors place disciple making at the heart of the church, this is applicable to disciple-making thinkers because they do the same thing.

characteristics are rather subjective since each person is unique. Bob Biehl suggests a discipler or mentor look for nine characteristics in a potential protégé. First, the mentor needs to feel the protégé is capable of living up to his fullest potential. Second, the protégé needs to be an individual whom the mentor finds naturally likable and enjoys being with both formally and informally. Third, the protégé should be a person whom the mentor finds it easy to keep helping, even if the individual does not say *thank you*. Fourth, the protégé is a person whom the mentor sees as part of the family. The mentor desires the protégé does well in all things. Fifth, the person needs to be teachable and eager to learn. Sixth, the mentor should sense the protégé has respect and admiration for the mentor. Seventh, the protégé should be an individual who is a self-motivator. Eighth, the mentor and protégé need to feel comfortable around each other. Since the disciple-maker has a strong grasp on systematic theology, the person knows that God is sovereign. Finally, the mentor realizes God may want him to disciple someone who does not necessarily meet the first eight characteristics. Sometimes the person who the Lord wants us to disciple does not stand out as potential protégé. Biehl notes that, "Sometimes the protégé God lays on a mentor's heart is the person who will not make it if someone doesn't care."[26]

The mentor thinks "systematically concerning objectives and methods."[27] The individual can adapt the typical approach and methods preferred to suit better those who require a different structure to achieve the desired goal. In other words, the disciple-maker develops a strategy to make disciples; furthermore, the person assists others in doing the same. When the body of Christ neglects to disciple a newborn believer, nobody seems to notice. Leroy Eims is convinced that "when a person comes to Christ, he needs someone to feed him and help him learn how to feed himself from the Word of God."[28] The disciple-maker sees the necessity of having a strategy in place. There are three primary methods for making disciples: large group, one-on-one, and small group.

In the large-group method, the communicator uses a shotgun approach. The speaker tells the group what they should believe and why. This approach is the main weakness of using a large-group method for

---

26. Biehl, *Mentoring*, 122–25. See also Eims, *Lost Art*, 83–86; Hull, *Disciple-Making Pastor*, 146–89. For additional insights into mentoring, see Kreider, *Authentic Spiritual Mentoring*; Lawless, *Making Disciples*.

27. Hull, *Disciple-Making Pastor*, 105.

28. Eims, *Lost Art*, 151.

discipling Christians. Furthermore, this method lacks a personal intimacy and individual accountability.

The one-on-one method has the personal intimacy and accountability factors in it. This method also has its weaknesses. The one-on-one approach is not the most sufficient use of the discipler's time. There will be times, however, when this method is going to be the best one to use. For example, it would be wise to use this method when a person knows an individual is preparing for the ministry.

The small group approach seems to be the most effective method for making disciples. Jesus Christ, himself, used the small group method when making disciples. Hence, this approach allows the disciple-maker to follow Christ's method. Alexander B. Bruce in his classic work, *The Training of the Twelve*, speaks of the three calls of Christ. The first call is found in John 1:39: "come and see." Mark 1:16–20 reveals the second call, "come and follow me." "Come and be with me" is the third call found in Mark 3:13–14.[29] Bruce comments that when Christ spoke the words "follow me, and I will make you fishers of men," Jesus was indicating that from the very beginning of his ministry he desired not only to have disciples but to have men whom he could train to make other disciples.[30]

There are six basic discipling principles Christ followed to train the twelve where they would become effective, reproducing disciples. The first thing Christ did in the discipling process of the twelve was to tell them the what, that is, what they needed to know. Next, Christ told the twelve the why behind the what; he wanted to make sure the disciples realized the meaning behind what he was teaching them. Christ, then, showed the twelve how to minister to others. In the next stage of the process, Christ had the twelve join him in doing what he just showed them, where they could have hands-on experience. When Christ felt the disciples were ready, he sent them out to do what they witness and experienced under Christ's leadership. Unleashing the twelve permanently was the final step of the process.[31]

There are several reasons why the small group system is the best way for making disciples, besides the fact it was the way Christ used with the

---

29. Bruce, A., *Training of the Twelve*, 11–18. For more on Christ's method of discipleship, see Hull, *Jesus Christ, Disciplemaker*. Hull picks up on Christ's three calls that Bruce notes in his work.

30. Bruce, A., *Training of the Twelve*, 13.

31. This is an assessment of the works of Bruce and of Arn and Arn.

twelve. The small group setting provides a controlled environment. The group is not too large while not necessarily being too small. This group setting allows personal intimacy and fosters accountability within the group.[32]

The disciple-making thinker accepts Christ's mandate to make disciples. Not only does the individual model discipleship, the person trains others how to make disciples. The disciple-maker sees Ephesians 4:11–16 as a key passage as defining the purpose behind mentoring others. We must be convinced that it is our God-given responsibility to equip those whom God as placed under our care for the "work of ministry, for building up of the body of Christ" (Eph 4:12). Since mentors have a biblical view of discipleship, they know God will equip and train others, and they are to be part of the ongoing process.

PRINCIPLES ON DISCIPLESHIP FOR THE CHRISTIAN THINKER

The following principles on discipleship apply to any teaching situation, regardless of its orientation. They are applicable because the focus is on the *context* rather than the *content*. They stress the importance of "developing an environment in which teachers nourish relationships with students so that spiritual growth takes place."[33]

It is important to recognize that God has appointed and equipped certain individuals to serve as spiritual leaders of his flock throughout history. In the Old Testament, the Levites were called to care for the tabernacle and later the temple. God raised up prophets to speak out against Israel's wandering away from God. In the New Testament, Jesus called twelve men to serve as his first disciples; later eleven of these men became the first leaders of the church, with Matthias (Acts 1:12–26) and Paul (Acts 9) being added later. When a new church began, spiritual leaders were appointed to have oversight over the new congregation (Acts 14:23; 2 Cor 8:19; Titus 1:5). Churches do the same thing today. Each local congregation of believers appoints individuals to serve as their spiritual leaders.

Spiritual leaders are to keep watch over the souls and minds of those entrusted to them (Heb 13:17). Peter exhorts spiritual leaders to "shepherd the flock of God that is among you, exercising oversight, not under compulsion, but willingly, as God would have you; not for shameful gain, but

---

32. For more on the advantages of small groups, see Tubbs, *Systems Approach*.
33. Slaughter, "Teacher as Discipler," 258.

eagerly; not domineering over those in your charge, but being examples to the flock" (1 Pet 5:2–3). The disciple-making thinker is in certain respects one of God's undershepherds. As a spiritual leader, the mentor is to protect, feed, lead, and care for the students' spiritual needs as well as their intellectual pursuits. It is crucial the thinker teaches respective subjects from a Christian perspective so that the students can see the mysteries of God in all things. As an undershepherd of God, disciple-makers are to assist in the spiritual formation of those under their care.

Furthermore, it is vital we, as mentors, foster an environment in which students feel comfortable around us. Slaughter correctly notes there is often an unhealthy distance in the mentor-student relationship. There are several possible reasons why this unhealthy distance exists. Both the students and the mentor can contribute to this unhealthy atmosphere in the disciple-making process. The student may put the mentor on an unnecessary pedestal since the student is in *awe* of the teacher's vast experience and knowledge. Likewise, the disciple-maker can contribute to the situation if the individual appears standoffish and impersonal. For the mentors to be effective in making disciples, they must seek to establish a healthy environment for discipleship to flourish.[34]

The educator must exhibit authentic love and care for those who are being discipled. We must follow Christ's example (John 13:1). Christ loved his disciples so much that he was willing to wash their feet (John 13:2–11). Christ told his disciples that they must have the same love for others (John 13:34–35). The disciple-maker must manifest Christ's love through him to others.

The disciple-making thinker serves as a servant.[35] One of the best ways for us to show love and care for our students is to be a servant to them. Being a servant to our students, we not only model what it means to be a servant but teach them how to become servants. Christ's entire life reveals he came to serve others and not to be served. Christians are called to follow Christ's example.[36]

Mark 10:32–45 is the clearest passage in Scripture to illustrate this fact. The passage describes Christ's final journey to Jerusalem where he will

34. Slaughter, "Teacher as Discipler," 260.

35. Parts of this point comes from an unpublished sermon written for one of my preaching classes at The Southern Baptist Theological Seminary in 2001, which was titled: "Christ is the Suffering Servant: Mark 10:32–45."

36. For a concise overview of Christ being a servant, see Pentecost, "Disciple as Servant," 89–95.

be delivered into the hands of the Roman authorities to be crucified (Mark 10:32–34). Those closest to Christ misunderstood what Christ was telling them (Mark 10:35–37, 39, 41). Then in Mark 10:42–45, Christ clarifies his purpose:

> And Jesus called them to him and said to them, "You know that those who are considered rulers of the Gentiles lord it over them, and their great ones exercise authority over them. But it shall not be so among you. But whoever would be great among you must be your servant, and whoever would be first among you must slave of all. *For even the Son of Man came not to be served but to serve*, and to give his life as a ransom for many." (emphasis added)

From God's perspective "servanthood marks true greatness, and characterizes the true disciple."[37] Christ models servant-leadership perfectly.

Since Christ emphasized the importance of being a servant, can the disciple-making thinker do anything less? Pupils learn best when the mentor creates a healthy atmosphere for learning. The atmosphere is one where the educator does not lord over the students by abusing authority. For us to properly teach our students, we correct our students when they error or misunderstand. But we do so with love and in the best interest of the students.

Also, the disciple maker is still a disciple. One knows that one ought to continue to grow towards godliness, just as one strives to convey to one's disciples the need to mature in the Christian faith.[38] The Christian walk is not mastered in a day; it is a life-long journey. Since the disciple-maker is a disciple, the person can share individual experiences and shortcomings with others. The point of sharing is to aid in relating with our students, to show how we at times struggle along the way and must rely on Christ to carry us.

CONCLUSION

It is Christ who said the following statements:

> "If anyone would come after me, let him deny himself and take up his cross daily and follow me" (Luke 9:23). Whoever does not

---

37. Slaughter, "Teacher as Discipler," 264.
38. See Packer, *Quest for Godliness*, for more on how God's children are to grow in godliness.

> carry his own cross and come after me cannot be my disciple (Luke 14:27). "Why do you call me, 'Lord, Lord,' and not do what I tell you?" (Luke 6:46). Go therefore and make disciples of all the nations. (Matthew 28:19)

Jesus desires his followers are genuine disciples who are willing to deny themselves and take up their crosses daily to follow him. Jesus desires his disciples are willing to be obedient to what he has said. Jesus expects his followers to be faithful to go out and make disciples of all nations.

Christ did not give his followers an option or a suggestion to make disciples. Christ commanded and commissioned his disciples and followers to do it. Making disciples is *the essential* part of the Great Commission. For evangelism, for discipleship, and for witnessing of the kingdom to be done, we must be faithful and obedient to the commands of Christ. For us to be faithful and obedient, God's undershepherds must model the Christian walk.

The disciple-making thinker is to lead, equip, and empower others to carry out the Great Commission. We are to model what a disciple looks like. We, as mentors, are to keep the vision of disciple making. We are to proclaim this vision through our teaching and interactions with others.

The twenty-first-century church is to follow the biblical mandate to make disciples. Jesus told his disciples, "you will receive power when the Holy Spirit has come upon you, and you will be my witnesses in Jerusalem and in all Judea and Samaria, and to the end of the earth" (Acts 1:8). There are still nations that have not heard the good news of the gospel. There are still individuals in local areas that have not heard the message of Christ's crucifixion and resurrection. The disciple-making thinker realizes the task at hand is not complete.

The issue at hand is not about whether Christians are supposed to be making disciples. The issue at hand is: are God's undershepherds being faithful in fulfilling the Great Commission? Mentors have a great responsibility to watch over the souls of God's children who sit under them. Thus, we are going to be held accountable for the type of disciples we reproduce.

Authentic biblical Christianity goes far beyond the confines of John 3:16. It moves beyond the privatization of faith and mere personal salvation.[39] True Christianity entails a framework for understanding all of life and reality—Christianity is a biblical worldview. A biblical worldview in its most simplistic definition is as Glenn R. Martin notes, "the recognition

---

39. This motif is the basic premise for Colson and Pearcey, *How Now Shall We Live?*

that God is [the] Alpha and Omega and that He applies to all of life."[40] Essential to any worldview is the implementation of it into practical, real-life situations.

It is essential we do not see ourselves as being part of two separate communities—that of the church and that of the world.[41] For the disciple-making mentors, it is crucial we do not divorce our biblical worldview from everyday life. We are to reveal to our students how Christ is related to all areas of study. David Noebel correctly points out: "God manifests Himself in the form of Christ in such a way as to underline the significance of each discipline [of study]."[42] For example, for the theologian, Christ is the "fullness of the Godhead" (Col 2:9). Christ is the Logos of God for the philosopher (John 1:1). For the historian, Christ is the "fullness of times" (Gal 4:5). And for the educator, Christ is the master Rabbi (Matt 8:19). Christ is the Alpha and Omega, the beginning and the end (Rev 1:8; 21:6; 22:13).[43]

---

40. Martin, G. R., "Biblical Christian Education."
41. Ganssle, "Two Communities"; Ganssle, "Doxastic Community Approach."
42. Noebel, *Understanding the Times*, 30.
43. For additional titles and symbols of Christ, see Large, *Titles & Symbols*.

PART FOUR

So What Now

11

Concluding Thoughts
Only Scratching the Surface

> "The Preacher sought to find words of delight,
> and uprightly he wrote words of truth."
> —Ecclesiastes 12:10

Our journey here draws to an end. But because it comes to a closing, do not presume all is truly over. To think such a thought is the furthest thing from the truth. Mastery of any subject matter takes years, at minimum, if not decades or a lifetime to master. *Philosophy, Who Needs It?* is only a brief glimpse into the study of philosophy. So much more can be discussed on the topic and has been said on it since its beginning. This project is only a layman's introduction.

Philosophy contains a vast wealth of knowledge. Simply defined, philosophy is the pursuit of seeking truth and its application. Christopher Rowe proclaims, "philosophers are *lovers* of the truth, because truth is the only sure guide for the conduct of life, and a successful life is something that we all want."[1] Pursuing truth likewise is what we as Christians ought to be doing as well. We, however, already know where truth is found, which means we should not have years of wandering in a wasteland looking for it.

1. Rowe, "Plato," 429.

As we mature in our faith, we should be growing in godliness and becoming more Christlike. This process is a life-long journey.

During my first academic course in philosophy over twenty years ago now, one of the requirements for the course was to read through the books of Proverbs and Ecclesiastes at least once each month of the semester in addition to reading the required textbook, which was Boethius's *The Consolation of Philosophy*.[2] In the annals of history, Boethius's work had a profound influence. For several centuries, *The Consolation of Philosophy* served as the primary textbook on philosophy and theology during the Middle Ages. It not only was influential on philosophers and theologians, the work had profound impact upon the thoughts and writings of authors such as Geoffery Chaucer, Dante, and J. R. R. Tolkien. Its influence also appears in musical compositions and operas during the twentieth century. This is quite remarkable since Boethius wrote the text in AD 523.[3] Boethius is still well worth the read.

SO WHERE DO WE GO FROM HERE?

Reading through Proverbs and Ecclesiastes is a great place to begin. Both of these biblical books are not only philosophical in nature, they are both very revelant to everyday life. These two books, however, can be challenging to read and to understand. There are great tools and resources to assist us with how to understand them properly. This is one of the great blessings living when we do.

Gaining Wisdom from Proverbs

What is knowledge? What is wisdom? These are just two of the questions Solomon answers in the book of Proverbs. Knowledge is an accumulation of facts of a specific type—raw data. Wisdom, on the other hand, is the ability of applying learned knowledge to everyday life. Proverbs touches upon nearly every aspect of life. Within this collection of wise sayings, we can find acumen on the following topics: ambition, business, charity, debt,

---

2. With the age of the work, people can find the work online for free since it is now considered public domain. Here is one website where Boethius's work can be found in PDF format: http://www.exclassics.com/consol/consol.pdf. Of course, the work is still available in print form.

3. Marenbon, "Anicius Manlius Severinus Boethius."

discipline, family issues—including raising children, personal behavior and conduct, politics, sexual relations, wealth, and many more.

Solomon continually exhorts his readers to seek, get, and understand wisdom throughout Proverbs. It is within this book we learn that the fear of the Lord is the beginning of wisdom (Prov 1:7; 9:10). The wisdom that we are told to desire and grasp finds its fulfillment in the locus of Christ (Col 2:3). The apostle Paul in 1 Corinthians 1:18–31 continues a theme found in Solomon's thoughts: wisdom of the world is folly and leads to foolishness and ultimately takes people down a road leading to death (Prov 14:12; 16:25). God's ways are not the wandering ways of the world through the substantial wasteland (Prov 3:7). Jesus' brother James fathoms the magnitude of individuals lacking wisdom and urges those people to do one task: "Now if any of you lacks wisdom, he should ask God, who gives to all generously and without criticizing, and it will be given to him" (Jas 1:5, HCSB). Seek out wisdom. Get wisdom. And understand wisdom.[4]

Gleaning Lessons on Life from Ecclesiastes

I venture to say that the majority of Christians find it much easier to read and understand the book of Proverbs when compared to the book of Ecclesiastes. While I was working on my first doctorate, I was part of a group of men that gathered once a week for a Bible study. The group preferred to do our study working through books of the Bible in a systematic approach where we studied the material verse-by-verse. Over the course of the study, we worked our way through several Old and New Testament books. One of those books we studied was Ecclesiastes since some the group did not understand its content.

Ecclesiastes can be challenging to grasp its depth of riches as one reads through it the first time or two. To truly enjoy the wealth of wisdom found within its pages, an individual needs to read through it several times over several months. As a freshman in college, I did not grasp all there is to be gained and learned from Solomon the first, second, or third time of reading

---

4. Proverbs contains such a wealth of knowledge and wisdom that it is impossible to adequately elaborate upon all of its riches here. Thankfully, there are individuals whom God gifted to share its astuteness in writing. For further insights into the book of Proverbs, see Atkinson, *Message of Proverbs*; Boa and Burnett, *Pursuing Wisdom*; Kidner, *Proverbs*; Kidner, *Wisdom of Proverbs*; Kitchen, *Proverbs*; Koptak, *Proverbs*; Phillips, *Exploring Proverbs*; Wiersbe, *Be Skillful*.

through Ecclesiastes. I am not sure that I can say I have mastered the book yet. Lessons to be learned remain.

If I were asked to describe Ecclesiastes in a single word, perspective would be it. As an individual reads through the book, it will not take the reader long to realize its author is the one who experiences the lessons found within Ecclesiastes. Solomon, however, is unique—being the wisest of all humanity yet at times lacking common sense or incapable of using his wisdom. We learn the author goes by the name Preacher.

Essentially, we can live vicariously through the Preacher. Instead of being content, he strives to live his life as he pleases with no restraints. As he does this, he realizes that all of life encompasses vanity. Its theme repeats itself explicitly and implicitly throughout the book—"vanity of vanities, all is vanity" (Eccl 1:2; 12:8). As the Preacher lives out his hedonistic and party lifestyle, he realizes his carefree behavior is not liberating as he imagined. Frustration manifests itself to some degree in the Preacher's attitude. Lessons he learned are applicable for us today. He seeks out to experience nearly all forms of worldly pleasure possible. Over time he comes to the realization of how these pleasures fail to give him a sense of lasting satisfaction and meaning in life.

> All things are wearisome; man is unable to speak. The eye is not satisfied by seeing or the ear filled with hearing. What has been is what will be, and what has been done is what will be done; there is nothing new under the sun. Can one say about anything, "Look, this is new"? It has already existed in the ages before us. There is no remembrance of those who came before; and of those who will come after there will also be no remembrance by those who follow them. I, the Teacher, have been king over Israel in Jerusalem. I applied my mind to seek and explore through wisdom all that is done under heaven. God has given people this miserable task to keep them occupied. I have seen all the things that are done under the sun and have found everything to be futile, a pursuit of the wind. (Eccl 1:8–14, HCSB)

Our pursuit of fleshly desires only give us temporary gratification despite what we think. Some pleasures may last longer than others. But all of them are fleeting. At some point during his pleasure-seeking, the Preacher acknowledges that only faith in God provides meaning and purpose in life. Without God life is meaningless and lacks purpose. Without God truth does not exist. In chapters 8 through 12 of Ecclesiastes, the Preacher gives his defense on how people should live their lives. Everything he says in these four chapters can be summarized by two phrases found in the closing chapter of the book: remember your creator from the days of youth (12:1) and follow God's will (12:13–14).[5]

MAKE SURE YOU HAVE A FIRM FOUNDATION

Having a solid, firm foundation for a Christian is essential. Christ points out how building on the wrong foundation can lead to destruction (Matt 7:24–27). Placing our beliefs on the wrong foundation will cause us to crumble when trouble comes our way. The story of the Three Little Pigs comes to mind. While the story focuses on the building materials for the houses and not the foundations they were built on, a similar principle appears in it. We would not build a house out of materials we know will not withstand the various stresses that will be put upon the house. We naturally want our house to provide shelter and security from countless storms for years to come. Likewise, we would not want to build our home on an inferior foundation. If the foundation is not solid, we would not want to build there. The same goes for our personal beliefs and convictions. We must make sure they are based off of truth.

Know What You Believe

As followers of Christ, we need to know what our beliefs and convictions are. If we were to look through the formation of the early church, we would discover the early church fathers held this same conviction. As a direct result of their conviction, they set out to establish creeds that conveyed the core beliefs of the Christian faith. These confessions of faith also express the basis for the formulation of Christian theology.

God does not ask for us to have blind faith, and he does not ask for us to life as if we have blind faith. In his treatise concerning the predestination of the saints, Christian philosopher and theologian Augustine writes:

> And, therefore, commending that grace which is not given according to any merits, but is the cause of all good merits, he says,

---

5. Like the book of Proverbs, so much can be said about the gleanings of the philosophy and wisdom found in Ecclesiastes. I, however, cannot expound on all of its treasures. For further study on the book, see Eaton, *Ecclesiastes*, Kidner, *Message of Ecclesiastes*; Kidner, *Wisdom of Proverbs*; Kreeft, *Three Philosophies*; Provan, *Ecclesiastes, Song of Songs*; Ryken, *Why Everything Matters*; Wiersbe, *Be Satisfied*.

"Not that we are sufficient to think anything as of ourselves, but our sufficiency is of God" [2 Cor 3:5]. Let them give attention to this, and well weigh these words, who think that the beginning of faith is of ourselves, and the supplement of faith is of God. For who cannot see that thinking is prior to believing? *For no one believes anything unless he has first thought that it is to be believed.* For however suddenly, however rapidly, some thoughts fly before the will to believe, and this presently follows in such wise as to attend them, as it were, in closest conjunction, it is yet necessary that everything which is believed should be believed after thought has preceded; although even belief itself is nothing else than to think with assent. *For it is not every one who thinks that believes, since [sic] many think in order that they may not believe; but everybody who believes, thinks—both thinks in believing, and believes in thinking.* Therefore in what pertains to religion and piety (of which the apostle was speaking), if we are not capable of thinking anything as of ourselves, but our sufficiency is of God, we are certainly not capable of believing anything as of ourselves, since we cannot do this without thinking; but our sufficiency, by which we begin to believe, is of God. Wherefore, as no one is sufficient for himself, for the beginning or the completion of any good work whatever—and this those brethren of yours, as what you have written intimates, already agree to be true, whence, as well in the beginning as in the carrying out of every good work, our sufficiency is of God—so no one is sufficient for himself, either to begin or to perfect faith; but our sufficiency is of God. Because if faith is not a matter of thought, it is of no account; and we are not sufficient to think anything as of ourselves, but our sufficiency is of God.[6] (emphasis added)

As believers, our sufficiency rests in God and his Son—Jesus Christ. Our faith, however, is not a blind one. Reasons exist for why we believe Christianity as true. In fact, Christian faith is a warranted belief and worldview. Os Guinness accurately proclaims, "Thinking is a crucial part of believing, for we should only believe what is believable."[7]

During my teenage years, God put key individuals in my life to aid in my growth as a Christian. I was introduced to a number of Christian authors. Some of these individuals had a profound impact on my Christian walk; I still consult a handful of the books I read during those years.

---

6. Augustine, *Praed. sanct.*, chapter 5.
7. Guinness, *Fool's Talk*, 249.

Concluding Thoughts

Thankfully, someone introduced me to the works of Paul E. Little. I am glad to see that InterVarsity Press still has some his works in print forty years after Little went to his eternal home. Little held the conviction that Christians had to know what they believe.[8] But simply knowing what we believe is not enough.

Know Why You Believe

Knowing what you believe is only the starting point. We must also know why we believe what we believe. Another work of Paul E. Little focuses on this very issue.[9] If we are not able to explain and defend the beliefs that we believe, how are we going to be able to share successfully them with others, especially if a question comes up by someone we are talking with?

Knowing what and knowing why we believe are crucial. These two factors work together. Being able to share your beliefs with others can be uncomfortable for certain individuals. This is completely understandable. We all have different gifts and abilities. Some people hate speaking to large groups of people while they are fine speaking one-on-one with others. Further, it is not the end of the world if you are asked a question that you do not know the answer. There is nothing wrong with admitting that you do not know. Do not get discouraged if this occurs. I have experienced each of those situations, and I am confident others have as well.

Another work that Paul E. Little wrote that had an impact on me during my teenage years dealt with how to share one's Christian faith with other people.[10] I have witnessed a handful of evangelistic fads and methodologies come and go through the past twenty-five years. And I have been trained in a number of the various methods, which were popular at different intervals during this period.[11] While each one of these systems have merits, every believer needs to develop their own method for sharing the

---

8. Little, *Know What You Believe*.
9. Ibid.
10. Little, *How to Give Away Your Faith*.
11. Two examples are Fay, *Share Jesus Without Fear*; Kennedy, *Evangelism Explosion*. But there are many others, such as F.I.R.E. and F.A.I.T.H. For more on this topic, see Thomas P. Johnston's website: www.evangelizology.org. Make sure to view the Writings and Notes tabs. When you get to the Notes tab, you will see a massive work that Johnston compiled. Chapter 30 of that project gives a great overview of a number of evangelistic resources and methods that have been used to share the gospel of Christ. I am indebted to my pastor, James Albers, for drawing my attention to this website.

gospel of Christ. What I am comfortable doing may not be for someone else. Additionally, what works well for an individual may not work well for me or others. Each of us are placed in different circumstances. Likewise, we each have different skill sets and life experiences. I will be more effective with certain people struggling with key issues than my pastor or my wife. On the other hand, my pastor will be able to talk with people who may not connect with me. Without a doubt my wife can reach individuals who neither my pastor nor I would ever be able to minister. This is perfectly fine and should be expected. Paul points out in Romans 12:3–8, 1 Corinthians 12, and Ephesians 4:1–16 that each member of the body of Christ has a role to play in carrying out the Great Commission mandate.

As we share the gospel of Christ, we should have nothing to worry about because "the Bible is both rational and experiential, propositional as well as relational, so that genuinely biblical arguments work in any age and with any person."[12] Os Guinness makes perhaps one of the best presentations I have seen regarding how believers do not need to worry if we do fail to present and defend the gospel message perfectly.

> *If the Christian faith is true, it is true even if no one believes it, and if it is not true, it is false even if everyone believes it. The truth of the faith does not stand and fall with our defense of it.*
>
> A good or bad defense of the faith may be helpful or unhelpful, but in each case that is only corroborative. The Christian faith is not true because someone argues for it brilliantly, nor is it false because someone defends it badly. Christian faith is true or false regardless of anyone's defense of the faith. Faith's certainty lies elsewhere than in the rapier sharp logic or the sledgehammer power of the apologist. At the end of the day, full certainty comes from the conviction of the Holy Spirit.[13] (emphasis in original)

Thankfully, God uses people regardless of their giftedness or their lack of it. Do you know what Moses told God when God was calling him to lead the chosen flock out of Egypt? The events are recorded for us in Exodus 3 and 4. Moses told God that he was not eloquent speaker and was, in fact, "slow of speech and of tongue" (Exod 4:10). God knew this about Moses, and he did not care. God calls and uses those who are not perfect to carry out his purposes and will.

12. Guinness, *Fool's Talk*, 34.
13. Ibid., 58.

Concluding Thoughts

Another aspect that Os Guinness speaks out against is Christians trying to separate apologetics and evangelism from each other too neatly. When we look at the two, we ought to see apologetics and evangelism working together hand-in-hand. Apologetics is simply addressing questions and concerns about key features or points of Christianity before we can present the good news of the gospel to an individual. In other words, apologetics equals pre-evangelism. On the other hand, evangelism is the actual sharing of the means by which sinners can be restored to having a personal relationship with the Creator and master. Without one the other is weakened.[14] Be authentic and yourself when opportunities arise where you can convey truth concerning God, his standards, humanity's state of being, Jesus, and our eternal hope.

Avoid Common Pitfalls

Beyond the basic introduction I give in a few of my courses, I encourage students to do further independent research into informal logical fallacies. Learning what and how to recognize these logical fallacies is very beneficial. Once you learn them, you will be amazed at how many people commit one or more of these fallacies in everyday conservation. When I discuss critical thinking strategies in my courses, I provide a list of the more common informal fallacies with their descriptions. Then, I show the classes several videos that are stored on YouTube where individuals have taken the time to insert the informal fallacies that newscasters committed in their broadcasts. Students immediately think of one particular news channel. I reveal to them the news channel that they mention does, in fact, have videos that appear on YouTube pointing out various examples of these fallacies being committed. But I also point out this news channel is not the only one committing them. Additionally, I inform the classes we can also find these errors being committed in political speeches as well.

Some valuable resources exist out there to assist us in learning these fallacies. With the advancements with technology, having access to numerous sources with a few clicks of the mouse and typing keywords into a search engine is a huge blessing. I still prefer holding books in my hands instead of reading an electronic book. All of us are human, and as a result of that fact, we all err. So when you look into the various informal fallacies,

---

14. Ibid., 110.

a high probability exists you will realize that you have committed a number of them through the years. I know I have done so.

Several of the fallacies go by several different names. And the list below is by no means exhaustive. But these are a handful of the more common ones that I see individuals committing consistently.

- **Ad Hominem**—attacking the person rather than dealing with the merits of the person's position.
- **Bandwagon**—since the majority holds this belief, it must be true and so you should as well.
- **Begging the Question**—at least one of the premises of an argument presupposes the truth of its conclusion. Another way of stating this fallacy is the argument takes for granted what it is trying to prove.
- **False Dilemma**—only providing two options in an argument when more alternatives are available.
- **Red Herring**—drawing the attention away from the main issue being discussed by bringing up material not related to the argument.
- **Cherry Picking**—ignoring, omitting, or rejecting any evidence that supports the opposing side of the position being argued.
- **Straw Man**—overstating or misrepresenting an opponent's argument to make it more easily refuted or destroyed. This particular fallacy is extremely popular in theological debates on controversial issues.

Even those who are well aware of these and other informal fallacies make them occasionally. Committing an informal fallacy can be done intentionally to show the absurdity of another position since it can point out its logical conclusion quickly.[15]

---

15. See the following sources for more information on informal logical fallacies: Bluedorn and Bluedorn, *Fallacy Detective*; Damer, *Attacking Faulty Reasoning*; Engel, *Fallacies and Pitfalls*; Engel, *With Good Reason*; Stearns, "22 Common Fallacies"; Vleet, *Informal Logical Fallacies*. Paul Stearns's "22 Common Fallacies" is a YouTube video. I do realize that anyone with a computer can make a video and upload it to YouTube. This video, however, is a reliable resource. Its maker, Paul Stearns, is a philosophy professor who teaches at Blinn College, which is in Brenham, Texas.

Concluding Thoughts

DEVELOPING A CHRISTIAN MIND

It is crucial that Christians develop their minds intellectually. There are numerous reasons why believers need to develop their minds. Here is one of those reasons: developing the Christian mind is crucial for believers because they are called to be different from the world in their thinking. Christians are to have a different worldview from that of the world. And the only way that followers of Christ can have a distinctly different worldview from the world is to develop their minds. Reading through the Bible in a systematic and expositional method is the best way to begin the process of developing the Christian mind. In addition to reading Scripture, the Christian mind can be developed by reading the biblically sound Christian books and authors. Do not just read modern authors. Pick up and read the Puritans and the Reformers. Read the writings of the great theologians, such as Augustine and Aquinas. Read the works of Christian apologists and philosophers.

Developing the Christian mind is not optional. Believers are commanded to develop and renew their minds. Furthermore, we are to have the mind of Christ. Do not think that you are exempt from developing and renewing your mind from thinking as the world. Scripture clearly states all Christians are to have a distinctly different mindset than the world.

God wants believers to use their minds. First, we are to use our minds in serving God (Matt 22:37; Mark 12:30; Luke 10:27). Second, the mind is to be used in seeking to discern God's will (1 Cor 7:37). Third, the mind is to be used in worship (Mark 12:28–34). Furthermore, God wants to renew the mind (Jer 31:33; Rom 12:1–2; Eph 4:23; Heb 10:16). Our minds ought to be correctly focused (Rom 8:5–6; Phil 4:6–7; Col 3:2). Scripture stresses that the minds of believers must be shaped by the knowledge and love of God, as our ways of thinking and acting become more like the pattern set out in Jesus Christ.

God's pattern of thought and attitude of heart is holy, righteous, and good. It is expressed in his law and his word, and also in the outworking of his mercy, but it is, ultimately, beyond our understanding and comprehension. God's mind is expressed in his law and his word (Exod 20:1–17; Deut 4:1–2; 6:1, 24–25; Ps 119:4, 34, 66, 89, 105, 130). God's mind is holy, righteous, and good (Deut 4:8; Num 23:19; 1 Sam 15:29; 2 Sam 22:31; Pss 18:30; 19:7–10; 119:68, 75, 137–38, 142; Prov 30:5; John 17:17; Rom 7:7, 12). God's mind is expressed in his merciful acts (Neh 9:31; Ps 123:2; Isa 55:7; Dan 9:18; Hos 11:8; Mic 7:18; Luke 1:78; Rom 9:18; 11:32; 12:1; Eph

2:4–5; 1 Pet 1:3; 2:10). God's mind is, ultimately, beyond human understanding and comprehension because of God's greatness (Isa 40:13–14, 28; 44:6–7; 55:8–9; Rom 11:33–36; 1 Cor 2:16) and of human lowliness (Eccl 5:1–2; 7:23–25).

The center of Christ's thought, understanding, and motivation is characterized by a total dedication to God. Christians are called upon to have the same mind as Christ. Since Christians are to have the mind of Christ, it is important that believers know what the mind of Christ looks like. Christ's mind is pure (Heb 7:26). One can see the purity of Christ's mind being declared by his words and actions and by his oneness with God, the Father. Christ used his mind to overcome temptation (Matt 4:4; 27:42; Mark 15:32; Luke 4:4; 23:37) and to overcome opposition (Matt 22:18–22; Mark 12:15–17; Luke 20:22–26).

Christ's is more than mere intellect. Christ's thinking is supported by prayer (Matt 26:39; Mark 14:35–36; Luke 5:16; 6:12–13; 22:41–43). Christ's thinking is tempered by understanding (Matt 9:35–36; Luke 4:22; John 2:24–25). Christ's mind experiences anguish (Matt 26:38; 27:46; Mark 14:34; Luke 12:49–50; 22:44; John 12:27; 13:21). Christ's mind is extraordinary. Christ has unusual insight (Matt 9:4; 12:25; Mark 2:8; Luke 5:22; 6:8; 9:47; 11:17; John 1:47–48; 4:17–18; 11:4). Christ understands the future (Matt 16:21; 26:21; Mark 8:31; 14:18; Luke 9:22; 22:34, 37; John 3:14; 4:49–50; 13:33; 18:4). Christ's mind did not know all things (Matt 8:10; Mark 9:21; 13:32; Luke 7:9). The mind of Christ discloses the mind of God in relation to righteousness, holiness, and the law (Matt 5:17; John 14:9–11; 15:10; 1 Cor 1:30) and in mercy (Matt 9:12–13; 23:23; Mark 2:17; Luke 5:31–32; 1 Tim 1:15–16; Jude 1:21). The mind of Christ is made known to believers by the Holy Spirit (John 14:26; 16:12–15; Rom 8:9; 1 Cor 2:11–13). Knowledge of the mind of Christ leads to holiness (1 Cor 2:14–16; Phil 2:5–11; 1 Pet 4:1–2). This is by far only a brief examination into the mind of Christ.

On account of its inner orientation, the fallen mind is in conflict with the mind of God and the mind of Christ. It is nevertheless capable of knowing God, being changed, and renewed by him. The human mind is the seat of reason and decision-making (1 Chr 17:2; 2 Chr 7:11; Neh 5:7; Job 12:1–3; Pss 19:14; 49:3; Prov 15:28; 19:21; Eccl 2:3; 8:16; Dan 4:16; 5:12; 7:1; Rom 10:10; 14:5; 1 Cor 14:14–15; 1 Pet 1:13; Rev 17:9). The fallen human mind is fatally flawed by sin (Gen 6:5; 8:21; 2 Chr 12:14; Pss 5:9; 64:6; 73:7; Isa 32:6;

Jer 17:1, 9; Rom 8:5–8; Eph 4:17–18). The fallen mind tends to confuse the Creator with his creation (Isa 44:16–18; Rom 1:21–25).

There are consequences of the human mind's sinfulness. First, sinful attitudes lead to sinful words and actions (Matt 15:19; Mark 7:21–22; Rom 1:28–32; Eph 4:17–19; Col 2:18; 1 Tim 6:5; 2 Tim 3:8). Second, sinfulness leads to death (Rom 2:5; 6:23; Col 1:21). Third, sinfulness leads to both doubt and instability (Jas 1:6–8).

There is, however, great news. God can change the attitudes of the sinful human mind. Our fallen minds can be convicted of sin (1 Kgs 2:44; Ps 5:13; John 16:8–11). Our fallen minds can be changed (2 Chr 32:26; Job 42:6; Ps 119:36; Acts 2:37; 26:17–18; 1 Thess 1:9). Our fallen minds are only enlightened by God (Deut 29:4; 2 Cor 4:6). God may withhold understanding, however (1 Sam 10:9; Job 38:36; Isa 32:4; Jer 24:7; 31:33; 32:39; Ezek 11:19; 18:31; 36:26–27; Rom 2:4; 2 Cor 3:14). It is God who renews the human mind (Ps 51:10; Titus 3:3–7).

Christians have had their minds enlightened, but we cannot stop there. We are called to renew our minds continually and to have the same mind as Christ. The renewal of the mind brings knowledge of God (Col 1:9–10). Renewal of the mind brings peace (Isa 26:3; Phil 4:7). Renewal of the mind leads to obedience (Jer 31:33; Rom 7:25; 8:5; 12:1–2; Col 1:10; 3:1–2; 1 Pet 1:13; Heb 8:10; 10:16). The believer's mind needs growth and renewal (Rom 7:22–23; 2 Cor 11:3; Eph 1:17; Col 1:9). Through the renewal of the believer's mind, the Christian's mind should become more and more like Christ's mind. We ought to have the same mind as Christ in our attitude (Isa 40:12; 1 Cor 2:16; Phil 2:5; 3:8; Col 2:2–3; 1 Pet 4:1). We should have the same mind as Christ in our knowledge of Scripture (Matt 7:28–29; 22:29; Luke 2:47; 24:27; John 5:39). We should have the same mind as Christ in our awareness of God (John 8:16, 28, 55; 14:10–11; 17:1, 6). Furthermore, we should be able to show the same love that Christ's mind exercised (Luke 11:42; John 14:23; 1 Cor 13:2).[16]

---

16. The material found within the following sources are definitely thought provoking, some more so than others. As with the majority of books that I read, I do not necessarily agree 100 percent with all of the content found in them. Each book listed here, however, is worth reading because they contain insightful information. For more on this subject, see Blamires, *Christian Mind*; Blamires, *Recovering the Christian Mind*; Blamires, *Post-Christian Mind*; Bloom, A., *Closing the American Mind*; Boice, *Renewing Your Mind*; DeMar, *Thinking Straight*; Gill, *Opening the Christian Mind*; Holmes, *Making a Christian Mind*; Hughes, *Vocation of a Christian*; Hunt, *Mind of Christ*; Jones, P., *Capturing the Pagan Mind*; Kinlaw, *Mind of Christ*; LaHaye and Noebel, *Mind Seige*; Lockerbie, *Thinking and Acting*; MacArthur, *Thinking Biblically*; Moreland, *Love the Lord*; Noll, *Scandal of the*

Part Four: So What Now

A DEPARTING CHALLENGE

From the opening page to the closing page of this work, I have conveyed the importance for the body of Christ not to be afraid and fearful of philosophy. I have also encouraged believers to take time to study it. There is a specific type of philosophy which Christians are to avoid and flee from—deceitful and empty philosophy (Col 2:8). Philosophy has its benefits. Philosophy has its challenges too. Studying philosophy can be difficult at times. I do not want to misrepresent philosophy to you as being easy to grasp. Certain aspects are much easier than others, even for me and those who have been studying and teaching it for years. To be honest with you, there are areas within philosophy that I do not enjoy studying; for example, the philosophy of science is one of those areas. But I do not let it discourage me from enjoying areas that I love to study, such as philosophy of religion. As you learn more on the topic, you will naturally find those topics you love. Do not give up before you find them.

Truth matters. In our society today, truth is under attack. This fact alone should be enough for followers of Christ to be encouraged and compelled to study philosophy alongside of theology. We need to be able to defend our beliefs and to be able to explain to others why we hold those convictions. If you do not think that truth matters, please take time to read the Johannine writings—the Gospel of John, the Epistles of John, and Revelation. For example, in the first four verses of 2 John, the word truth is mentioned five times. Then as we read further, we come to:

> Many deceivers have gone out into the world; they do not confess the coming of Jesus Christ in the flesh. This is the deceiver and the antichrist. Watch yourselves so you don't lose what we have worked for, but that you may receive a full reward. Anyone who does not remain in Christ's teaching but goes beyond it, does not have God. The one who remains in that teaching, this one has both the Father and the Son. If anyone comes to you and does not bring this teaching, do not receive him into your home, and don't say, "Welcome," to him; for the one who says, "Welcome," to him shares in his evil works. (2 John 1:7–11, HCSB)

Evangelical; Piper, *Think: Life of the Mind*; Sire, *Discipleship of the Mind*; Sire, *Habits of the Mind*; Stott, *Your Mind Matters*; Veith, *Loving God*; White, J. E., *Mind for God*; Williams, *Life of the Mind*. I truthfully hope that the books I have listed here will be found helpful for those who decide to pursue further research on this vital topic.

Concluding Thoughts

The Christian church is to be "the pillar and foundation of the truth" (1 Tim 3:15). If we are unable to distinguish truth from falsehood, how can we be the pillar and foundation for truth, Jesus Christ the Logos? For the sake of the gospel message, develop your mind so that you are capable to differentiate between falsehood and truth.[17] To God be the glory.

---

17. For more on the importance of this task, see Holmes, *All Truth is God's*; MacArthur, *Truth War*.

Bibliography

Allen, Diogenes. *Philosophy for Understanding Theology*. Atlanta, GA: John Knox, 1985.
Althaus, Paul. *The Theology of Martin Luther*. Translated by Robert C. Schultz. Philadelphia: Fortress, 1966.
Anderson, James F. *Natural Theology: The Metaphysics of God*. Milwaukee: Bruce, 1962.
Anselm. *Cur Deus Homo*. In *A Scholastic Miscellany: Anselm to Ockham*, edited and translated by Eugene R. Fairweather, 100–183. Philadelphia: Westminster, 1982.
———. *Proslogion*. In *A Scholastic Miscellany: Anselm to Ockham*, edited and translated by Eugene R. Fairweather, 69–93. Philadelphia: Westminster, 1982.
Aristotle. *An. post.* In *The Complete Works of Aristotle: The Revised Oxford Translation*, edited by Jonathan Barnes, 1:114–66. Princeton: Princeton University Press, 1984.
———. *Metaph.* In *The Complete Works of Aristotle: The Revised Oxford Translation*, edited by Jonathan Barnes, 2:1552–1728. Princeton: Princeton University Press, 1984.
———. *Poet.* In *The Complete Works of Aristotle: The Revised Oxford Translation*, edited by Jonathan Barnes, 2:2316–40. Princeton: Princeton University Press, 1984.
———. *Pol.* In *The Complete Works of Aristotle: The Revised Oxford Translation*, edited by Jonathan Barnes, 2:1986–2129. Princeton: Princeton University Press, 1984.
Arn, Win, and Charles Arn. *The Master's Plan for Making Disciples*. Grand Rapids: Baker, 1988.
Atkinson, David. *The Message of Proverbs: The Bible Speaks Today*. Downers Grove, IL: InterVarsity, 1996.
Augustine. *Civ.* New York: Modern Library, 1993.
———. *Fid. symb.* In *Augustine: Earlier Writings*, edited and translated by J. H. S. Burleigh, 349–69. Louisville, KY: Westminster John Knox, 2006.
———. *Lib.* In *Augustine: Earlier Writings*, edited and translated by J. H. S. Burleigh, 102–217. Louisville, KY: Westminster John Knox, 2006.
———. *Mag.* In *Augustine: Earlier Writings*, edited and translated by J. H. S. Burleigh, 64–101. Louisville, KY: Westminster John Knox, 2006.
———. *Praed. sanct.* In *NPNF1: Augustin: Anti-Pelagian Writings*, edited by Philip Schaff, 5:499–500. Buffalo, NY: Christian Literature, 1887.
———. Sermon 43. Villanova University, Augustinian Studies. August 27, 2003. Accessed July 6, 2007. http://www.augustinian.villanova.edu/AugustinianStudies/texts/sermo43.htm.
———. *Trin.* In *Augustine: Later Works*, edited and translated by John Burnaby, 17–181. Louisville, KY: Westminster John Knox, 2006.

Bibliography

———. *Trin.* In *NPNF1: Augustin: On the Holy Trinity, Doctrinal Treatises, Moral Treatises*, edited by Philip Schaff, 3:1–228. Buffalo, NY: Christian Literature, 1887.

———. *Util. cred.* In *Augustine: Earlier Writings*, edited and translated by J. H. S. Burleigh, 284–323. Louisville, KY: Westminster John Knox, 2006.

———. *Ver. rel.* In *Augustine: Earlier Writings*, edited and translated by J. H. S. Burleigh, 218–83. Louisville, KY: Westminster John Knox, 2006.

Badcock, Gary D. *The Way of Life: A Theology of Christian Vocation*. Grand Rapids: Eerdmans, 1998.

Baker, Hunter. *Political Thought: A Student's Guide*. Wheaton, IL: Crossway, 2012.

Barna, George. *Growing True Disciples*. Colorado Springs, CO: Waterbrook, 2001.

Barton, Bruce B., et al. *1 & 2 Peter and Jude*. Life Application Bible Commentary. Grant Osborne, series ed. Wheaton, IL: Tyndale, 1995.

Bavinck, Herman. *The Philosophy of Revelation: The Stone Lectures for 1908–1909, Princeton Theological Seminary*. New York: Longmans, Green, 1909.

———. *Reformed Dogmatics: Prolegomena*. Vol. 1. Edited by John Bolt. Translated by John Vriend. Grand Rapids: Baker Academic, 2007.

Beasley-Murray, Paul. *The Message of the Resurrection: The Bible Speaks Today*. Downers Grove, IL: InterVarsity, 2001.

Becker, O. "peithomai." In *NIDNTT*, 2:588–93.

Becker, Siegbert W. *The Foolishness of God: The Place of Reason in the Theology of Martin Luther*. 2nd ed. Milwaukee, WI: Northwestern, 1999.

Beckwith, Francis J., and Gregory Koukl. *Relativism: Feet Firmly Planted in Mid-Air*. Grand Rapids: Baker, 1998.

Bendtz, N. Arne. "Faith and Knowledge in Luther's Theology." In *Reformation Studies: Essays in Honor of Roland H. Bainton*, edited by Franklin H. Littell, 21–29. Richmond, VA: John Knox, 1962.

Bergvall, Ake. "Reason in Luther, Calvin, and Sidney." In *Sixteenth Century Journal* 23 (Spring 1992) 115–27.

Berkhof, Louis. "Man as the Image of God." In *Systematic Theology*, 202–10. 1939. Reprint, Grand Rapids: Eerdmans, 1988.

———. *Systematic Theology*. 4th ed. Grand Rapids: Eerdmans, 1941.

———. *Systematic Theology: Combined Edition*. Grand Rapids: Eerdmans, 1996.

Berkouwer, Gerrit Cornelis. *General Revelation*. Grand Rapids: Eerdmans, 1955.

Biehl, Bob. *Mentoring*. Nashville: Broadman & Holman, 1996.

Blamires, Harry. *The Christian Mind: How Should a Christian Think?* Vancouver, CAN: Regent College, 2005.

———. *The Post-Christian Mind*. Vancouver, CAN: Regent College, 2004.

———. *Recovering the Christian Mind: Meeting the Challenge of Secularism*. Downers Grove, IL: InterVarsity, 1988.

Bloesch, Donald G. *Holy Scriptures: Revelation, Inspiration, & Interpretation*. Downers Grove, IL: InterVarsity, 1994.

———. *Jesus Christ: Savior & Lord*. Downers Grove, IL: InterVarsity, 1997.

Bloom, Allen. *The Closing of the American Mind*. New York: Simon and Schuster, 1998.

Bloom, Harold. *Where Shall Wisdom be Found?* New York: Riverhead, 2004.

Bluedorn, Nathaniel, and Hans Bluedorn. *The Fallacy Detective: Thirty-eight Lessons on How to Recognize Bad Reasoning*. Muscatine, IA: Christian Logic, 2009.

Boa, Kenneth, and Robert M. Bowman. *Faith Has Its Reasons: An Integrative Approach to Defending Christianity*. Colorado Springs, CO: NavPress, 2001.

Bibliography

Boa, Kenneth, and Gail Burnett. *Pursuing Wisdom: A Biblical Approach from Proverbs*. Colorado Springs, CO: Navpress, 1999.

Boethius, Anicius Manlius Severinus. *The Consolation of Philosophy*. New York: Penguin, 1999.

Boice, James Montgomery. *Renewing Your Mind in a Mindless World: Learning to Think and Act Biblically*. Grand Rapids: Kregel, 2001.

Bonevac, Daniel. *Simple Logic*. New York: Oxford University Press, 1990.

Bonhoeffer, Dietrich. *Ethics*. New York: Macmillan, 1955.

Bonjour, Laurence, and Ann Baker. *Philosophical Problems: An Annotated Anthology*. New York: Pearson Education, 2005.

Boole, George. *The Laws of Thought*. 1854. Reprint, Mineola, NY: Dover, 1958.

Boyce, James Petigru. *Abstract of Systematic Theology*. Philadelphia: American Baptist Publication Society, 1887.

Braisby, Nick, and Angus Gellatly. *Cognitive Psychology*. New York: Oxford University Press, 2005.

Bray, G. L. "Image of God." In *NDBT*, edited by T. Desmond Alexander and Brian S. Rosner, 575–76. Downers Grove, IL: InterVarsity, 2000.

Breen, Quirinus. "The Twofold Truth Theory in Melanchthon." In *Christianity and Humanism: Studies in the History of Ideas*, 69–92. Grand Rapids: Eerdmans, 1968.

Brown, Colin. *Christianity & Western Thought: A History of Philosophers, Ideas & Movements from the Ancient World to the Age of Enlightenment*. Vol. 1. Downers Grove, IL: InterVarsity, 1990.

———. *Philosophy and the Christian Faith: An Introduction to the Main Thinkers and Schools of Thought from the Middles Ages to the Present Day*. London: Tyndale, 1969.

———. "phōs." In *NIDNTT* 2:490–96.

Brown, Francis, et al. *Hebrew and English Lexicon of the Old Testament*. Peabody, MA: Hendrickson, 1999.

Brown, Harold O. J. *Heresies: Hersey and Orthodoxy in the History of the Church*. 1984. Reprint, Peabody, MA: Hendrickson, 1998.

Bruce, Alexander Balmain. *The Training of the Twelve*. Grand Rapids: Kregel, 1971.

Bruce, Frederick Fyvie. *The Canon of Scripture*. Downers Grove, IL: InterVarsity, 1988.

———. *The Epistles to the Colossians, to Philemon, and to the Ephesians*. Grand Rapids: Eerdmans, 1984.

———. *Jesus: Lord and Savior*. Downers Grove, InterVarsity, 1986.

———. *Jesus Past, Present & Future: The Work of Christ*. Downers Grove, IL: InterVarsity, 1998.

Brunner, Emil. *Revelation and Reason: The Christian Doctrine of Faith and Knowledge*. Philadelphia: Westminster, 1946.

Bultmann, Rudolf. "ginōskō, gnōsis, epiginōskō, epignōsis." In *TDNT*, 1:689–719.

Burnyeat, M. F. "Aristotle on Understanding Knowledge." In *Aristotle on Science, the "Posterior Analytics" Proceedings of the Eighth Symposium Aristotelicum Held in Padua from September 7 to 15, 1978*, by Enrico Berti. Studia Aristotelica 9. Padova, ITA: Editrice Antenore, 1981.

Butler, Hiram Erastus. "The Idea of God." In *Seven Creative Principles*, 1–19. Applegate, CA: Esoteric Fraternity, 1913.

Calvin, John. *Institutes of the Christian Religion*. Vol. 1. Edited by John T. McNeill. Louisville, KY: Westminster John Knox, 2006.

Carus, Paul. *The Idea of God*. Chicago: Open Court, 1896.

Bibliography

Casserley, J. V. Langmead. *The Christian in Philosophy*. London: Faber & Faber, 1949.

Charnock, Stephen. *The Existence and Attributes of God*. 2 vols. 1853. Reprint, Grand Rapids: Baker, 1996.

Chesterton, G. K. *The Everlasting Man*. New York: Dodd, Mead, 1925.

———. *Heretics/Orthodoxy*. Nashville: Thomas Nelson, 2000.

Cicero, Marcus Tullius. *Tusc*. Cambridge, MA: Harvard University Press, 1971.

Ciocchi, D. M. "Contradiction and Non-Contradiction." In *New Dictionary of Christian Apologetics*, edited by W. C. Campbell-Jack and Gavin McGrath, 176–79. Downers Grove, IL: InterVarsity, 2006.

Clark, Gordon H. *A Christian View of Men and Things*. Unicoi, TN: Trinity Foundation, 2005.

———. *Logic*. Unicoi, TN: Trinity Foundation, 2004.

———. *Thales to Dewey*. Jefferson, MD: Trinity Foundation, 1985.

Clines, D. J. A. "The Image of God in Man." *Tyndale Bulletin* 19 (1968) 53–103.

Coffey, P. *Ontology, or the Theory of Being: An Introduction to General Metaphysics*. New York: P. Smith, 1938.

Cole, Michael, and Sheila R. Cole. *The Development of Children*. 2nd ed. New York: Scientific American, 1997.

Coleman, Robert E. *The Master Plan of Discipleship*. Grand Rapids: Revell, 1987.

Collins, C. John. *The God of Miracles: An Exegetical Examination of God's Action in the World*. Wheaton, IL: Crossway, 2000.

Colson, Chuck, and Nancy Pearcy. *How Now Shall We Live?* Wheaton, IL: Tyndale, 1999.

Cook, E. D. "Epistemology." In *NDT*, edited by Sinclair B. Ferguson and David F. Wright, 225–26. Downers Grove, IL: InterVarsity, 1988.

Copleston, Frederick. *A History of Philosophy*. Mahwah, NJ: Paulist, 1950.

Corduan, Winfried. *Handmaid to Theology: An Essay in Philosophical Prolegomena*. Grand Rapids: Baker, 1981.

———. *Reasonable Faith: Basic Christian Apologetics*. Nashville: Broadman & Holman, 1993.

Cosgrove, Mark P. *Foundations of Christian Thought: Faith, Learning, and the Christian Worldview*. Grand Rapids: Kregel, 2006.

Craig, William Lane, and Paul M. Gould. *The Two Tasks of the Christian Scholar: Redeeming the Soul, Redeeming the Mind*. Wheaton, IL: Crossway, 2007.

Damer, T. Edward. *Attacking Faulty Reasoning: A Practical Guide to Fallacy-Free Arguments*. Boston: Wadsworth, Cengage Learning, 2013.

Davids, Peters H. *The First Epistle of Peter*. Grand Rapids: Eerdmans, 1990.

Davis, Jimmy H. "Faith and Learning." In *Shaping a Christian Worldview: The Foundations of Higher Education*, edited by David S. Dockery and Gregory Alan Thornbury, 129–48. Nashville: Broadman & Holman, 2002.

Davis, John Jefferson. *Evangelical Ethics: Issues Facing the Church Today*. Phillipsburg, NJ: P & R, 1993.

Davis, Stephen T. "Revelation and Inspiration." In *The Oxford Handbook of Philosophical Theology*, edited by Thomas P. Flint and Michael C. Rea, 30–53. New York: Oxford University Press, 2009.

DeMar, Gary. *Thinking Straight in a Crooked World: A Christian Defense Manual*. Powder Springs, GA: American Vision, 2001.

Demarest, Bruce A. *General Revelation: Historical Views and Contemporary Issues*. Grand Rapids: Zondervan, 1982.

Bibliography

———. "Revelation, General." In *EDT*, edited by Walter A. Elwell, 944–45. Grand Rapids: Baker, 1995.

Dew, James K., Jr., and Mark W. Foreman. *How Do We Know? An Introduction to Epistemology*. Downers, Grove, IL: InterVarsity, 2014.

Dewey, John. *How We Think*. Amherst, NY: Prometheus, 1991.

Diogenes Laërtius. *Lives of Eminent Philosophers*. Vol. 1. Books 1–5. Cambridge, MA: Harvard University Press, 1925.

Dockery, David S. *Renewing Minds: Serving Church and Society through Christian Higher Education*. Nashville: Broadman & Holman, 2007.

Dockery, David S., and Greg Thornbury. *Shaping a Christian Worldview: The Foundations of Christian Higher Education*. Nashville: Broadman & Holman, 2002.

Dorman, Ted M. *Faith for All Seasons: Historic Christian Belief in Its Classical Expression*. 2nd ed. Nashville: Broadman & Holman, 2001.

———. "*Fides Quaerens Intellectum*: The Soul of a Christian University." *SBJT: The Promise of Christian Higher Education* 1 (Fall 2003) 58–67.

Dulles, Avery. "Can Philosophy Be Christian?" In *First Things* 102 (April 2000) 24–29.

Eaton, Michael A. *Ecclesiastes*. Tyndale Old Testament Commentary 16. Downers Grove, IL: IVP Academic, 2009.

Eavey, C. B. *Principles of Teaching for Christian Teachers*. 7th ed. Grand Rapids: Zondervan, 1940.

Eichler, J. "logizomai." In *NIDNTT*, 3:822–26.

Eims, Leroy. *The Lost Art of Disciple Making*. Grand Rapids: Zondervan, 1978.

Engel, S. Morris. *Fallacies and Pitfalls of Language: The Language Trap*. New York: Dover, 1994.

———. *With Good Reason: An Introduction to Informal Fallacies*. Boston: Bedford / St. Martin's, 2004.

English Standard Version. Wheaton, IL: Crossway Bibles, 2001.

Enns, Paul. *The Moody Handbook of Theology*. Chicago: Moody, 1989.

Erickson, Millard J. *Christian Theology*. 2nd ed. Grand Rapids: Baker, 1998.

———. *God the Father Almighty: A Contemporary Exploration of the Divine Attributes*. Grand Rapids. Baker, 1998.

———. *How Shall They Be Saved? The Destiny of Those Who Do Not Hear of Jesus*. Grand Rapids: Baker, 1996.

———. "The Image of God in the Human." In *Christian Theology*, 2nd ed., 517–36. Grand Rapids: Baker, 1998.

———. *Making Sense of the Trinity: Three Crucial Questions*. Grand Rapids: Baker, 2000.

Erickson, Millard J., and Sandra McMaken. *Does It Matter What I Believe? What the Bible Teaches and Why We should Believe It*. Grand Rapids: Baker, 1992.

Evans, C. Stephen. "The Calling of the Christian Scholar-Teacher." In *Faithful Learning and the Christian Scholarly Vocation*, edited by Douglas V. Henry and Bob R. Agee, 26–49. Grand Rapids: Eerdmans, 2003.

Evans, C. Stephen, and R. Zachary Manis. *Philosophy of Religion: Thinking about Faith*. Downers Grove, IL: IVP Academic, 2009.

Evans, Tony. *The Transforming Word*. Chicago: Moody, 2004.

Fackre, Gabriel, et al., eds. *What About Those Who Have Never Heard? Three Views on the Destiny of the Unevangelized*. Downers Grove, IL: IVP Academic, 1995.

Fay, William. *Share Jesus Without Fear*. Nashville: LifeWay, 1997.

Fee, Gordon D. *The First Epistle to the Corinthians*. Grand Rapids: Eerdmans, 1987.

Bibliography

Fee, Gordon D., and Douglas K. Stuart. *How to Read the Bible for All Its Worth*. Grand Rapids: Zondervan, 2003.

Feinberg, Charles Lee. "The Image of God." *Bibliotheca Sacra* 129 (1972) 235–46.

Ferguson, Sinclair B. "Image of God." In *NDT*, edited by Sinclair B. Ferguson and David F. Wright, 328–29. Downers Grove, IL: InterVarsity, 1988.

Fischer, Robert H. "A Reasonable Luther." In *Reformation Studies: Essays in Honor of Roland H. Bainton*, edited by Franklin H. Littell, 30–45. Richmond, VA: John Knox, 1962.

Fisher, Alec. *The Logic of Real Arguments*. 2nd ed. New York: Cambridge University Press, 2004.

Foster, Richard J. "Study." In *Celebration of Discipline: The Path to Spiritual Growth*, 62–76. San Francisco: HarperSanFrancisco, 1998.

Frame, John M. *Apologetics: A Justification of Christian Belief*. Phillipsburg, NJ: P & R, 2015.

———. *Apologetics to the Glory of God: An Introduction*. Phillipsburg, NJ: P & R, 1994.

———. *The Doctrine of God*. Phillipsburg, NJ: P & R, 2002.

———. *The Doctrine of the Word of God*. Phillipsburg, NJ: P & R, 2010.

———. "Is Natural Revelation Sufficient to Govern Culture?" 2006. Accessed February 8, 2011. http://www.frame-poythress.org/frame_articles/2006NaturalRevelation.htm.

Fürst, D. "dialogizomai." In *NIDNTT*, 3:820–21.

Ganssle, Gregory. "A Doxastic Community Approach for Christian Scholarship." Accessed March 20, 2008. http://ai.clm.org/articles/ganssle_doxastic.html.

———. "The Two Communities of the Christian Scholar." Accessed January 11, 2008. http://www.leaderu.com/real/ri9902/ganssle.html.

Garber, Daniel. "Rationalism." In *CDP*, 2nd ed., edited by Robert Audi, 771–72. New York: Cambridge University Press, 1999.

Geisler, Norman L., ed. *Baker Encyclopedia of Christian Apologetics*. Grand Rapids: Baker, 1999.

———. *The Battle for the Resurrection*. Nashville: Thomas Nelson, 1989.

———. "Beware of Philosophy: A Warning to Biblical Scholars." In *JETS* 42 (March 1999) 3–19.

———. *Christian Apologetics*. 1976. Reprint, Peabody, MA: Prince, 2003.

———. *Christian Ethics: Options and Issues*. Grand Rapids: Baker, 1989.

———. "Fideism." In *Christian Apologetics*, 47–64. 1976. Reprint, Peabody, MA: Prince, 2003.

———. *Inerrancy*. Grand Rapids: Zondervan, 1980.

———. "Rationalism." In *Christian Apologetics*, 29–46. 1976. Reprint, Peabody, MA: Prince, 2003.

———. *Reasons for Faith: Making a Case for the Christian Faith*. Wheaton, IL: Crossway, 2007.

———. *Systematic Theology*. Vols. 2–3. Minneapolis: Bethany, 2003–4.

———. "Why I Believe Truth is Real and Knowable." In *Why I Am a Christian*, edited by Norman L. Geisler and Paul K. Hoffman, 15–45. Grand Rapids: Baker, 2001.

Geisler, Norman L., and Peter Bocchino. *Unshakable Foundations: Contemporary Answers to Crucial Questions about the Christian Faith*. Minneapolis: Bethany, 2001.

Geisler, Norman L., and Ronald M. Brooks. *Come, Let Us Reason: An Introduction to Logical Thinking*. Grand Rapids: Baker, 1990.

Bibliography

———. *When Skeptics Ask: A Handbook on Christian Evidences*. Wheaton, IL: Victor, 1990.

Geisler, Norman L., and Winfried Corduan. *Philosophy of Religion*. 2nd ed. Grand Rapids: Baker, 1998.

Geisler, Norman L., and Paul D. Feinberg. *Introduction to Philosophy: A Christian Perspective*. Grand Rapids: Baker, 1980.

Geisler, Norman L., and Thomas Howe. *When Critics Ask: A Popular Handbook on Bible Difficulties*. Grand Rapids: Baker, 1992.

Geisler, Norman L., and William D. Watkins. *Worlds Apart: A Handbook on World Views*. Grand Rapids: Baker, 1989.

George, Timothy. *Is the Father of Jesus the God of Muhammad?* Grand Rapids: Zondervan, 2002.

———. *Theology of the Reformers*. Nashville: Broadman, 1988.

Gill, David W. *The Opening of the Christian Mind: Taking Every Thought Captive to Christ*. Downers Grove, IL: InterVarsity, 1989.

Glanzberg, Michael. "Truth." 2013. Accessed October 15, 2015. Plato.stanford.edu/entries/truth/.

Goetzmann, J. "synesis." In *NIDNTT*, 3:130–34.

Goldstein, E. Bruce. *Cognitive Psychology: Connecting Mind, Research, and Everyday Experience*. 2nd ed. Belmont, CA: Thomson/Wadsworth, 2007.

GotQuestions.org. "What is Truth?" 2015. Accessed October 3, 2015. http://www.gotquestions.org/what-is-truth.html.

Gould, Paul M. "The Two Tasks Introduced: The Fully Integrated Life of the Christian Scholar." In *The Two Tasks of the Christian Scholar: Redeeming the Soul, Redeeming the Mind*, 17–54. Wheaton, IL: Crossway, 2007.

Green, Brad. "Theological and Philosophical Foundations." In *Shaping a Christian Worldview: The Foundations of Higher Education*, edited by David S. Dockery and Gregory Alan Thornbury, 62–91. Nashville: Broadman & Holman, 2002.

Groothuis, Douglas R. *Christian Apologetics: A Comprehensive Case for Biblical Faith*. Downers Grove, IL: IVP Academic, 2011.

———. *Truth Decay: Defending Christianity against the Challenges of Postmodernism*. Downers Grove, IL: InterVarsity, 2000.

Grudem, Wayne. "The Creation of Man." In *Systematic Theology: An Introduction to Biblical Doctrine*, 439–53. Grand Rapids: Zondervan, 1994.

———. *Politics According to the Bible: A Comprehensive Resource for Understanding Modern Political Issues in Light of Scripture*. Grand Rapids: Zondervan, 2010.

———. *Systematic Theology: An Introduction to Biblical Doctrine*. Grand Rapids: Zondervan, 1994.

Guinness, Os. *The Call: Finding and Fulfilling the Central Purpose of Your Life*. Nashville: Word, 1998.

———. *Fit Bodies, Fat Minds: Why Evangelicals Don't Think and What to Do About It*. Grand Rapids: Hourglass, 1994.

———. *Fool's Talk: Recovering the Art of Christian Persuasion*. Downers Grove, IL: IVP, 2015.

Gurnall, William. *The Christian in Complete Armour: A Treatise of the Saints' War against the Devil*. Unabridged ed. 1662–65. Reprint, Carlisle, PA: Banner of Truth, 1995.

Habermas, Gary R., et al. *Did the Resurrection Happen? A Conversation with Gary R. Habermas and Anthony Flew*. Downers Grove, IL: IVP, 2009.

Habermas, Gary R., and Mike Licona. *The Case for the Resurrection*. Grand Rapids: Kregel, 2004.

Halverson, Dean C. "World Religions Overview." In *The Compact Guide to World Religions*, edited by Dean C. Halverson, 13–36. Minneapolis: Bethany, 1996.

Halverson, William H. *A Concise Introduction to Philosophy*. New York: Random, 1967.

Hanegraaff, Hank. *Resurrection*. Nashville: Word, 2000.

Hankey, Wayne J. "Ratio, Reason, Rationalism." In *Augustine Through the Ages: An Encyclopedia*, edited by Allan D. Fitzgerald, 696–702. Grand Rapids: Eerdmans, 1999.

Harder, G. "nous." In *NIDNTT*, 3:122–30.

Hardwick, J. "Deism Defined." 2010. Accessed January 23, 2011. http://moderndeism.com/html/deism_defined.html.

Harris, Murray J. *From Grave to Glory: Resurrection in the New Testament*. Grand Rapids: Academie, 1990.

Hasker, William. "Evidentialism." In *CDP*, 2nd ed., edited by Robert Audi, 294. New York: Cambridge University Press, 1999.

———. *Metaphysics: Constructing a World View*. Downers Grove, IL: InterVarsity, 1983.

Hastings, James. *The Christian Doctrine of Faith*. New York: Charles Scribner's Sons, 1919.

Hazelton, Roger. *Renewing the Mind: An Essay in Christian Philosophy*. New York: MacMillan, 1949.

Helm, Paul. *Faith and Reason*. New York: Oxford University Press, 1999.

———. *Faith with Reason*. New York: Oxford University Press, 2000.

Hendricks, Howard G., and William D. Hendricks. *Living by the Book*. Chicago: Moody, 1991.

Hendriksen, William. *Matthew*. Oxford: Banner of Truth, 1973.

Henry, Carl F. H. *God, Revelation and Authority*. Vols. 1, 3. Wheaton, IL: Crossway, 1999.

———. "Image of God." In *EDT*, edited by Walter A. Elwell, 545–48. Grand Rapids: Baker, 1984.

———. "The Image of God in Man." In *God, Revelation and Authority*, vol. 2, 124–42. Wheaton, IL: Crossway, 1999.

———. "The Rejection of Natural Theology." In *God, Revelation and Authority*, vol. 2, 104–23. Wheaton, IL: Crossway, 1999.

Hodge, Charles. *Commentary on the Epistle to the Romans*. London: Religious Tract Society, 1838.

———. "Proper Office of Reason in Matters of Religion and Relation of Philosophy and Revelation." In *Systematic Theology*, 1:49–59. 1871. Reprint, Grand Rapids: Eerdmans, 1997.

Hoekema, Anthony A. *Created in God's Image*. Grand Rapids: Eerdmans, 1986.

Hoeksema, Herman. "Man, Created in the Image of God." In *Knowing God & Man*, 77–86. Jenison, MI: Reformed Free, 2006.

Holden, Joseph M., and Norman L. Geisler. *The Popular Handbook of Archaeology and the Bible: Discoveries That Confirm the Reliability of Scripture*. Eugene, OR: Harvest, 2012.

Holman Christian Standard Bible. Nashville: Holman Bible, 2003.

Holmes, Arthur F. *All Truth is God's Truth*. Grand Rapids: Eerdmans, 1977.

———. *Contours of a World View*. Grand Rapids: Eerdmans, 1983.

———. *Ethics: Approaching Moral Decisions*. Downers Grove, IL: InterVarsity, 1984.

Bibliography

———. *Faith Seeks Understanding: A Christian Approach to Knowledge*. Grand Rapids: Eerdmans, 1971.

———. *The Idea of a Christian College*. Grand Rapids: Eerdmans, 1987.

———. *The Making of a Christian Mind: A Christian Worldview & the Academic Enterprise*. Downers Grove, IL: InterVarsity, 1985.

Holtz, Traugott. "apokalyptō, apokalypsis." In *EDNT*, 1:130–32.

Howard, David M., Jr. "glh." In *NIDOTTE*, 1:861–64.

Hughes, Richard T. *The Vocation of a Christian Scholar: Or How Christian Life Can Sustain the Life of the Mind*. 2nd ed. Grand Rapids: Eerdmans, 2005.

Hull, Bill. *The Disciple-Making Church*. Grand Rapids: Revell, 1990.

———. *The Disciple-Making Pastor*. Grand Rapids: Revell, 1998.

———. *Jesus Christ, Disciplemaker*. 1984. Reprint, Grand Rapids: Baker, 2004.

Hunt, T. W. *The Mind of Christ: The Transforming Power of Thinking His Thoughts*. Nashville: B&H, 1997.

Internet Encyclopedia of Philosophy. "English Deism." April 25, 2001. Accessed January 23, 2011. http://www.iep.utm.edu/deismeng/.

James, William. *The Varieties of Religious Experience*. New York: Barnes & Noble, 2004.

Jensen, Peter. *The Revelation of God*. Downers Grove, IL: InterVarsity, 2002.

John Paul II. *Fides et Ratio: On the Relationship Between Faith and Reason*. Boston: Pauline, 1998.

Johnson, Gregory. "The Inadequacy of General Revelation for the Salvation of the Nations." Spring 1996. Accessed February 8, 2011. http://gregscouch.homestead.com/files/Generalrev.html.

Johnston, Thomas P. "Evangelism Unlimited." 2015. www.evangelizology.org.

Jones, G. C. *1000 Illustrations for Preaching and Teaching*. Nashville: Broadman & Holman, 1986.

Jones, Peter. *Capturing the Pagan Mind: Paul's Blueprint for Thinking and Living in the New Global Culture*. Nashville: B&H, 2003.

Kennedy, D. James. *Evangelism Explosion*. Wheaton, IL: Tyndale, 1996.

Kidner, Derek. *The Message of Ecclesiastes: The Bible Speaks Today*. Downers Grove, IL: InterVarsity, 1989.

———. *Proverbs*. Tyndale Old Testament Commentary 17. Downers Grove, IL: IVP Academic, 2008.

———. *The Wisdom of Proverbs, Job and Ecclesiastes: An Introduction to Wisdom Literature*. Downers Grove, IL: InterVarsity, 1985.

Kinlaw, Dennis F. *The Mind of Christ*. Nappanee, IN: Francis Asbury, 1998.

Kirkham, Richard L. *Theories of Truth: A Critical Introduction*. Cambridge, MA: MIT Press, 1995.

Kitchen, John. *Proverbs: A Mentor Commentary*. Fearn, ROC: Christian Focus, 2006.

Koptak, Paul. *Proverbs: NIV Application Commentary*. Grand Rapids: Zondervan, 2003.

Koukl, Greg. *Tactics: A Game Plan for Discussing Your Christian Convictions*. Grand Rapids: Zondervan, 2009.

———. "The Value of Philosophy." Stand to Reason, 1994. Accessed May 16, 2008. http://www.str.org/articles/the-value-of-philosophy#.VKHPSV4AKA.

Kreeft, Peter. *Three Philosophies of Life*. San Francisco: Ignatius, 1989.

Kreeft, Peter, and Ronald K. Tacelli. *Handbook of Christian Apologetics*. Downers Grove, IL: InterVarsity, 1994.

Kreider, Larry. *Authentic Spiritual Mentoring*. Ventura, CA: Regal, 2008.

Bibliography

Kuntz, John Kenneth. *The Self-Revelation of God*. Philadelphia: Westminster, 1967.
Kvanvig, Jonathan L. *The Intellectual Virtues and the Life of the Mind: On the Place of the Virtues in Epistemology*. Savage, MD: Rowman & Littlefield, 1992.
———. *The Value of Knowledge and the Pursuit of Understanding*. New York: Cambridge University Press, 2003.
LaHaye, Tim, and David Noebel. *Mind Seige: The Battle for the Truth in the New Millennium*. Nashville: Thomas Nelson, 2001.
Large, James. *Titles & Symbols of Christ: 280 Clear and Powerful Images of Christ Revealed in the Scriptures*. 1888. Reprint, Chattanooga, TN: AMG, 1994.
Lawless, Chuck. *Discipled Warriors: Growing Healthy Churches that are Equipped for Spiritual Warfare*. Grand Rapids: Kregel, 2002.
———. *Making Disciples through Mentoring*. Elkton, MD: Church Growth Institute, 2002.
Lawless, Chuck, and John Franklin. *Spiritual Warfare*. Nashville: LifeWay, 2001.
Leahy, Thomas Hardy, and Richard Jackson Harris. *Learning and Cognition*. 4th ed. Upper Saddle River, NJ: Prentice Hall, 1997.
Lear, Jonathan. *Aristotle: The Desire to Understand*. New York: Cambridge University Press, 1988.
Letham, Robert. *The Work of Christ*. Downers Grove, IL: InterVarsity, 1993.
Lewis, C. S. *Abolition of Man, or, Reflections on Education with Special Reference to the Teachings of English in the Upper Forms of Schools*. New York: Simon & Schuster, 1996.
———. *Miracles: A Preliminary Study*. New York: MacMillan, 1947.
———. *The Weight of Glory*. 1949. Reprint, New York: HarperOne, 2001.
Little, Paul E. *How to Give Away Your Faith*. Downers Grove, IL: InterVarsity, 2008.
———. *Know What You Believe*. Downers Grove, IL: InterVarsity, 2008.
———. *Know Why You Believe*. Downers Grove, IL: InterVarsity, 2008.
Lloyd-Jones, David Martyn. *The Christian Solider: An Exposition of Ephesians 6:10–20*. Grand Rapids: Baker, 1977.
———. *The Christian Warfare: An Exposition of Ephesians 6:10–13*. Grand Rapids: Baker, 1977.
———. *Studies in the Sermon on the Mount*. One-volume ed. Grand Rapids: Eerdmans, 1976.
Lockerbie, D. Bruce. *Thinking and Acting Like a Christian*. Portland, OR: Multnomah, 1989.
Lockyer, Herbert. *All the Miracles of the Bible: The Supernatural in Scripture, Its Scope and Significance*. Grand Rapids: Zondervan, 1961.
Luther, Martin. *First Lectures on the Psalms II: Psalms 76–126*. Luther's Works 11. Edited by Hilton C. Oswald. St. Louis, MO: Concordia, 1976.
———. *Sermons on the Gospel of St. John: Chapters 6–8*. Luther's Works 23. Edited by Christopher B. Brown et al. St. Louis, MO: Concordia, 1955.
Lutzer, Erwin W. *Who Are You to Judge? Learning to Distinguish Between Truths, Half-Truths and Lies*. Chicago: Moody, 2002.
MacArthur, John F. *1 Corinthians*. Chicago: Moody, 1984.
———. "The Only Source of Wisdom." 2003. Accessed June 15, 2008. http://www.gty.org/resources/articles/A299/the-only-source-of-wisdom.
———. *1 Peter*. Chicago: Moody, 2004.
———. *Thinking Biblically: Recovering a Christian Worldview*. Wheaton, IL: Crossway, 2003.

Bibliography

———. *The Truth War: Fighting for Certainty in an Age of Deception.* Nashville: Thomas Nelson, 2007.
MacGregor, Geddes. "Epistemology." In *DRP*, 220–21. New York: Paragon, 1989.
———. "Fideism." In *DRP*, 250. New York: Paragon, 1989.
———. "Rationalism." In *DRP*, 524–25. New York: Paragon, 1989.
Machen, J. Gresham. *The Christian View of Man.* 1937. Reprint, Carlisle, PA: Banner of Truth, 2002.
MacLeod, Donald. *The Person of Christ.* Downers Grove, IL: InterVaristy, 1998.
Malik, Charles Habib. *A Christian Critique of the University.* 2nd ed. Waterloo, ON: North Waterloo Academic, 1987.
———. *The Two Tasks.* Westchester, IL: Cornerstone, 1980.
Marenbon, John. "Anicius Manlius Severinus Boethius." 2010. Accessed November 16, 2015. http://plato.stanford.edu/entries/boethius/.
Marsden, George M. *The Outrageous Idea of Christian Scholarship.* New York: Oxford University Press, 1997.
———. *The Soul of the American University: From Protestant Establishment to Established Nonbelief.* New York: Oxford University Press, 1994.
Martin, G. W. "Faith." In *NDT*, edited by Sinclair B. Ferguson and David F. Wright, 246–47. Downers Grove, IL: InterVarsity, 1988.
Martin, Glenn R. "Biblical Christian Education: Liberation for Leadership." Address, Indiana Wesleyan University Faculty Conference, Indiana Wesley University, Marion, IN, August 30, 1983; and Azusa Pacific Fall Faculty Conference, Azusa Pacific University, October 29, 1993.
Mauro, Philip. "Modern Philosophy." In *The Fundamentals: A Testimony to the Truth*, 4 vols., edited by R. A. Torrey, 4:5–29. 1917. Reprint, Grand Rapids: Baker, 1998.
McComiskey, Thomas. "emphanizō." In *NIDNTT* 2:488–90.
McDowell, Josh. *Evidence that Demands a Verdict: Historical Evidences for the Christian Faith.* Vols. 1–2. Nashville: Thomas Nelson, 1979.
———. *A Ready Defense.* Nashville: Thomas Nelson, 1993.
———. *The Resurrection Factor.* San Bernardino, CA: Here's Life, 1981.
McDowell, Josh, and Bob Hostetler. *Don't Check Your Brains at the Door.* Nashville: Thomas Nelson, 1992.
McDowell, Josh, and Sean McDowell. *Evidence for the Resurrection.* Grand Rapids: Baker, 2008.
McDowell, Josh, and Bill Wilson. *He Walked Among Us: Evidence for the Historical Jesus.* 1988. Reprint, Nashville: Thomas Nelson, 1993.
McGinn, Colin. "The Problem of Philosophy." Accessed June 14, 2008. http://www.nyu.edu/gsas/dept/philo/courses/consciousness97/papers/ProblemOfPhilosophy.html.
McGrath, Alister E. *Luther's Theology of the Cross: Martin Luther's Theological Breakthrough.* Oxford / New York: B. Blackwell, 1985.
———. *Mere Apologetics: How to Help Seekers & Skeptics Find Faith.* Grand Rapids: Baker, 2012.
Michel, O. "pistis." In *NIDNTT*, 2:593–606.
Miller, Eddie L. "Faith in Search of Understanding." In *God and Reason: An Invitation to Philosophical Theology*, 2nd ed., 134–37. Englewood Cliffs, NJ: Prentice Hall, 1992.
Mitchell, Basil. *The Justification of Religious Belief.* New York: Oxford University Press, 1981.

Bibliography

Mitchell, C. Ben. *Ethics and Moral Reasoning: A Student's Guide*. Wheaton, IL: Crossway, 2013.

Mitchell, Joshua. "Through a Glass Darkly: Luther and Calvin and the Limits of Reason." In *Early Modern Skepticism and the Origins of Toleration*, edited by Alan Levine, 21–50. New York: Lexington, 1999.

Moberly, R. W. L. "'mn." In *NIDOTTE*, 1:427.

Mohler, R. Albert, Jr. "'Evangelical': What's in a Name?" In *The Coming Evangelical Crisis*, edited by John Armstrong, 29–44. Chicago: Moody, 1996.

Molloy, Michael. *Experiencing the World's Religions: Tradition, Challenge, and Change*. 6th ed. New York: McGraw-Hill, 2013.

Moreland, J. P. *Love the Lord Your God with All Your Mind: The Role of Reason in the Life of the Soul*. Colorado Springs, CO: Navpress, 1997.

Moreland, J. P., and William Lane Craig. *Philosophical Foundations for a Christian Worldview*. Downers Grove, IL: InterVarsity, 2003.

Moreland, J. P., and Kai Nielsen. *Does God Exist? The Debate between Theists & Atheists*. Amherst, NY: Prometheus, 1993.

Morey, Robert A. *Exploring the Attributes of God: An Apologetic for the Biblical Doctrine of God*. Iowa Falls, IA: World Bible, 2001.

———. *The Trinity: Evidence and Issues*. Grand Rapids: World, 1996.

Morris, Leon. *The Apostolic Preaching of the Cross*. Grand Rapids: Eerdmans, 1965.

———. *The Atonement: Its Meaning and Significance*. Downers Grove, IL: InterVarsity, 1983.

———. *The Biblical Doctrine of Judgment*. Grand Rapids: Eerdmans, 1960.

———. *The Cross of Jesus*. Carlisle, CMA: Paternoster, 1994.

———. *The Gospel According to Matthew*. Grand Rapids: Eerdmans, 1992.

———. *The Lord of Heaven: A Study of the New Testament Teaching on the Deity and Humanity of Jesus Christ*. Downers Grove, IL: InterVarsity, 1974.

Morris, Thomas V. *The Logic of God Incarnate*. Eugene, OR: Wipf & Stock, 2001.

Moser, Paul K. "Epistemology." In *CDP*, 2nd ed., edited by Robert Audi, 273–78. New York: Cambridge University Press, 1999.

Muck, Terry C., and Frances A. Adeney. *Christianity Encountering World Religions: The Practice of Mission in the Twenty-first Century*. Grand Rapids: Baker Academic, 2009.

Müller, D. "dokeō." In *NIDNTT*, 3:821–22.

Muller, Richard A. "Crede, ut intelligas." In *DLGTT*, 85. Grand Rapids: Baker, 1985.

———. "Credo, ut intelligam." In *DLGTT*, 86. Grand Rapids: Baker, 1985.

———. "Finitum non capax infiniti." In *DLGTT*, 119. Grand Rapids: Baker, 1985.

Mundle, W. "apokalyptō, apokalypsis." In *NIDNTT*, 3:310–16.

Munson, Paul Allen. *Art and Music: A Student's Guide*. Wheaton, IL: Crossway, 2014.

Murray, John. *Principles of Conduct: Aspects of Biblical Ethics*. Grand Rapids: Eerdmans, 1957.

Nash, Ronald H. "The Christian Rationalism of St. Augustine." In *The Word of God and The Mind of Man*, 79–90. Phillipsburg, NJ: P & R, 1982.

———. *The Concept of God*. Grand Rapids: Zondervan, 1983.

———. *Faith and Reason: Searching for a Rational Faith*. Grand Rapids: Academie, 1988.

———. "Gordon Clark's Theory of Knowledge." In *The Philosophy of Gordon H. Clark: A Festschrift*, edited by Ronald H. Nash, 125–75. Philadelphia: Presbyterian & Reformed, 1968.

Bibliography

———. *Life's Ultimate Questions: An Introduction to Philosophy*. Grand Rapids: Zondervan, 1999.

———. *The Light of the Mind: St. Augustine's Theory of Knowledge*. Lima, OH: Academic Renewal, 2003.

———. *Worldviews in Conflict: Choosing Christianity in a World of Ideas*. Grand Rapids: Zondervan, 1992.

Naugle, David K. *Worldview: The History of a Concept*. Grand Rapids: Eerdmans, 2002.

Netland, Harold A. *Dissonant Voices: Religious Pluralism and the Question of Truth*. Grand Rapids: Eerdmans, 1991.

Netland, Harold A., and Keith E. Johnson. "Why is Religious Pluralism Fun—and Dangerous?" In *Telling the Truth*, edited by D. A. Carson, 47–67. Grand Rapids: Zondervan, 2000.

New International Version. Grand Rapids: Zondervan, 2011.

Nicole, Roger R. "The Biblical Concept of Truth." In *Scripture and Truth*, edited by D. A. Carson and John D. Woodbridge, 287–98. Grand Rapids: Baker, 1998.

———. "How to Deal with Those Who Differ from Us: The Necessity of Godly Disputation." 4 Parts. *IIIM Magazine Online* 4:24–27 (June 19 to July 17, 2002).

———. "Polemic Theology, or How to Deal with Those Who Differ from Us." *JBC* 19 (Fall 2000) 5–12.

Noebel, David A. *Understanding the Times: The Religious Worldviews of Our Day and the Search for Truth*. Eugene, OR: Harvest, 1994.

Noll, Mark. *The Scandal of the Evangelical Mind*. Grand Rapids: Eerdmans, 1994.

Obitis, Stanley R. "Philosophy, Christian View of." In *EDT*, edited by Walter A. Elwell. Grand Rapids: Baker, 1984.

Oepke, Albrecht. "apokalyptō, apokalypsis." In *TDNT*, 3:563–92.

Oliphint, K. Scott. *Christianity and the Role of Philosophy*. Philadelphia: Westminster Seminary Press / Phillipsburg, NJ: P&R, 2013.

Orr, James. *God's Image in Man and Its Defacement in the Light of Modern Denials*. Grand Rapids: Eerdmans, 1948.

Packer, J. I. *Concise Theology: A Guide to Historic Christian Beliefs*. Wheaton, IL: Tyndale, 1993.

———. *Knowing God*. Downers Grove, IL: InterVarsity, 1993.

———. *A Quest for Godliness: A Puritan Vision of the Christian Life*. Wheaton, IL: Crossway, 1990.

Pannenberg, Wolfhart. "How to Think About Secularism." *First Things* (June/July 1996). Accessed July 6, 2007. http://www.firstthings.com/article.php3?id_article=3890.

Pascal, Blaise. *Pensées*. Translated by A. J. Krailsheimer. New York: Penguin, 1995.

Pearcey, Nancy R. *Finding Truth: 5 Principles for Unmasking Atheism, Secularism, and Other God Substitutes*. Colorado Springs, CO: David C. Cook, 2015.

———. *Total Truth: Liberating Christianity from Its Cultural Captivity*. Wheaton, IL: Crossway, 2005.

Peels, Rik. "The Effects of Sin upon Human Moral Cognition." *Journal of Reformed Theology* 4 (2010) 42–69.

Pentecost, J. Dwight. "The Disciple as Servant." In *Design for Discipleship*, 89–95. Grand Rapids: Zondervan, 1971.

Phillips, John. *Exploring Proverbs*. 2 vols. Grand Rapids: Kregel, 2002.

Pink, Arthur W. *The Attributes of God*. Grand Rapids: Baker, 1975.

Bibliography

Pinnock, Clark H. *A Wideness in God's Mercy: The Finality of Jesus Christ in a World of Religions*. Grand Rapids: Zondervan, 1992.

Piper, John. "Faith and Reason." Desiring God, March 15, 2007. Accessed July 11, 2007. http://www.desiringgod.org/conference-messages/faith-and-reason.

———. *Think: The Life of the Mind and the Love of God*. Wheaton, IL: Crossway, 2010.

Plantinga, Alvin. "How to be an Anti-Realist." *Proceedings and Addresses of the American Philosophical Association* 56 (1982) 47–70.

———. "The Reformed Objection to Natural Theology." *Christian Scholar's Review* 11 (1982) 187–98.

———. *Warranted Christian Belief*. New York: Oxford University Press, 2000.

Plantinga, Alvin, and Nicholas Wolterstorff, eds. *Faith & Rationality: Reason and Belief in God*. Notre Dame, IN: University of Notre Dame Press, 1983.

Plato. *Pol*. In *Plato: Complete Works*, edited by John M. Cooper, 294–358. Indianapolis, IN: Hackett, 1997.

———. *Resp*. In *Plato: Complete Works*, edited by John M. Cooper, 971–1223. Indianapolis, IN: Hackett, 1997.

———. *Theaet*. In *Plato: Complete Works*, edited by John M. Cooper, 157–234. Indianapolis, IN: Hackett, 1997.

Porter, Stanley E. *John, His Gospel, and Jesus: In Pursuit of the Johannine Voice*. Grand Rapids: Eerdmans, 2015.

Poythress, Vern S. *Logic: A God-Centered Approach to the Foundation of Western Thought*. Wheaton, IL: Crossway, 2013.

Provan, Iain. *Ecclesiastes, Song of Songs: NIV Application Commentary*. Grand Rapids: Zondervan, 2001.

Quine, Willard V. *Methods of Logic*. 4th ed. Cambridge, MA: Harvard University Press, 2006.

———. *Philosophy of Logic*. 2nd ed. Cambridge, MA: Harvard University Press, 2006.

Reynolds, Christopher. "The Quest for Knowledge: A Study of Descartes." 1999. Accessed June 13, 2008. http://www.global-logic.net/descarte.htm.

Robbins, Jerry K. "Luther on Reason: A Reappraisal." In *Word & World* 13 (1993) 191–202.

Rood, Rick. "Is Jesus the Only Way to God? A Defense of the Exclusive Claims of Jesus Christ." In *The Compact Guide to World Religions*, edited by Dean C. Halverson, 235–51. Minneapolis: Bethany, 1996.

Rowe, Christopher. "Plato: Aesthetics and Psychology." In *Routledge History of Philosophy*. Vol. 1, *From the Beginning to Plato*, edited by C. C. W. Taylor, 395–419. New York: Routledge, 1997.

Russell, Bertrand. "The Value of Philosophy." In *The Problems of Philosophy*, 107–13. 1912. Reprint, New York: Barnes & Noble, 2004.

Ryken, Philip. *Why Everything Matters: The Gospel in Ecclesiastes*. Fearn, ROC: Christian Focus, 2015.

Ryrie, Charles C. *Basic Theology*. Wheaton, IL: Victor, 1986.

Samples, Kenneth Richard. "Faith and Reason." *Connections* 8 (October 2006). Reasons to Believe. Accessed July 11, 2007. http://www.reasons.org/articles/faith-and-reason.

Sanders, John. *No Other Name: An Investigation into the Destiny of the Unevangelized*. Grand Rapids: Eerdmans, 1992.

Saucy, Robert. *Scripture: Its Power, Authority, and Relevance*. Nashville: Word, 2001.

Schaeffer, Denise. "Wisdom and Wonder in Metaphysics A:1–2" *The Review of Metaphysics* 52 (1999) 641.

Bibliography

Schaeffer, Francis A. *Art and the Bible*. 2nd ed. Downers Grove, IL: IVP, 2006.

———. "The Church at the End of the Twentieth Century." In *The Complete Works of Francis A. Schaeffer: A Christian Worldview*, vol. 4, *A Christian View of the Church*, 2nd ed., 3–110. Wheaton, IL: Crossway, 1985.

———. *He is There and He is Not Silent*. Wheaton, IL: Tyndale, 1972.

———. *How Should We Then Live?* Old Tappan, NJ: F.H. Revell, 1976.

Schmithals, W. "ginōskō." In *EDNT*, 1:248–51.

Schmitz, E. D. "ginōskō." In *NIDNTT*, 2:392–406.

Schreiner, Thomas R. *1, 2 Peter, Jude*. New American Commentary 37. Nashville: Broadman & Holman, 2003.

———. *Romans*. Baker Exegetical Commentary on the New Testament 6. Grand Rapids: Baker Academic, 1998.

Shedd, William G. T. *Orthodoxy & Herterodoxy*. Birmingham, AL: Solid Ground Christian, 2007.

Sherlock, Charles. "Focus 1: Made in the Image of God." In *The Doctrine of Humanity: Contours of Christian Theology*. Downers Grove, IL: InterVarsity, 1996.

Showers, Renald. "The Foundations of Faith: A Definition and Kinds of Divine Revelation." *Israel My Glory* 53 (1999).

Sire, James W. *Discipleship of the Mind: Learning to Love God in the Ways We Think*. Downers Grove, IL: InterVarsity, 1990.

———. *Habits of the Mind: Intellectual Life as a Christian Calling*. Downers Grove, IL: InterVarsity, 2000.

———. *Naming the Elephant: Worldview as a Concept*. Downers Grove, IL: InterVarsity, 2004.

———. *The Universe Next Door: A Basic Worldview Catalog*. 3rd ed. Downers Grove, IL: InterVarsity, 1997.

Skillen, James W. *The Good of Politics: A Biblical, Historical, and Contemporary Introduction*. Grand Rapids: Baker Academic, 2014.

Slaughter, James R. "The Teacher as Discipler." In *The Christian Educator's Handbook on Teaching*, edited by Kenneth O. Gangel and Howard G. Hendricks, 257–68. Wheaton, IL: Victors, 1988.

Smith, Gordon T. *Courage and Calling: Embracing Your God-Given Potential*. Downers Grove, IL: IVP, 1999.

Smith, Robin. "Aristotle's Logic." *Stanford Encyclopedia of Philosophy*. December 14, 2007. Accessed June 12, 2008. http://plato.stanford.edu/entries/aristotle-logic/.

Socrates. In Plato's "*Apol.*" In *Plato: Complete Works*, edited by John M. Cooper, 17–36. Indianapolis, IN: Hackett, 1997.

Sproul, R. C. *Consequences of Ideas: Understanding the Concepts that Shaped Our World*. Wheaton, IL: Crossway, 2000.

———. *Defending Your Faith: An Introduction to Apologetics*. Wheaton, IL: Crossway, 2003.

———. *Essential Truths of the Christian Faith*. Wheaton, IL: Tyndale, 1992.

Sproul, R. C., et al. *Classical Apologetics: A Rational Defense of the Christian Faith and a Critique of Presuppositional Apologetics*. Grand Rapids: Zondervan, 1984.

Stearns, Paul. "22 Common Fallacies." YouTube. Teachphilosophy, August 28, 2015. Accessed November 20, 2015. https://www.youtube.com/watch?v=NUO2asxV-Jo.

Stewart, Matthew. *The Courtier and the Heretic: Leibniz, Spinoza, and the Fate of God in the Modern World*. New York: W. W. Norton, 2006.

Bibliography

Stott, John R. W. *The Cross of Christ*. Downers Grove, IL: InterVarsity, 1986.

———. *Your Mind Matters: The Place of the Mind in the Christian Life*. Downers Grove, IL: InterVarsity, 1972.

Strange, Daniel. "General Revelation: Sufficient or Insufficient?" In *Faith Comes by Hearing: A Response to Inclusivism*, edited by Christopher W. Morgan and Robert A. Peterson, 40–77. Downers Grove, IL: InterVarsity, 2008.

Tarnas, Richard. *The Passion of the Western Mind: Understanding the Ideas that have Shaped Our World View*. New York: Ballantine, 1991.

Taylor, Charles. *A Secular Age*. Cambridge, MA: Belknap Press of Harvard University Press, 2007.

Tertullian. *Praescr*. In *ANF: Latin Christianity: Its Founder, Tertullian*, edited by Alexander Roberts et al., 3:243–65. Buffalo, NY: Christian Literature, 1885.

TeSelle, Eugene. "Faith." In *Augustine Through the Ages: An Encyclopedia*, edited by Allan D. Fitzgerald, 347–50. Grand Rapids: Eerdmans, 1999.

Thiessen, Gesa Elsbeth. *Theological Aesthetics: A Reader*. Grand Rapids: Eerdmans, 2005.

Thiessen, Henry Clarence. *Lectures in Systematic Theology*. Grand Rapids: Eerdmans, 1979.

Thiselton, A. C. "Truth." In *NIDNTT*, 3:874–83.

Thomas, R. Murray. *Counseling and Life-Span Development*. Newbury Park, CA: Sage, 1990.

Thompson, Loren J. *Habits of the Mind: Critical Thinking in the Classroom*. Lanham, MD: University Press of America, 1995.

Tidball, Derek. *The Message of the Cross: Wisdom Unsearchable, Love Indestructible*. Downers Grove, IL: InterVarsity, 2001.

Tidman, Paul, and Howard Kahane. *Logic and Philosophy*. 9th ed. Belmont, CA: Wadsworth, 2003.

Tiessen, Terrance L. *Who Can Be Saved? Reassessing Salvation in Christ and World Religions*. Downers Grove, IL: IVP Academic, 2004.

Tozer, A. W. *The Attributes of God*. Vol. 1, *A Journey into the Father's Heart*. Camp Hill, PA: Christian, 1997.

———. *The Attributes of God*. Vol. 2, *Deeper Into the Father's Heart*. Camp Hill, PA: Christian, 2001.

———. *The Knowledge of the Holy: The Attributes of God: Their Meaning in the Christian Life*. San Francisco: Harper & Row, 1978.

Trevethan, Thomas L. *The Beauty of God's Holiness*. Downers Grove, IL: InterVarsity, 1995.

Tubbs, Stewart L. *A Systems Approach to Small Group Interaction*. 5th ed. New York: McGraw-Hill, 1995.

Turner, David L. "Image of God." In *EDBT*, edited by Walter A. Elwell, 325–27. Grand Rapids: Baker, 1996.

Vleet, Jacob E. Van. *Informal Logical Fallacies: A Brief Guide*. Lanham, MD: University Press of America, 2011.

Veith, Gene Edward. *Loving God with All Your Mind: Thinking as a Christian in the Postmodern World*. Wheaton, IL: Crossway, 2003.

Vuletic, Mark I. "What is Philosophy?" May 22, 2008. Accessed July 1, 2008. http://www.vuletic.com/hume/ph/philosophy.html.

Walls, David, and Max Anders. *I & II Peter, I, II & III John, Jude*. Nashville: Broadman & Holman, 1999.

Walvoord, John. *Jesus Christ Our Lord*. Chicago: Moody, 1969.

Bibliography

Warfield, Benjamin B. "Augustine's Doctrine of Knowledge and Authority." In *The Works of Benjamin B. Warfield*, vol. 4, *Studies in Tertullian and Augustine*, 135–225. 1932. Reprint, Grand Rapids: Baker, 1978.

———. *Inspiration and Authority of the Bible*. Phillipsburg, NJ: P&R, 1948.

———. *The Person and Work of Christ*. Phillipsburg, NJ: P&R, 1950.

Wason, P. C., and P. N. Johnson-Laird, eds. *Thinking and Reasoning*. Baltimore, MD: Penguin, 1968.

Watts, Isaac. *Logic or the Right Use of Reason in the Inquiry After Truth*. 1825. Reprint, London: Elibron Classics, 2005.

Weaver, Richard M. *Ideas have Consequences*. Chicago: University of Chicago Press, 1984.

Westcott. *The Spectator* (November 25, 1916). Quoted in *The Christian Doctrine of Faith*, by James Hastings. New York: Charles Scribner's Sons, 1919.

White, James Emery. *A Mind for God*. Downers Grove, IL: InterVarsity, 2006.

White, James R. *The Forgotten Trinity*. Minneapolis: Bethany, 1998.

Whitney, Donald S. *Spiritual Disciplines for the Christian Life*. Colorado Springs, CO: Navpress, 1991.

Wiersbe, Warren W. *Be Satisfied*. Wheaton, IL: Victor, 1990.

———. *Be Skillful*. Wheaton, IL: Victor, 1995.

Willard, Dallas. *The Great Omission: Reclaiming Jesus's Essential Teachings on Discipleship*. San Francisco: HarperSanFrancisco, 2006.

Williams, Clifford. *The Life of the Mind: A Christian Perspective*. Grand Rapids: Baker Academic, 2002.

Williamson, Timothy. *Knowledge and Its Limits*. New York: Oxford University Press, 2000.

Wood, W. Jay. *Epistemology: Becoming Intellectually Virtuous*. Downers Grove, IL: InterVarsity, 1998.

World Union of Deists. "Welcome to Deism, Deism Defined, Deist Glossary, and FAQ." Accessed January 23, 2011. http://www.deism.com/deism_defined.htm.

Wright, N. T. *Simply Christian: Why Christianity Makes Sense*. San Francisco: HarperSanFrancisco, 2006.

Subject Index

Abelard, Peter, 34n68
absoluteness of truth, 77, 86–88, 89, 90, 93–94
accountability for knowledge, 74–75, 101
Adeney, Frances S., 105–6
ad hominem, 164
aesthetics, 15
alētheia (truth), 71
Analogy of Faith, 28n37
analysis, 13–14
Anders, Max, 129–130
Anselm of Canterbury, 32n60, 34, 35
antichrist, 168
apokalupto (revelation), 53
apologetics, 41, 163
Apostle's Creed, 63
Aquinas, Thomas, 32n60, 34n68
Aristotle, 6, 8, 81n18, 92–93. *See also* Ancient Documents Index
assensus, 26
atheism, 108
Augustine of Hippo
  impact on philosophy, 32–33
  on predestination, 159–160
  six attributes of truth, 75, 76, 78, 80, 90, 112
  solution to faith-reason conflict, 32–34
  use of *Crede ut intelligas*, 33–34
  See also Ancient Documents Index
authorities, 128–130
authority, 33
axiology, 15

bandwagon, 164
Barna, George, 143
Barnabas, 55–56
Barth, Karl, 55n25
begging the question, 11, 164
Bereans, 17n2
Bible. *See* Ancient Documents Index; New Testament; Old Testament; Scriptures
biblical language, 70–72
Biehl, Bob, 145
Bloom, Harold, 7
Boethius, Anicius Manlius Severinus, 156
Boice, James Montgomery, 32n60
Bonevac, Daniel, 109
boss-employee relationship, 130–31
Brooks, Ronald, 97
Brown, Colin, 39–40
Bruce, Alexander B., 146
Bryant, James W., 110–11
Buddhism, 79, 107
Bush, Randall, 15n47

Calvin, John, 32n60, 34
cause and effect, 109
Chaucer, Geoffery, 156
cherry picking, 164
Christian apologetics, 41
Christianity
  alignment with philosophy, 38–39
  challenges to, 103–4
  common objections against, 115–19
  exclusivity of, 63, 79, 84, 86, 106, 119–120

189

Subject Index

Christianity *(continued)*
  importance of truth, as way to God
  as only true religion, 79
  reception of, 119–120
  trustworthiness of, 117
  as truth, 88
  truth claims of, 62–63, 84, 86, 100, 106, 119–120
Christian leadership, 125
Christians
  attitude toward authorities, 128–130
  attitude when witnessing to gospel, 119–120
  blessings of, 132
  challenge of philosophy, 37
  challenges to, 168–69
  character of God of, 48
  citizenship of, 126
  defense of Christianity, xxi–xxii, 18
  developing Christian mind, 165–67
  discernment of, xxii, 12, 38–39
  discipleship, 138–39
  example for, 126, 131–32, 148–49
  foundation of faith, 159–164
  gifts of, 139, 140
  growth into godliness, 156
  hypocrisy of, 116–17
  impact of universities, 137–38
  judgment of others, 108–9
  knowing why you believe, xxi, 39, 161–63
  knowledge of non-Christian religion, 104–5
  life in pagan culture, xxi, 116–17, 123–135
  mindset of, xxi–xxii, 119, 133, 147, 165
  obedience to Christian precepts, 113–14
  persecution of, 25, 128, 129, 131, 132–33, 144
  philosophy's challenge to, 12–13
  poor use of logic, 12
  readiness to give account, xxi–xxii, 132, 133–35, 168–69
  refutation of unsound doctrine, 18
  renewal of mind, xxi, 17, 22, 40, 165–67
  response to trials, 25
  study of philosophy, 168
  tasks of, 137–38
  trust in Christ, 132–33
  worldview of, 150–51, 165
  See also disciple-making thinkers; disciples
Christian scholarship, 136–37
Christian theology, 41, 159
Christian thinker
  as discipler, 141
  goal of, 142–47
  Great Commission and, 140–41
Christian View of Men and Things, A (Clark), 75
Christian witness
  effects of inconsistent life, 116–17
  effects of sinful desires, 127
  goal of, 137
  knowing why you believe, 161–63
  method of sharing faith, 161–62
  nature of, 137
  in persecution, 128, 129
  pitfalls, 163–64
  readiness to give account, xxi–xxii, 132, 133–35, 168–69
  submission to authorities, 129, 130
  suffering and, 131–32
  See also evangelism; Great Commission
circular reasoning, 11
Clark, Gordon H.
  on attributes of truth, 75, 76, 77, 78, 80
  on truth of contradictory statements, 95
coherence theory of truth, 96–98, 101
Colson, Charles, 124
communication
  between God and man, 50
  of the gospel, 139–140
  philosophy's function in, 43
  See also revelation
communication skills, 14
Confucianism, 79, 107
conscience, 135
Consolation of Philosophy, The (Boethius), 156

Subject Index

context of Scripture, 27–28
convictions, 159–161
Corduan, Winfried, 32, 38–39, 91n1, 113
correspondence theory of truth, 96, 99–100
correspondence view of truth, 63
Cowan, Steve, 70n10
Cramer, Thomas, 32n60
creation, revelation of God in, 21, 29, 31, 51, 54–57, 59–60
Crede ut intelligas (believe in order to understand), 33–34
Credo ut intelligam (believe to understand), 34
creeds, 159
critical thinking, 10–11
crucified life, 139, 149–150
curiosity, 6–8

Daniel, 84, 129
Dante Alighieri, 156
David (king of Israel), 86
Davis, Stephen T., 48
deception, 90, 91. *See also* falsehood
definitions, 10, 65
deism, 47–48
Demarest, Bruce A., 56
dialectics, 14, 15
discernment, xxii, 17, 38–39, 91, 144
disciple-making thinkers
    choice of disciples, 144–45
    creation of learning atmosphere, 149
    goals and preparation, 141–44, 149
    methods of, 145–46
    mindset of, 147
    principles for, 146, 147–49
    relationship with disciples, 148–49
    responsibility of, 150
    as undershepherds, 148
    worldview of, 150–51
disciples
    abilities of, 142
    characteristics of, 144–45
    relationship with mentor, 148–49
discipleship
    as crucified life, 149–150
    current trends, 138–39
    extent of, 150
    goal of, 142–47
    methods of, 145–47
    principles of, 146, 147–49
    resistance to, 143–44
    teachers' responsibility, 140–49
discovery, 53–54
doctrine of internal relations, 97
doctrine of the Trinity, 111
Dorman, Ted M., 34

early church formation, 159–160
Eavey, C. B., 140
Ecclesiastes, 157–59
education, 137–39
Edwards, Jonathan, 32n60
Eims, Leroy, 145
Elihu, 55
'emet (truth), 70–71
employee-boss relationship, 130–31
epistemology, 15, 18n5
Essays in Radical Empiricism (James), 111–12
eternality
    as gift from God, 88
    of God, 51, 80, 86, 87
    of Jesus, 37
    of truth, 78, 86, 87, 89, 90
    of Word of God, 86
ethical philosophy, 14
evangelism, 163–64. *See also* Christian witness; Great Commission; testimony
exclusivity
    of Christianity, 63, 79, 84, 86, 106, 119–120
    of God, 87
    of Judaism and Islam, 79
    of truth, 79–80, 84, 87, 90
existence
    of God, 4, 42, 47, 55, 56, 63, 75, 80, 82
    of truth, 62, 76, 88, 89, 90, 93
existential viability, 113–15
external correspondence, 111–13
Ezekiel, 118

Subject Index

faith
  biblical reflection on, 22–25
  Christian defense of, 133–35, 162
  defined, 23, 26–27
  facets of, 26
  foundation of, 159–164
  growth of, 24
  integration in academia, 136–37
  knowing what you believe, 159–161
  knowing why you believe, 161–63
  as means to truth, 31
  method of sharing, 161–62
  object of, 23–24
  origin of, 24, 160
  pitfalls in sharing, 163–64
  readiness to give account of, xxi–xxii, 132, 133–35, 168–69
  Scriptural roots of, 30
  as source of knowledge, 25
  as source of purpose in life, 158
  testing of, 24–25
  as way of life for Christians, 17
faithfulness, 71–72
faith-reason relationship
  biblical basis for study of philosophy, 18–25
  biblical reflection on, 35–37
  biblical reflection on faith, 22–25
  biblical reflection on reason, 20–22
  faith against reason, 19, 27–30
  faith and reason, 19, 30–31
  faith plus reason, 19, 31–32
  faith supports reason, 17–18, 19, 32–35
fallacious reasoning, 11, 97, 163–64
fallacy of infinite regress, 97
Fall of Adam and Eve, 21–22, 37, 117–18
false dilemma, 164
falsehood
  constraints on, 92–96
  defined, 72
  discernment of, 78, 90–102, 169
  See also deception
fear, 132–33
Feinberg, Paul D., 12, 99n15
Fideists, 19

fides quaerens intellectum (faith seeking understanding), 35
fiducia, 26
finitum non capax infiniti (finite cannot comprehend infinite), 20–21, 51–52
freedom, 13, 41, 129–130
Frege, Gottlob, 81n18

galah (revelation), 53
Gautama, Siddhartha, 79
Geisler, Norman L., 12, 39, 63, 66n8–9, 97, 99n15
general revelation, 21, 29, 31, 48, 51, 54–57, 59–60
God
  acceptance in philosophy, 4
  aid to Christians, 25
  attributes of, 80, 82–83, 87–88, 117–19
  as Christian's sufficiency, 160
  communication with man, 139–140
  faith in, 23–24
  greatness of, 107
  illumination of believers, 35–36
  knowledge of, 20, 86
  mind of, 165
  nature of, 56, 80
  as only true God, 24
  punishment of sin, 117–19
  renewal of believers' minds, 22
  revelation in creation, 21, 29, 31, 51, 54–57, 59–60
  self-revelation of, 23, 24, 47–51, 57–59
  as source of faith, 24
  as source of purpose in life, 158
  as source of truth, 8, 75, 80–81, 84, 88, 90
  as truth, 80–84, 87–88, 112, 158
  various religious beliefs concerning, 95
  wisdom of, 134
Great Commission, 138–149. *See also* Christian witness; disciple-making thinkers; discipleship; testimony
Greek philosophy, 4

Subject Index

Groothuis, Douglas, 70n10, 76, 78–79, 100, 109
Guinness, Os, 65, 140, 160, 162–63

Halverson, Dean C., 107
hardness of heart, 21
Hebrew Bible, 112–13
He is There and He is Not Silent (Schaeffer), 47
hell, 117–19
Henry, Carl F. H., 26, 50, 64, 76
hermeneutics, 27–28
Hinduism, 79, 107
Hodge, Charles, 43
Holmes, Arthur, 75, 80
Holy Spirit
 renewal of believers' minds, 22
 as revealer of truth, 83
 as source of Christian power, 150
 as truth, 88
hope, 133–35
Hosea, 101
How Now Shall We Live? (Colson and Pearcey), 124
How Shall We Then Live? (Schaeffer), 124
Hull, Bill, 142
human conscience, 56
humans
 communication with others, 50
 creation in God's image, 20–21, 37, 50, 51
 effects of fallen state, 21–22, 37, 117–18
 finite nature of, 51–52
 knowledge of God, 20–21, 82
 nature of, 117–19
 quest for God, 48–49
 transgression of the law, 56
 See also mind
humility, 134

immutability
 of God, 87
 of truth, 77, 86–88, 89, 90, 93
Intelligo ut credam (understand to believe), 34
intolerance, 108n9

is, uses of, 80–81
Isaiah, 84, 86, 118, 123. *See also* Ancient Documents Index
Islam, 79, 107

James, brother of Jesus, 125, 140, 157. *See also* Ancient Documents Index
James, son of Zebedee, 144
James, William, 111–12
Jeremiah, 82, 118. *See also* Ancient Documents Index
Jesus Christ
 admonition to persecuted, 133
 atonement for sin, 118
 on believers' mindset, xxi
 calling of disciples, 138, 144, 146, 147
 as Christian's sufficiency, 160
 discipling method of, 146–47
 as example for Christians, 126, 131–32, 148–49
 final journey to Jerusalem, 148–49
 on foundation of faith, 39, 159
 as God's means of communication with man, 139–140
 on judgment of others, 108
 as Logos, 37
 mind of, 166
 oneness with God, 111
 parable of evil and faithful servants, 101
 parable of the sower, 36
 relationship with disciples, 148–49
 as revelation of God, 57, 58–59, 60, 83
 roles of, 151
 scriptural testimony to, 59
 sending of Holy Spirit, 150
 Sermon on the Mount, 107
 as source of truth, 134
 suffering of, 131
 as theme of revelation, 59
 as truth, 83, 86, 87–88
 truth as freedom, 41
 as way to God, 62–63, 84, 86, 106, 119–120
 witness to truth, 61

Subject Index

Jesus Christ *(continued)*
  work of as object of faith, 23
John, Apostle, 83, 85, 144. *See also* Ancient Documents Index
John Paul II (pope), 19
Judaism, 79
judgment, 108–9

knowability
  of God, 20, 86
  of truth, 78, 85–86, 87, 89, 90, 101
knowledge
  acquisition of, 40–41
  defined, 156
  from general revelation, 54–57
  of God, 82
  precondition for, 26, 34–35
  responsibility to and accountability for, 74–75, 101
  from revelation vs. discovery, 53–54
  search for, 7–8
  source of, 134
  through general revelation, 54–59

large-group method of discipleship, 145–46
law of bivalence, 63–64, 91
law of identity, 91–92
law of non-contradiction
  application to truth, 84, 91, 94–96
  application to truth claims, 110
  concept of, 64, 92
  equality of religions and, 115–16
law of the excluded middle
  application to truth, 91, 93–94
  application to truth claims, 110
  concept of, 64, 92
learning, 90
legalism, 48
Levites, 147
Lewis, C. S., 18
lies. *See* falsehood
Lincoln, Abraham, 13
Little, Paul E., 161
Lloyd-Jones, D. Martyn, 20, 21–22
logic
  application of laws, 104
  application to truth claims, 90–91
  defined, 15
  fallacious reasoning, 11, 97, 163–64
  law of bivalence, 63–64, 91
  law of identity, 91–92
  law of non-contradiction, 64, 84, 91, 92, 94–96, 110, 115–16
  law of the excluded middle, 64, 91, 92, 93–94, 110
logical consistency, 109–11
logical fallacies, 11, 97, 163–64
logical thinking, 10–11
Luther, Martin, 32n60. *See also* Ancient Documents Index

MacArthur, John, 51–52
Machen, J. Gresham, 32n60
Malik, Charles, 137–38
Martin, Glenn R., 150–51
Matthias, 147
Mauro, Philip, 3
mentor. *See* disciple-making thinkers
metaphysics, 14
mind
  Christian uses of, 165–66
  developing Christian mind, 165–67
  enlightenment of, 22
  of fallen man, 21–22, 166–67
  of God, 165
  maturity of, 6–8
  renewal of believers' minds, 40, 165–67
  as seat of reason, 20
  truth's preexistence to, 78
miracles, 57, 58
missionaries, 104–5
'*mn* (truth), 70–71
Moberly, R. W. L., 70
Mohler, R. Albert, Jr., 85
Moreland, J. P., 28
Moses, 162
Muck, Terry C., 105–6

Nahum, 107
Nash, Ronald H., 76, 95–96
natural philosophy, 14
natural theology, 48, 85, 104, 105–6
necessary conditions, 109–10
Nero, 128

Subject Index

New Testament, 70, 71–72, 82, 112–13. See also Ancient Documents Index; Scriptures
Nicole, Roger, 71
nihilism, 48–49
Noebel, David, 151
nominal definition, 65
non-Christian religions
    Christians' knowledge of, 104–5
    criteria for evaluation of truth claims of, 108–15
    truth claims of, 94–95
    truth in, 106–8
notitia, 26

objectivity
    of God, 87
    of truth, 78–79, 85, 87, 89, 90
Ockham's Razor, 98
Oepke, Albrecht, 53
Old Testament, 70, 82, 112–13. See also Ancient Documents Index; Scriptures
Oliphint, K. Scott, 9
one-on-one method of discipleship, 146
Otto, Rudolf, 55n25
Owen, John, 32n60

Packer, J. I., 32n60
Pascal, Blaise, 32, 32n60
Paul, Apostle
    admonitions concerning unsound doctrine, 18
    argument for resurrection of Christ, 100
    on aspects of philosophy, 12
    calling as apostle, 147
    on Christian life, 125
    on closeness of God, 107
    on confrontation with truth, 104
    defense of Christianity, 119
    on faith-reason relationship, 35
    on fallen state of man, 21
    on general revelation of God, 55–56
    on gifts of Holy Spirit, 140
    God's revelation on Damascus Road, 54
    on importance of gospel message, xxii
    on knowledge of God, 82
    on philosophy and deception, 27–29, 38, 39
    on renewing of the mind, 40
    on responsibility and accountability with knowledge, 74
    on roles of Christians, 162
    on sin, 118
    on spiritual battle, 124–135
    struggle with sin, 117, 127
    on suppression of truth, 91
    on taking thoughts captive, xxi
    teaching on conscience, 56
    teaching on submitting to authorities, 107
    on truth, 63, 85
    on unbelievers, 134
    on unknown God, 106
    on use of freedom, 130
    use of reason, 22
    on wisdom, 157
    See also Ancient Documents Index
Pearcey, Nancy, 124
persecution, 128, 129, 131, 132–33
Peter, Apostle. See also Ancient Documents Index
    on believers' mindset, xxi
    on Christian life, 124–135
    description of God's acts, 58
    on faith and reason, 31
    on salvation, 119
    time with Jesus, 144
philosophers, 7, 9, 109
philosophy
    acceptance of religious beliefs, 4, 9
    acquiring deeper understanding of, 9–15
    aid in polemics, 42–43
    biblical basis for study of, 18–25
    biblical justification for, 17–37
    challenge of, 9–13, 37
    Christian, 134
    Christianity's alignment with, 38–39
    defined, 3–9, 15–16, 155
    dynamic nature of, 8–9

195

Subject Index

philosophy *(continued)*
    function in communication of Christian faith, 43
    functions in service of Christianity, 40–41
    impact on Christian apologetics, 41
    influence on Christian theology, xxiii, 41, 159
    major branches of, 14–15
    pragmatism's influence on, 98
    preparation of account of Christian hope, 134
    purpose of, 8, 43–44
    source of, 6–8
    study of, 16, 18–25, 168
    of this world, 133–34
    value of, xxii–xxiii, 13–14
    See also reason
philosophy of divine revelation, 47–60
philosophy of religion, 18n5
physic, 14
Pilate, Pontius, 61, 62–63
Piper, John, 21, 35–36
pistos (faithfulness), 71–72
Plantinga, Alvin, 75, 76, 80
Plato, 81n18
polemics, 41
political correctness, 104
Porter, Stanley, 83
pragmatic theory of truth, 96, 98–99, 101, 113
pragmatism, 66–67, 77, 98–99
Pragmatism (James), 112
problem solving, 13
propaganda, 13
prophecy, 58
prophets, 147
propositions, 90, 92, 93
Protagora of Abdera, 62
Proverbs, 156–57
Pythagora of Samos, 3

Rahner, Karl, 55n25
Rationalism, 19, 39
real definition, 65
reality
    interpretation of, 43, 91
    philosophy's description, 9

    religious beliefs' external correspondence with, 111–13
    truth's correspondence with, 62–63, 64, 69–70, 84, 85, 87, 88, 89, 90
    wisdom as application of knowledge about, 4
reason
    biblical reflection on, 20–22
    effects of the Fall of man, 21–22
    explanation of religious beliefs, 110
    faith-reason relationship, 17–37
    as means of knowing God, 51
    as means to truth, 31
red herring, 164
relativism
    coherence theory and, 101
    precepts of, 48
    view of religions, 116
    view of truth, 62, 77, 78, 88–89, 93–94
religious beliefs
    acceptance in philosophy, 4, 9
    consistency and coherence of, 109–11
    equality of all religions, 115–16
    existential viability of, 113–15
    external correspondence, 111–13
    issues covered, 113
    knowledge of, 159–161
    See also specific religion
religious skeptics, 12, 115–16
research, 13
responsibility for knowledge, 74–75, 101
revelation
    defined, 53–54
    general, 21, 29, 31, 48, 51, 54–57, 59–60. *See also* creation
    modes of, 54–59
    necessity of, 50–52
    purpose of, 47–49, 52
    rationale of, 49–50
    special, 31, 54, 57–60, 86. *See also* Jesus Christ; miracles; Scriptures; theophanies
ritualism, 48
Rood, Rick, 110
Rowe, Christopher, 155

Subject Index

salvation
  certainty of, 124
  consequences of, 124
  by faith, 23–24
  in Jesus alone, 62–63, 84, 86, 106, 119–120
  non-Christian religions and, 107
  sufficient conditions for, 23, 26, 109, 110
Saucy, Robert, 58
Saul. *See* Paul, Apostle
saving faith, 23, 26
Schaeffer, Francis A., 47, 57, 103–4, 124
Schleiermacher, Friedrich, 55n25
Scholasticism, 34n68
Schreiner, Thomas, 129
Scriptures
  commitment to, 142
  interpretation of, 27
  reading and study of, 165
  as revelation of God, 57, 58
  as source of truth, 24
  as testimony to Jesus, 59
  See also Ancient Documents Index
servanthood, 148–49
Shinto, 79
sin
  abstaining from sinful desires, 127
  consequences of, 118–19, 123–24, 167
  defined, 24
  effect on relationship with God, 52
  impact on knowledge of truth, 85
  impact on reason, 21–22, 91
Sire, James W., 11
skepticism, 12, 115–16
Slaughter, James R., 141, 148
slaves, 130–31
small group method of discipleship, 146–47
social-political philosophy, 15
Socrates, 9–10
Solomon, 5, 41, 82, 156–57, 158
special revelation, 31, 54, 57–60, 86
spiritual disciplines, 40–41
spiritual leaders, 147–48
spiritual warfare, 143–44

Stearns, Paul, 164n15
Stewart, Matthew, 7
stipulative definition, 65
straw man, 164
submission to authorities, 128–130
suffering
  Buddhists' acknowledgement of, 107
  Christian walk during, 124, 125, 126, 131–32
  of Jesus, 131
  need for understanding of, 113
  unbelievers' objections concerning, 117
sufficient conditions, 109, 110

teachers
  call of, 140–41
  as disciplers, 141–49
  goal of, 142–47
  principles for, 147–49
  responsibility to students, 137–39
Tertullian, 19
testimony
  effects of inconsistent life, 116–17
  effects of sinful desires, 127
  goal of, 137
  knowing why you believe, 161–63
  method of sharing faith, 161–62
  nature of, 137
  in persecution, 128
  pitfalls, 163–64
  readiness to give account, xxi–xxii, 132, 133–35, 168–69
  submission to authorities, 129, 130
  suffering and, 131–32
  See also Great Commission
testing of faith, 24–25
theology, xxiii, 41
theophanies, 57–58
theories of truth
  coherence theory of truth, 96–98, 101
  correspondence theory of truth, 96, 99–100
  pragmatic theory of truth, 96, 98–99, 101, 113
Thiessen, Henry Clarence, 54
thinking, 160

Subject Index

Tillich, Paul, 55n25
Tolkien, J. R. R., 156
touchstone proposition, xxii n2
Training of the Twelve, The (Bruce), 146
truth
    attacks on, 168
    attributes of biblical perspective, 75–81
    biblical language and, 70–72
    constraints on, 92–96
    correspondence with reality, 62–63, 64, 69–70, 84, 85, 87, 88, 89, 90
    defense of, 65–66
    defined, 8, 69, 71–73
    degrees of, 97
    demand for confrontation, 103–4
    discernment of falsehood and, 90–102
    discovery of, 20
    as divine revelation, 54
    enigma of nature of, 65–72
    eternality and universality of, 78, 86, 89, 90
    exclusivity of, 79–80, 84, 89, 90
    existence of, 62, 76, 88, 89, 93
    freedom through, 41, 74–89
    God as, 8, 75, 80–84, 87–88, 89, 158
    human interpretation of, 22
    immutability and absoluteness of, 77, 86–88, 89, 90, 93–94
    Jesus as, 61
    knowability of, 78, 85–86, 89, 90, 101
    magnitude of the nature of, 62–65
    in non-Christian religions, 106–8
    objectivity of, 78–79, 85, 89, 90
    philosophy's search for, 8
    proper interpretation of, 22
    relativism and, 62, 88–89
    search for, 74
    source of, 8, 30, 31, 75, 80–81, 84, 87–88, 90, 134
    suppression of, 85
    verification of, 90–91
    views of, 88–89
    what it is not, 66–69
    See also theories of truth
truth-claims
    of Christianity, 62–63, 84, 86, 100, 106, 119–120
    consistency and internal coherence, 109–11
    correspondence with reality, 111–13
    equality of, 115–16
    existential viability of, 113–15
    external correspondence, 111–13
    of non-Christian religions, 94–95, 106–8
    reality and, 90
Truth Decay (Groothuis), 70n10, 76
truth-value, 92

unbeliever's mind, 104, 133–34
understanding, 7–8
universality
    of God, 87
    of truth, 78, 86, 87, 89, 90
universities, 137–39
unrighteousness. *See* sin

Varieties of Religious Experience, The (James), 111, 112

Walls, David, 129–130
Warfield, Benjamin B., 32n60
Wesley, John, 116, 125
Westcott, Bishop, 23
Willard, Dallas, 138–39
wisdom
    acquisition of knowledge and, 41
    defined, 4–6, 156
    of disciple-makers, 144
    of God, 134
    in Proverbs, 156–57
Word of God. *See* Ancient Documents Index; New Testament; Old Testament; Scriptures
worldly pleasures, 158–59
worldview
    Christian impact on affairs, 138
    of Christians, 150–51, 165
    Christians' ability to critique, 134–35
    defined, 11, 12, 150–51

establishing Christian worldview, 13, 37
existential viability of, 113–15
external correspondence with reality, 111–13

issues covered, 113
questions of, 11–12
See also religious beliefs

Wright, N. T., 62

Ancient Documents Index

OLD TESTAMENT

Genesis

1:1	82
1:1–2:25	89
1–2	50
1:26	82
1:26–27	20
1:27	58, 105, 117
1:28	50
1:31	117
2:18	50
3.	117
3:1–24	21
3:8	50
6:5	118, 166
6:5–6	21
8:21	21, 118, 166
9:6	20
11:1–9	48n4
15:15	24
15:17	57
16:9–13	57
17:1	58
18	57
18:1–2	57
18:22	57
19	57
20:3	58
22	58
22:12	70
26:24	58
28:12	57
28:12–16	58
31:24	58
32:1–2	57
32:24–30	57
35:9	58
37	58
46:2	58

Exodus

3:1–6	57
3:2	57
3:2–4	57
3–4	162
4:4	58
4:10	162
4:12	58
6:2	58
12:12	58
12:23	58
14:15	24
17:6	58
19:9ff	57
20:1–17	165
24:16	57
32:1–10	48n4
32:14	87
33:18ff	57
33:20	51
34:4 7	57
34:5–7	70

Ancient Documents Index

Numbers

9:15–23	57
11:17	57
11:25	57
12:5	57
12:6	58
12:6–8	58
14:6–9	24
14:10–12	57
15:27–31	101
17:7	57
20:16	57
23:4	58
23:5	58
23:16	58
23:19	83, 84, 87, 165

Deuteronomy

3:21–22	24
4:1–2	165
4:8	165
4:39	82
5:29	70
6:1	165
13:1	58
24–25	165
29:4	22, 167
29:29	51
30:1–10	56
31:15	57
33:23	57

Joshua

5:13–15	57
6:2–5	24

Judges

7:13–14	58
13:3–23	57
16:11–24	57

1 Samuel

3:4–14	58
3:21	58
10:9	22, 167
15:11–29	87
15:29	83, 87, 165
17:34–37	24

2 Samuel

5:24	58
22:31	23, 165

1 Kings

2:44	22, 167
3:5	58
9:2	58
17:17–18	25
17:24	84
22:16	84

2 Kings

4:1	25
4:17–28	25
18:19–25	25

1 Chronicles

16:25	107
17:2	166

2 Chronicles

7:11	20, 166
12:14	21, 166
15:3	82
18:15	84
32:7–8	24
32:10–15	25
32:26	22, 167

Nehemiah

5:7	20, 166
6:6	84
9:31	165

Job 107

2:7	25
9:4	52
9:10	52
11:7	51, 52

11:7–9	20
12:1–3	20, 166
12:20	20
12:23	56
12:24–25	20
23:3–9	52
26:14	52
28:28	3, 31, 70
31:35	49
32:3	20
32:8	82
32:11–12	20
33:14–15	58
33:23	57
36:22	55
36:22–26	55
36:26	52
36:27–37:13	55
36–37	55
37:5	52
37:14–22	55
37:23	52
38:36	22, 167
38:36–37	20
38–39	55
42:2–6	51
42:6	22, 167

Psalms

5:9	21, 166
5:13	167
8:3–8	20
9:10	24
12:6	83
18:2–6	23
18:7–15	55
18:30	165
19	56
19:1–6	31, 51, 55, 56, 59
19:2	58
19:4	24
19:7–10	165
19:12–13	101
19:14	20, 166
20:27	23
22:27	106
25:1–2	23
25:5	84, 90
26:1	23
26:3	84
27:13–14	23
29:3	58
31:5	83
33:4	83
33:9	58
33:11	87
37:3–5	24
40:10–11	83
41:13	87
43:3	84
46:1–3	24
47:7–8	56
49:3	166
51:3	22
51:4	24, 83
51:5	118
51:10	22, 167
58:3	118
64:6	21, 166
66:7	56
66:10–12	25
73:7	21, 166
86:11	84
90:2–4	87
91:1–4	24
91:1–6	85
91:14–15	25
95:7	24
96:4	107
96:13	83
105:1	57
111:10	31
115:2–11	24
118:9	23
119:4	165
119:30	83
119:34	165
119:36	22, 167
119:42	165
119:43–44	83
119:66	165
119:68	165
119:75	165
119:89	86, 165
119:105	165

Psalms (continued)

119:130	165
119:137–138	165
119:142	83
119:151	83
119:160	83
123:2	165
139:6	51, 52
145:3	20, 52

Proverbs

	156–157
1:5	41
1:7	xxii, 31, 134, 157
3:7	157
4:1–27	5
8:7	84
9:9	41
9:10	31, 41, 157
10:14	41
12:17	84, 103
14:12	157
15:28	20, 166
15:33	31
16:13	84
16:25	157
18:15	41
19:21	20, 166
28:36	23
29:25	23
30:5	165

Ecclesiastes

	157–159
1:2	158
1:8–14	158
1:9	xxii
1:18	74
2:3	20, 166
3:11	20, 52
3:11–22	82
5:1–2	166
7:23–25	166
8–12	158
8:16	20, 166
8:16–17	20

9:3	21
12:1	159
12:10	155
12:13	31
12:13–14	159

Isaiah

1:18	29, 38
1:18–20	20
5:20	123
7:9	24, 33
8:12–13	132
10:5–13	56
12:2	24
26:3	167
26:4	24
28:26	58
29:14	20
32:4	22, 167
32:6	21, 166
36:4–10	25
40:8	86
40:12	167
40:13	20
40:13–14	52, 166
40:28	20, 52, 166
42:17	23
43:2	25
43:10–11	82
44:6–7	166
44:16–18	21, 167
45:5–6	82
45:14	82
45:19	83, 84
45:21	82
46:9–11	87
48:10	25
50:4	58
50:10	24
51:16	58
52:7	24
55:7	165
55:8–9	20, 51, 166
59:2	52
64:6	48, 118
65:16	83, 84

Jeremiah

1:9	58
9:7	25
10:6	107
10:10	82
14:22	24
17:1	21, 167
17:5–6	24
17:9	21, 118, 167
24:7	22, 167
31:33	22, 165, 167
32:39	22, 167
38:36	167
42:5	83

Lamentations

3:19–24	24

Ezekiel

1:1	58
11:19	22, 167
18:31	22, 167
24:14	87
26–28	58
33:10	123
36:25–27	118
36:26–27	22, 167

Daniel

1.	129
2:21	56
2:31–35	56
4:16	20, 166
5:12	20, 166
6:10–12	25
7:1	20, 166
7:1–28	56

9:13	84
9:18	165
9:24–27	56
10:21	83

Hosea

3:4–5	56
4:1–3	101
10:13	23
11:8	165

Amos

4:13	59

Micah

7:18	165
7:20	83

Nahum

1:2–7	107
1:2–8	55
1:7	24

Habakuk

2:4	17
2:18–20	24

Zechariah

8:16	84
13:9	25
14:9	82

Malachi

3:2–3	25
3:6	87

NEW TESTAMENT

Matthew

1:20	58
2:13	58
2:19	58
4:4	166
4:19	138
5–7	107
5:11	132n9

Matthew (continued)

5:17	166
5:18	83
5:45	56
6:28–30	24
7	108
7:1	108
7:15–23	108
7:24–27	39, 159
7:28–29	167
8:10	24
8:19	151
8:26	24
9:4	166
9:12–13	166
9:20–22	24
9:24	25
9:35–36	166
10:22	128
10:28	133
12:14	83
12:25	166
13:18–23	36
13:20–21	25
15:19	167
15:28	24
16:8	24
16:15–17	24
16:21	166
17:20	24
22:15–22	129
22:16	83
22:18–22	166
22:29	167
22:32	107
22:37	17, 165
23:23	166
23:37–25:46	56
26:38	166
26:39	166
27:42	166
27:46	166
28:18–20	138
28:19	111, 150
28:19a	136

Mark

1:15	24
1:16–20	146
2:8	166
2:17	166
3:13–14	146
4:16–17	25
4:40	24
5:25–34	24
5:35–36	25
5:40	25
7:20–23	118
7:21–22	167
7:29	24
8:31	166
9:21	166
9:24	24
10:32–34	149
10:32–45	148
10:35–37	149
10:39	149
10:41	149
10:42–45	149
11:27	51
12:15–17	166
12:17	129
12:28–34	165
12:30	xxi, 17, 22, 29, 134, 165
13:32	166
14:18	166
14:34	166
14:35–36	166
15:32	166
16:4	24

Luke

1:49	107
1:78	165
2:32	24
2:47	167
4:4	166
4:22	166
4:24	83
5:16	166
5:22	166
5:31–32	166
6:8	166

Ancient Documents Index

6:12–13	166
6:40	142, 144
6:46	150
7:9	24, 166
8:13	25
8:25	24
8:43–48	24
8:49–50	25
8:53	25
9:22	166
9:23	139, 149
9:47	166
10:27	165
11:17	166
11:42	167
12:27–28	24
12:35–48	101
12:47–48	101
12:49–50	166
13:1–9	107
14:27	150
17:5	24
20:21	83
20:22–26	166
22:31	25
22:32	25
22:34	166
22:37	166
22:41–43	166
22:44	166
23:37	166
24:27	167

John

	168
1:1	111, 151
1:1–14	37
1:1–18	58, 83
1:5	52
1:9	88
1:10–12	24
1:14	83
1:17	24, 83
1:18	51, 82
1:39	146
1:47–48	166
1:51	83
2:22	24
2:24–25	166
3:2	58
3:14	166
3:16	23, 150
3:18	23
3:19	118
3:33	83
3:36	23
4:17–18	166
4:23	88
4:41–42	24
4:42	23
4:49–50	166
5:39	59, 167
6:28–29	24
6:46	51
6:68–69	23
7:28	83
8:16	167
8:26	83
8:28	167
8:31–32	83, 85, 88
8:31–38	41
8:32	74
8:34	118
8:55	167
9:35–38	24
10:30	111
11:4	166
12:27	166
12:42–43	24
13:1	148
13:2–11	148
13:21	166
13:33	166
13:34–35	148
14:1	23
14:6	23, 41, 56, 83, 84, 85, 86, 106, 134
14:8–11	24
14:9–11	166
14:10–11	167
14:12	141
14:15	127
14:17	83
14:23	127, 167
14:26	166
15	108

John (continued)

15:10	166
15:18	128
15:26	83
16:8–11	22, 167
16:12–15	166
16:13	83
17:1	167
17:3	82, 88
17:5	87
17:6	167
17:17	165
17:20	24
18:4	166
18:37	61
18:37–38	83
18:38	61
19:38	24
20:26–28	24
20:29	23
20:30–31	24

Acts

1:8	150
1:12–26	147
2:22	58
2:25–26	24
2:37	22, 167
3:13	107
3:16	24
4:6	56
4:11–12	119
4:12	106
8:1–4	25
9.	147
9:4	58
11:19–21	24
14:8–13	55
14:14–15	55
14:14–17	18, 29
14:16–17	56, 82
14:17	55, 57
14:22	24, 25
14:23	147
14:27	24
15:13–18	56
16	58
16:30	48
16:30–31	24
17:2	18
17:2–4	22, 35
17:10–15	17
17:16–31	56
17:17	22, 35
17:22–23	20
17:22–31	18, 29
17:22–34	106
17:23	20
17:24	56
17:24–27	57
17:24–28	82
17:25a	56
17:25b	56
17:26	56
17:27	20, 55, 56, 107
17:28	56
18:4	22, 35
18:19	22, 35
18:27	24
19:4	24
19:8–9	22, 35
20:7–9	22, 35
20:21	24
20:30	88
24:25	22, 35
26:17–18	22, 167
27:23–25	24

Romans

1:5	24
1:7	17
1:11–12	24
1:16	119
1:18	21, 56, 85, 91
1:18–21	24, 56
1:18–32	52, 59, 82, 85, 133
1:19	56
1:19–20	20, 21, 106
1:20	51, 55, 56
1:20–21	56
1:20–23	104
1:21	21, 56
1:21–25	21, 167
1:21–32	xxii

1:28–32	167
2:1–15	51
2:4	22, 167
2:5	167
2:14–15	20, 56, 82
2:15	106
3:1–4	24
3:3–4	83
3:4	83, 84
3:7	83
3:9–18	118
3:10–11	52
3:17	22
3:18	xxii, 134
3:21–26	118
3:23	21, 119
4:18–21	24
5:3–4	25
6:23	119, 167
7.	118
7:7	165
7:12	165
7:13–25	127
7:22–23	167
7:25	167
8:1–17	117
8:5	167
8:5–6	165
8:5–8	21, 167
8:7	xxii
8:7–8	118
8:8	166
8:28	56
9–16	125
9:18	165
10:10	20, 166
10:14	56
10:14–17	24
10:17–18	24
11:13–29	56
11:32	165
11:33	51, 52
11:33–34	20
11:33–36	166
12:1	165
12:1–2	22, 35, 165, 167
12:2	xxi, 40
12:3	24
12:3–8	162
13	107
13:1–2	128–129
14:1–2	24
14:2	101
14:5	20, 166
14:19	141
14:23	24
15:8	83
16:25–27	24

1 Corinthians

	125
1–2	29
1:18	104, 119
1:18–2:16	27, 28
1:18–31	20, 134, 157
1:20–21	20
1:20–25	17
1:21	51
1:30	166
2:1–5	28
2:4–5	24
2:6	xxii
2:10–11	51
2:11–13	166
2:14	52, 91, 118
2:14–16	166
2:16	22, 35, 166, 167
3:1–3	117
3:1–4	xxi
3:18–23	17
4:6	22
4:7	24
7:37	165
8:1–13	24
9:19–23	130
10:13	25
11:7	20
11:14	55
12	162
12:9	24
13:2	167
13:11	6
14:9	22
14:14–15	20, 166
14:20	xxi

1 Corinthians (continued)

15	29, 100
15:14–19	63

2 Corinthians

3:5	160
3:14	21, 22, 52, 167
4:2	88
4:3–4	52
4:4	91, 118
4:6	167
4:18	23
5:16–6:10	140–141
7:5–7	25
8:19	147
10:3–5	142
10:3–6	143
10:5	xxi, 12, 17, 22, 35, 133
11:3	167
11:25–27	25
12:7–9	25

Galatians

1:6–2:10	xxii
2:5	88
3:11	17
4:5	151
5:19–21	127

Ephesians

1:13	88
1:17	167
1:19–20	107
2:1–5	48, 118
2:1–10	118
2:4–5	165–166
2:8	106
2:8–9	24
4:1–16	162
4:11–13	140
4:11–16	147
4:12	147
4:17–18	xxii, 52, 91, 134, 167
4:17–19	21, 167
4:17–24	35
4:18	21, 118
4:23	165
4:24	88
6:10–20	144
6:13–20	127

Philippians

1:7	18
1:29–31	24
2:5	167
2:5–11	166
3:8	167
3:20	126
4:6–7	165
4:7	167

Colossians

1:5	88
1:9	167
1:9–10	167
1:10	167
1:13	56
1:15–19	89
1:21	21, 133, 167
1:121	xxii
2:1–3	74
2:2–3	167
2:3	xxii, 75, 134, 157
2:6	xxii
2:8	17, 27, 28, 29, 35, 38, 38n1, 39, 168
2:9	58, 151
2:18–20	167
3:1–2	167
3:2	165
3:16	141
3:23–24	130

1 Thessalonians

1:8	141
1:9	82, 88, 167
1:19	22
3:2–3	25
3:4–5	25

2 Thessalonians

1:4	25

1 Timothy

1:2	88
1:15–16	166
2:3–4	88
2:5	106
3:2–3	24
3:10	24
3:15	24, 169
3:16	51
4:6	88
6:3–6	18
6:5	21, 167
6:11–16	18
6:19	88

2 Timothy

1:5	23
1:9	87
2:7	35
2:13	84
2:14–16	18
2:15	xxii, 142
2:18	88
3:8	167
3:16	47, 59
3:16–17	142
3:17	142
4:2	142
4:4	88

Titus

1:1	88
1:2	83, 88
1:5	147
1:9	18
1:12	84
3:1–8	125
3:2	88
3:3–7	22, 167

Hebrews

1:1–4	49
1:2	58
1:3	56
2:1–12	56
3:12–18	24
4:12	59
4:14–16	25
5:11–14	117
5:12–14	xxi
6:18	83, 84
7:26	166
8:2	88
8:10	167
9:24	88
10:1–18	119
10:16	165, 167
10:22	24
10:31	119
10:38	17
11:1	23
11:1–3	23
11:6	17, 23
11:7	23
11:17–19	20–21
11:27	23
11:29–30	24
11:35–38	25
12:1–3	25
12:2	37
12:8	88
13:17	147

James

	26, 125
1:2–4	24, 25
1:5	157
1:6–8	167
1:7	83
1:12	25
1:13	129
1:17	87
2:5	24
3:1	140
4:17	101
5:11	25
5:19	88

1 Peter

1:1–2	124
1:3	166
1:3–2:10	124

1 Peter (continued)

1:3–12	124
1:6–7	24, 25
1:11	131
1:13	xxi, 17, 20, 22, 166, 167
1:13–2:10	124, 126
1:21	23
2:1–2	117
2:2	xxi
2:5	144
2:9–10	126, 141
2:10	166
2:11–3:7	125
2:11–3:12	125
2:11–4:6	124
2:11–25	124, 125–126, 131
2:11a	126
2:11b	127
2:12	128, 129
2:12–20	127
2:13–3:7	128
2:13–17	128–130
2:15	129
2:17	130
2:18–20	130–131
2:21–25	127, 131–132
2:23	23
3:8	134
3:8–12	125
3:9	134
3:13–4:6	125
3:13–14a	132
3:13–17	124, 132
3:14b–15a	132–133
3:15	xxi, 18, 22, 42, 135, 141, 142
3:15a	133
3:15b–17	133–135
3:15c	134
3:16	134
3:17	135
3:18	135
4:1	167
4:1–2	166
4:7–5:11	125
4:7–11	125
4:12–13	25
4:12–15	132n9
4:12–19	125
4:13	127
4:17	25
4:19	25
5:1–4	125
5:2–3	148
5:5–11	125
5:10	25
5:12	88, 124
5:12–14	125

2 Peter

1:3–11	31
1:21	59
2:2	88
2:9	25

1 John

	26, 108, 168
1:8	118
2:5	88
2:8	88
3:1	107
3:19	88
3:23	24
4:1	xxii
4:6	83
4:12	51
5:6	83
5:11	106
5:20	83, 88

2 John

	168
1:7–11	168

3 John

	168

Jude

1:3	42
1:20	24
1:21	166

Revelation

1:8	82, 151
1:11	82
2:3	25
2:10	25
2:19	25
6:10	82
15:3	83
16:7	83
17:9	20, 166
19:2	83
19:9	88
19:11	83
21:6	151
21:24–26	106
22:13	151

GREEK AND LATIN TEXTS

Anselm

	32, 34, 35
Cur Deus homo 1.1.2	34n70
Proslogion	34
73	34, 34n67

Apostle's Creed

	63

Aquinas, Thomas

	34n68

Aristotle

Analytica posterior (Posterior Analytics)	
2.19	8n16
De civitate Dei (The City of God)	
	15n44
Metaphisca (Metaphysics)	
1:1:982b11–25	7n12, 11n29
1.1.98a21–27	6n6, 7n13
1.1.98a27–981a12	8n16
4.3.1005b14–33	92–93, 93n4
Poetica (Poetics)	15n43
Politica (Politics)	15n44

Augustine of Hippo

	15n47, 32n60, 76, 80, 90
De civitate Dei (The City of God)	42n11
De fide et symbolo (Faith and the Creed)	
	33n62
De libro arbitrio (Free Will)	33n62
1.2.4	33n63
2.6	33n63
134–69	75n3
II	75
III	75
De magistro (The Teacher)	33n62
xi.37	33n63
De praescriptione haereticorum (On the Predestinatin of the Saints)	160n6
De trinitate (The Trinity)	33n62
9.1.1	33n64
De utilitate credendi (The Usefulness of Believing)	33n62
De vera religione (True Religion)	
	33n62
xxiv, 45	33n65
Sermones	
43.7	33n62
43.9	32n60

Boethius

The Consolation of Philosophy	156

Cicero

Tusculanae disputations 5.3–4, 5.3–4	
	3n3

Diogenes Laërtius

	15n47
Lives of Eminent Philosophers	
1.1.8	3n3
1.1.13	14n40

Plato

Apologia (Apology of Socrates) 38a 15n47, 81n18
  10n24
Politicus (Statesman) 15n44
Theaetus 11n29

Protagoras of Abdera

62

Pythagoras

3

Socrates

10n24, 81n18

Tertullian

De Preaedestinatio Sanctorum (On the Predestination of the Saints) 19n9

REFORMATION TEXTS

Calvin, John

32
Institutes of the Christian
1:255–89 52n14
1:542–92 26n30
1.1–5 34, 34n71

Luther, Martin

Sermons on Gospel of John 23:99 19n8

www.ingramcontent.com/pod-product-compliance
Lightning Source LLC
Chambersburg PA
CBHW062016220426
43662CB00010B/1351